Best wishes

CW01661681

Doug [illegible]

Led Soldiers

The Second World War Diaries of a Royal Hussar

Doug Mayman

Dedication

When Churchill said: 'Never in the field of human conflict was so much owed by so many to so few' he was referring to the efforts of Battle of Britain fighter pilots. However, this statement could, with equal applicability, have been used to characterise Britain's other frontline forces, fighting on land and sea. While good leadership was essential, behind the leaders was a solid core of men that was willing and able to be led; hence the title *Led Soldiers*. All the names that appear in these diaries are those of real people, many of them friends and colleagues. Over the sixty odd years that have past since the end of the war we have lost touch and, in truth I don't know how many of them have passed away, but to me they will always be unsung heroes or, if you will 'led soldiers'.

Finally, I would also like to dedicate this book to my wife, Dorothy. While her war wasn't at the frontline, she, like so many loved ones, had to live with the ever-present fear that her husband-to-be would be one of the next victims of the war, a different, but equally fraught experience.

Acknowledgements

I must begin by thanking my editor and son-in-law, Patrick Murphy. When he volunteered to perform the duties of editor, I must confess that I had little idea about the amount of work this task would involve. Thank you Patrick. I would also like to thank my daughter, Joy, for typing the manuscript; my grandson, Thomas, for his assistance with the scanning of the maps and photographs, Andrew, my other son-in-law, for sharing the proof-reading burden, Lisa Heggs for her processing and formatting skills, Richard Linnett of AnchorPrint for his general advice and assistance and Carly Hudson, also of AnchorPrint, for her cover design. My final vote of thanks goes to Stephen Phillips, the Military Librarian of Aldershot Museum, for his help in locating Major Courage's book *The History of the 15/19 The King's Royal Hussars: 1939-1945.*

ISBN: 978-0-9556367-1-4
Published by Anchorprint Group Ltd

Distributed by Douglas Mayman
1st Printed in Great Britain 2007

Printed by AnchorPrint Group Limited,
www.anchorprint.co.uk

Contents

Foreword and editorial notes

The last entry Douglas Mayman made in his war diary was on Saturday 21st April 1945. How is it then that this two-volume diary comes to be published over sixty-two years later? Over most of this period it has lain, neglected and forgotten, in his loft. Some two years ago, when engaged in a rummaging exercise, he rediscovered them, dusted them down and presented them to his surprised daughters. The family perused them and decided that they should be published.

Doug Mayman was conscripted into the Army on September 3rd 1942. He decided to keep a diary on November 5th 1943 and his daily entries began on November 6th 1943 and continued until his return home from Germany on leave on April 21st 1945. These daily entries are preceded by a brief retrospective account of the first fourteen months of his army service. The diaries consist of two substantial, hardbound volumes and, notwithstanding their sixty-odd years of neglect, they remain in excellent condition. On opening them, the first thing that strikes one is the handwriting. Done in pen and ink, the style is uniformly elegant and clear. No doubt, such consistency would deserve to pass without comment had these diaries been written in the comfort of a study, but given the varied and, at times, primitive conditions under which some of the entries were made, this quality is quite remarkable. If, having to contend with onerous physical circumstances were not enough, some of the entries were made in the immediate aftermath of his friends and colleagues being killed or being badly burnt or suffering shattered limbs. The level of self-discipline and control involved in keeping this account can best be illustrated by reproducing an extract from the second diary; one that was written in the aftermath of a particularly traumatic episode. See *Figure 1*.

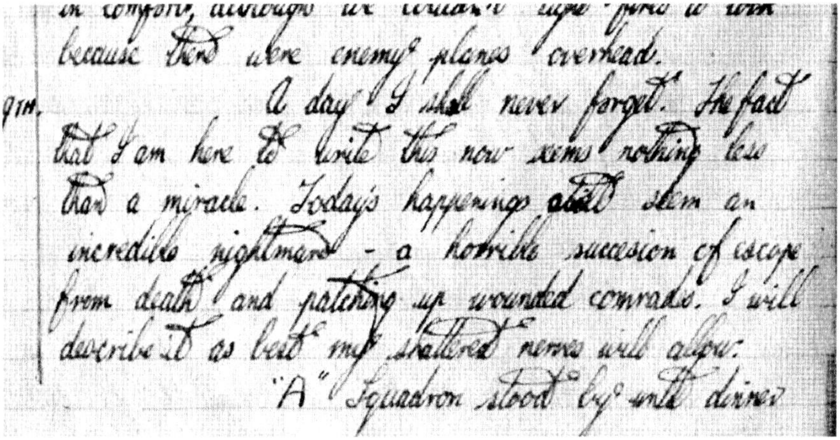
because there were enemy planes overhead.
9th. A day I shall never forget. The fact
that I am here to write this now seems nothing less
than a miracle. Today's happenings seem an
incredible nightmare - a horrible succession of escapes
from death and patching up wounded comrades. I will
describe it as best my shattered nerves will allow.
"A" Squadron stood by until dinner

Figure 1

An extract from the diaries that introduces a particularly bloody episode (for an extended account of this incident see Chapter 37:19th October 1944).

The diaries were written with a fountain pen and, therefore, once he had put pen to paper the entries were irrevocable. And yet, in the whole of the two volumes there is only the odd word crossed out and not one passage rewritten. The only retrospective elements that appear in the document are a few salutary notes in the margin that were made during the course of the war and were always dated. The fact that he has resisted the temptation to tamper with the text is not only admirable in itself, it also testifies to the fact that at no point did it undergo retrospective editing. At no point has he attempted to rewrite history. Apart from the opening months, his experiences are related on a daily basis in a matter-of-fact manner, while wrestling with what, at times, must have been a spectrum of emotions that ranged from the trauma of dealing with bloody battles and bereavements to interludes of boredom where the war almost passed him by, interspersed by fleeting visits to the cinema to relieve the tension. Over these events hangs the all-consuming wish to be done with it and return to the normality of home life; to pick-up the threads of his previous existence and pursue the personal and career aspirations that were so abruptly suspended by the onset of war and his conscription. As the war in Europe drew to a close, the heightened anxiety that the author experienced is something he undoubtedly shared with the vast majority of frontline troops. The imminent defeat of Germany only served to heighten their feelings of trepidation. Would they survive intact to enjoy the fruits of peace? It doesn't take too much imagination to empathise with the mental turmoil experienced by men who were already battle-weary, when they are informed that leave is due in a few weeks, but in the meantime they must go back into action.

The survival of the first diary was secured by the author's decision to take it home on his final leave before his embarkation to support the earlier D-day landings. The survival of the second diary is little short of miraculous. Firstly, it spent most of the time the author was on active service in the alcoves of a number of different tanks that suffered varying degrees of damage. The risk of it being destroyed, along with the tank and the crew, was never far away. On one occasion, when the crew were forced to bale out, the author returned to the smouldering tank to rescue his diary. Clearly, what he may have begun as almost an academic exercise had come to assume considerable symbolic value to him. Even if he didn't survive, he wanted to leave behind some kind of imprint. The second threat to the diary's existence came from his own-side. While some of his fellow troopers were aware that he was keeping a diary, he felt the need to conceal this fact from his officers. Understandably, they might have had reservations about the existence of a contemporaneous document that contained information on troop movements, tactics and references to troop morale combined with the possibility that it might fall into German hands. He too recognised this risk, but the compulsion to leave some account of the fact that he had passed this way outweighed the dangers.

As editor, first and foremost, my responsibility has been to remain as non-interventionist as possible. However, this characterisation of my role should not lead the reader to assume that I have adopted a purely passive stance. On the contrary, I took it upon myself to assume the responsibility of guardian of the text. On occasions, protecting the integrity of the text meant that I had to be quite assertive. My commitment to defending it was particularly tested by the author's opposition to the inclusion of the first diary on the grounds that it was 'too mundane; too boring' to impose upon the reader. The first diary covers his induction into the Army, his training and his assignment to the 15th /19th The King's Royal Hussars. It also covers his leisure time, periods of leave and the kind of activities and concerns that tend to fill the daily lives of all of us. In a word, it deals with the period prior to his firing a shot in anger. The second diary covers his landing in France and records on a day-by-day basis the horrors encountered during the drive through France, Belgium and Holland and then deep into Germany. I argued strongly for the inclusion of the first diary precisely because of the contrast in the content between it and the second diary. This link is not something peripheral to the work as a whole. The author's earlier experiences flow into and inform his responses to and interpretations of his active service. Together, the diaries tell the story of an ordinary man, coming from a loving family and secure community who was thrust into a situation that most of us cannot imagine in our wildest nightmares. I argued that an appreciation of the 'normality' of his previous existence and how ill-prepared he was, as were so many others like him, for the task that lay ahead and the experiences to which he would be exposed would add to the reading experience. The contrast between the relative tranquillity of life in a market town in the Yorkshire Dales and the sights, sounds and grotesque experiences of war that the author endured is, in my view, the most illuminating lens through which to read the diaries. The reader will, of course, form his/her own judgment.

As editor, I have seen my second task as being to place myself in the position of the reader. For the most part the original diaries take the form of a day-by-day unbroken text. For ease of reading and with the author's cooperation, I have broken his account down into chapters that are based on relatively self-contained episodes, although, of course, many of them tend to merge into one another. Some are quite short, while others run to nine or ten pages. With the one exception of *Figure 26*, all the figures included in this book were collected during the course of the author's military service and were attached to the associated page in the diaries. Given the circumstances under which some of this material was gathered, it is hardly surprising that the author has lost track of the sources of some of these data.

Also when providing insider accounts it is very difficult for authors to avoid conveying their thoughts in the argot of the insider culture. Terms, initials and expressions are used that tend to make unwarranted assumptions with regard to the knowledge of the reader. I have tried to read the diaries with a view to identifying the occasions when the author employs 'short-hand' or makes inappropriate assumptions. Where I have felt it necessary, I offer brief clarification. For example, the first time an organisation or a piece of weaponry is mentioned in the text I have included the abbreviation in brackets immediately afterwards. Thereafter, only the abbreviation is used. If the reader later encounters an abbreviation and cannot remember what the letters stand for, a list of abbreviations is provided in Appendix A. Again, when an expression or term can be clarified by a single word or short phrase I have done so in brackets in the text. Where I have felt that a little more elaboration might assist the reader's understanding, I have provided it in the form of footnotes that appear at the bottom of the page. The aim of this clarifying exercise has been to try to be as unobtrusive as possible.

To help provide the reader with some initial orientation, it may be useful to offer a thumbnail biography of the author. Douglas (Doug) Mayman was born in Skipton, Yorkshire on 29th October 1923. His father, Albert, originally of farming stock, was a canal transport agent, His mother, Kerry, died of tuberculosis at the age of twenty-five, when Doug was only three. For the next eleven years his father and his father's sister, Jessie, brought him up. In 1937 his father remarried and had two children with his new wife, Rose: Dennis in 1939 and Sylvia in 1941.

Notwithstanding straitened economic circumstances, at the age of eleven, he won a scholarship to Ermysted's Grammar school. He was a diligent student and also enjoyed rugby and tennis. However, financial exigencies led him to leave school in July 1939, at the age of fifteen, in order to seek employment.

Two months later, on September 3rd 1939, war was declared. His first job was as a wages clerk for Rycroft and Hartley Ltd, a local textiles company. However, his stay there was short-lived as he very quickly secured marginally more lucrative employment in a Royal Ordnance Factory in nearby Steeton. The factory manufactured aircraft shells. His boss there was Stanley Mason, an accountant and a man who was destined to have a considerable influence on his post-war career.

It was during this period in his life that he acquired a rudimentary drum kit and taught himself to play and he, together with some friends, formed a band that went under the name 'The New Rhythmists'. They played at social functions in the Yorkshire Dales and the resulting remuneration made a substantial contribution to his income. While his family were not particularly religious, church attendance was still felt to be appropriate and so he went to Methodist Sunday School, followed by Sunday evening Methodist chapel. He met his future wife, Dorothy, at a Methodist Youth Club meeting when they were both seventeen years of age.

Soon after starting his job at the Royal Ordnance Factory it became clear that there was a decision to be made. One option open to him was to register as being in a reserved occupation in the armaments industry. Alternatively, he could volunteer and go straight into the forces. He did apply to join the RAF on two occasions in January 1942, but was rejected on grounds of weak eyesight. Thereafter, he decided to let things take their course and to simply wait until he received the call to arms. When it came it constituted a radical break with his past. Prior to his conscription, apart from a trip to Liverpool with his father and a school trip to London with his junior school, he had hardly ventured much beyond the market town of Skipton.

Returning to the diaries themselves, at all times it should be borne in mind that this book is the work of someone in his late teens, early twenties. Some of the views expressed are aired under great emotional pressure; other opinions are those of a young adult still finding his way in the world. How many of us would wish to be held to account for things we said at this phase in our own lives, let alone for views expressed under conditions that are barely imaginable to most of us?

Finally, the reader can perhaps appreciate the strength of the temptation experienced by the author to begin this publication with a prologue in which he would rehearse the contents and, in the process, perhaps try to engage in retrospective rationalisations. I was of the view that if the author was given free rein to express his thoughts at this stage it might serve to colour the reader's interpretation of the text proper. A compromise was reached. He would write a *Postscript*, free of any editorial oversight, in which he would be able to express his thoughts and feelings on experiences that occurred almost a lifetime ago.

Patrick Murphy
Editor

Doug Mayman, aged 21, in Brussels 1944.

Led Soldiers
Part 1: The lull before the storm

I have decided to write a diary for many varied reasons, but mainly because I think that an account of army life will be both interesting and useful, even more so in the event of service overseas. January 1st is the orthodox time to start a diary, but I have never been a great believer in orthodoxy. And so, in my 20th year on this earth and my second in the army, I consign my activities to paper. But first of all, a brief sketch of my army career to date.

November 5th 1943

Chapter 1
From Name to Number

As an eighteen year-old rookie, full of ambitious ideas about promotion, I made my debut in the army at Victoria Barracks, Beverley, (Yorkshire) on September 3rd 1942, the third anniversary of the war. Consequently, it was an easy date to remember, although it was one that I couldn't have forgotten anyway. It would take too long to recall in detail that first eventful day in the army, a day on which everyone who has experienced it will never forget. From the comparative shelter of home life to being bang up against life in the raw; in other words, from Canal Wharf, Skipton to No.8 Primary Training Centre, Beverley. Small, apparently insignificant things about that first day are salient in one's memory. The first army meal without even a newspaper for a table cloth, from a collar and tie to the coarse texture of army shirts, the first march in step, the visit to the dentist, the unfriendly barrack-room, the intermingling with people from all walks of life, the usual issue of kit and the intricacies of web equipment,[1] but above all, the violent turmoil of thoughts about home, parents, new friends, new circumstances, forthcoming inoculations, reveille at 6.00am, the prospect of being in the Army for any length of time and once again, home. In one day - from a name to a number.

The first six weeks in A13 Platoon No.8 Primary Training Centre were, to say the least, hectic. They took the form of elementary infantry training and several intelligence tests, the results of which would determine to what job and to what corps we would be posted. Foot-drill, PT, route marches, field craft, distance judging, Bren[2] gun mechanism, rifle drill, security lectures and gas training were but part of the extensive curriculum. Altogether, we had five inoculations and vaccinations.

---

1. Web equipment refers to the various belts, straps, holsters and haversacks carried by soldiers.
2. A Bren gun is a submachine gun operated by gas pressure.

Chapter 2
The Royal Armoured Corps

After six weeks, on October 4th, I was posted to the 53rd Training Regiment, Royal Armoured Corps (RAC), which was then situated at Catterick Camp, near Richmond in Yorkshire. There, I was to be trained as a driver-operator and my training was to consist of five weeks general training, an eight-week wireless course, two weeks of gunnery, one week of mechanics, three weeks driving instruction and one week wireless revision; an aggregate of twenty weeks.

For the first five weeks we were engaged in RAC training that consisted of such components as pistol drill, tank compass, map reading etc. One day, while out map reading, I saw my first dead body. The squad was out in two fifteen-hundredweight lorries and I was in the rear one. We were proceeding at a moderate speed on a narrow lane up a slight gradient when two sergeant despatch riders came round the corner at about thirty miles an hour. They both saw us. The first fellow wobbled into the ditch, but the second one was not quite so fortunate and fell inwards. The first lorry ran over his head with a sickening crunch. Our lorry pulled up within ten yards of the poor fellow. I jumped out of the lorry to see if there was anything I could do, but before I knew it, a stream of vivid, red, steaming blood was pouring over my boots. The poor chap's head was crushed like an eggshell and grey matter was splattered on the road. One of his eyes was squashed out, a few inches from his head and covered in chippings. The wheel of his motorcycle was still spinning. At first, I felt violently sick, but I soon got over it. I learned later that the sergeant was forty-eight years of age and had a daughter of sixteen.

I remember clearly the first forty-eight hours leave I had from Catterick. It was the first time I had been home since I went into uniform. Dorothy was waiting for me at the station and I distinctly remember wondering if she was as excited as me. The return journey will take some forgetting. On arriving at the station to catch the 5:30pm Sunday train to Leeds, I found it had been taken out of service only the week before. The result was a big flapping effort. The only solution was to ask my uncle John to take me to Leeds on his motorcycle. I often wondered what monsoons were like, but I got an idea that night. When I eventually arrived in the barrack room, I was drenched to the skin. But such is the price of leave.

After five weeks general training, I had my first nine days leave. I remember very little about this leave, except that I had a deuce of a good time and was more than sorry to come back. Then came the eight-week wireless course, which was fairly extensive, covering as it did elementary electricity theory, theory of wireless waves, Morse code up to fifteen words per minute, flag signalling, radio telephone (R/T) procedure and, of course, operating. Wireless schemes[1] in utility vans continued in spite of several inches of snow and once, we were actually stuck in a snowdrift. Whatever the route of the scheme, we always seemed to find our way to the National Army Air Force Institute (NAAFI) at Scotch Corner. Our instructor was a former schoolteacher with an MA degree. He was an exceedingly nice fellow. On completing the course, we were given a simple test, which I passed with a fairly high percentage.

In the fortnight gunnery course, we delved into the intricacies of the Besa, six-pounder gun, Bren, Browning, Tommy gun[2] and Mills Grenade. The miniature range[3] was a great attraction and the RYPA[4] range another. The week's mechanics course was very elementary, but interesting. It was followed by a putting the theory into practice course with three weeks of driving and maintenance. It was then that I first learnt to drive and after three days 'on the concrete', I was passed fit for the road. I was lucky and never hit anything, although I did once run over a newly cemented road. Apart from that, my three weeks driving instruction went without incident and at the end of it I passed out as a more or less competent driver.

The week's wireless revision passed fairly quickly, experimenting with the '38 Infantry wireless set' and this completed my training in the 53rd Training Regiment. Several people in this Regiment are worthy of mention. I had several intimate friends. The first was Jim Cane, a former clerk of 4 Montreal Street, Dansom Lane in Hull. As he was also a driver-operator, we went through our training together and became firm friends. In fact, when he got married at the completion of our training, he asked me to be his best man, but circumstances made it impossible for me to accept. He was a competent pianist and had a basic knowledge of 'boogie-woogie', but couldn't 'busk' at all. I often accompanied him on drums on the stage of NAAFI. Next comes Graham Stewart, aged twenty-three. He came into the Army from Oxford University, where he was studying English and English Literature. A tall, handsome fellow of excellent physique, he enjoyed his pipe and was by nature slow and deliberate. His tastes in music were fairly extensive, but he favoured Bach and Beethoven. He introduced me to a lot of good literature and I used to be 'two up' on most of his books. His companion was Charlie Woolgar, a Londoner, about thirty-two years of age and an out-and-out Communist. One

1. The terms 'schemes' and 'exercises' are employed throughout as synonyms.
2. The Besa is a machine gun. A 'six-pounder' is the main tank gun. The Browning in question is a machine gun. The Tommy gun is a 45-calibre submachine gun.
3. The miniature range was the range used for practicing with small arms.
4. R.Y.P.A. stood for: 'Roll, Yaw, Pitch, Alteration'. It was related to instructional apparatus.

night, Graham and I went to a symphony concert at the Gaiety Theatre at the camp centre and by one of those remote coincidences that make the world seem such a small place, I bumped into Angus Dunn, an old Ermystedonian.[1] I saw Gus many times after that as we had the 'old school tie', our hometown and many things in common. Then, we met Jack Kirk, another 'old boy'. He was in the 60th Training Regiment, adjacent to ours. We had many good times together, usually meeting at the camp centre. Lance-Corporal Nye was, and as far as I know, still is, a very interesting character. He was older than the rest of us, approximately six feet tall and very handsome, behind a well-trimmed, black moustache. His father was a Lieutenant Colonel and he himself had served for four years as a CID sergeant in the Palestine Police. He had a fluent command of French and Arabic and his English was perfect. By nature, quiet and reserved, he was the perfect English gentleman with a unique store of knowledge and experience.

For three months of my time at the 53rd Training Regiment, I went to Officer Command Training Unit (OCTU) on a part-time basis. It involved elocution, general knowledge, speeches, drill, assault courses etc. Goodness knows how many interviews I had and how many testimonials I had to produce, but on the final War Office selection board, I was turned down as 'unsuitable for the present'. And so went my hopes of a Commission. It is perhaps just as well.
One of the best-spirited 'entertainment parties' it has ever been my privilege to be associated with was the 53rd Valentines, a male-voice choir concert, partly directed by Lance-Corporal Roy Darby. Versatility was their keynote, both in terms of acting and singing. As my drums had been forwarded from home, I was asked to play in a small band to support a musical comedy they were giving at Christmas. See *Figure 2* for the programme of the performance. The band combination was piano, drums, alto-sax and clarinet, doubling-accordion. The show ran for three successive nights and, after the last performance, we had a party at the NAAFI's expense. Two high spots of the show were swing reveille and drill to the bongos.

1. The old school in question was Ermysted's Grammar School.

(By kind permission of Lt.-Col. G. H. Phipps-Hornby)

THE VALENTINES

(The Male Voice Choir of 53rd Tng. Regt., R.A.C.)

Present an Apology for a Pantomime

"TROOPER IN WONDERLAND"

THE CHARACTERS—

TROOPER SMITH	Cyril Gregory
TROOPER BROWN	Ronald Britnell
TROOPER JONES	Gordon Heard
TROOPER GOLIGHTLY	Lou Davico
TROOPER SHORTHOUSE	Joe Ward
L/CPL. FAIREY	Cyril Smart
SGT. (BIG) CHOPPER	Robert Camp
CAPTAIN SPRATT, N.B.G. ...	Leslie Bristow
BLUEBELL	Dennis Eadon
BLANCO	Len Nichols
PRIVATE TUPPER	George Rix

THE DANCERS-Rex Harnan with Lou Davico, Cyril Gregory, David Thompson and Edward Wardle.

THE TROOPETTES - Anthony Allan, Joe Barker, Robert Camp, Dennis Eadon, Gordon Heard and George Rix.

Part One — A Barrack Room on Christmas Eve
Part Two — The Dream
Part Three — As Part One - Christmas Morning

Devised, written and produced by ROY DARBY

All characters and incidents in the play are entirely fictitious.

THE MUSIC—

'White Christmas' (Berlin), 'Soldiers' Chorus' (Gounod), 'Lullaby of Broadway' (Warren), 'When anybody plays or sings' (Straus), 'Louisiana Hay Ride' 'Donkey Seranade' (Stothart), 'Volga Boat Song' (Trad.), 'The Holly and the Ivy' and 'Silent Night' (Trad. Carols), 'Little Grey Home in the West' (Lohr), 'Johnny come down to Hilo' (Shanty) and 'Rose of England' (Novello)

and

'Oh, to be a Trooper,' 'It ain't much fun being a Fairy,' 'Bluebell and Blanco,' 'Madrigal,' and 'Madrigal in the Modern Manner' by Roy Darby, and 'I'm Bashful' (Yellen and Darby).

THE MUSICIANS—

Harry Crossland, Douglas Mayman, Robert Archer and Roy Darby at the Piano.

Stage Manager ... Geoffrey Hodgkinson
Dance Ensembles in Act Two by Arthur Franks
Wardrobe - Ted Grimshaw Makeup - Cliff Pett
Lighting Effects by the Wireless Wing Staff
Librarian and Production Asst. ... Stanley Smith

THE VALENTINES' WHO'S WHO—

Sergeants	Ainsworth, Barker and Swift.
Corporals	Allan, Badger, Bristow, Britnell, Camp, Clark, Eadon, Franks, Gregory (Secretary), Grimshaw, Harnan, Hodgkinson, Nicholas, Thompson, and Wardle.
L/Corporals	Darby, Nichols, Rix, Smart and Ward.
Troopers	Beal, Davico, Dibben, Heard and Smith.

Figure 2

The programme for 'Trooper in Wonderland' listing the author as one of the musicians. He was on the drums (Christmas 1942).

Christmas in the snow on the moors at Catterick was cheered up immensely by Dorothy's visit to Richmond. She stayed with a Mrs Waggett, a distant relative who dished up an excellent Christmas dinner. Unfortunately, on the morning of Dorothy's return, I was on church parade and, consequently, I was unable to see her to the train. In late February, Dorothy was operated on for appendicitis and, in early March, I went on leave. Dorothy had only been out of hospital just over a week, yet was able to get around marvellously well. I spent the usual enjoyable day at the Royal Ordnance Factory at Steeton where I used to work. There was nothing spectacular about this leave, but it was exceedingly enjoyable for its leisureliness all the same.

Chapter 3
Joining the Royal Hussars

On March 21st, I left Catterick to join the 15th/19th The King's Royal Hussars (KRH), then stationed in Helmsley, Yorkshire.[1] We were billeted in Nissen huts[2] in a wood in Duncombe Park, about a mile from the village of Helmsley, notorious for its lack of cinemas or, indeed, entertainment of any description. The squadron washhouse consisted of a table with a few bowls on it, in a rough shelter and the WCs were open to nature. On the second day, I was posted to A Squadron. One Saturday afternoon, in May, my right eye gradually closed up and on the Wednesday, the medical officer (MO) sent me by ambulance to York Military hospital. Here, oddly enough, I spent a very enjoyable fortnight with excellent food and plenty of free time. The abscess on my eye eventually burst, with the persuasion of hourly hot poultices and on my fourteenth day in Ward 7, I was sent to a rest home outside York for a week's recuperation. The house was in magnificent surroundings and, to say the least, I had a marvellous time there. Thus, my first experience of military hospitals was a very favourable one, made even more enjoyable by Dorothy visiting me there one afternoon.

After three weeks of leisure, I returned to the Regiment at Helmsley and went into the newly formed 5th Troop.[3] Soon after that, I started wireless classes under Sergeant Davies. Actually, we discussed dance bands more than we studied wireless theory. We moved under canvas at Sledmere, near Driffield, Yorkshire in early June and there I continued my wireless course. On completing it, I gained a Class II pass. For some unknown reason, there are only Class II and Class III at fifteen words per minute in Morse.

By this time, I was installed as (unofficial) drummer in the Regimental Band and played at several dances in the village. So-called passion trucks used to run every Saturday to Scarborough and Bridlington and I had some very enjoyable days there. I bought my first pipe in Scarborough.

Training at Sledmere, after the wireless course, consisted of two-day schemes, involving Squadron, Regimental and Brigade manoeuvres. The weather was consistently glorious and made life under canvas quite tolerable.

---

1. In the Hussars privates are called troopers.
2. The Nissen hut was invented and built as housing for troops in the Great War. Due to its semi-circular, corrugated-iron shape, the Nissen hut deflects shrapnel and bomb blast, making it an effective bomb shelter.
3. A Troop is the subdivision of a cavalry or armoured cavalry squadron. A squadron consists of two or more troops, HQ and supporting arms.

On July 1st came my second leave in the Army. Dorothy got the week off as her summer holidays and we tried to get lodgings at Blackpool and Morecambe, but without success. We spent the usual day in Leeds, but there were no good theatre shows on. We spent one day in Morecambe, but we couldn't see any variety shows as the last train went at 6:40pm. Another enjoyable day was spent at my old office. Like all good things, it soon came to an end and Dorothy saw me off at the station at 3:30pm on the Sunday express to London.

On July 11th I met my cousin, Ken, by arrangement on St Pancras Station and we had supper before going by tube to Victoria Station, where I caught my train to Crowborough. I was nineteen and this was my first adult visit to London, although I had been before with a party from Brougham Street Council School. I was surprised to see that St Pancras and Kings Cross were so near to one another. As I had to wait until 6.00am for my train, the Rail Transport Officer (RTO) directed me to the Gordon Services Club[1] and gave me a free chitty. There I met several other fellows from A Squadron who were returning from leave and we had a very enjoyable evening. Next morning, we were given a free and plentiful breakfast, before departing to catch our train.

Our first impressions of Crowborough and Crowborough West Camp were favourable, and this isn't the case with most camps. The billets were stone built bungalows with adjacent washhouses. Crowborough itself was approximately twenty minutes walk from camp and a very pleasant little town. It sported a cinema and a Women's Voluntary Services (WVS) canteen, both of which were always full. Its proximity and easy access to London made our short stay there a little brighter. One weekend I went to London on a thirty-six hour pass and stayed at the RAC Club, in Grovenor Square. I paid a surprise visit to Ken in Notting Hill Gate, but as he had to see Hannah, his fiancée, that night, I went to the London Pavilion in Piccadilly Circus to see Bob Hope in 'They've got me covered' and I also visited Petticoat Lane. The afternoon was spent watching a baseball game in Hyde Park and looking round the well-known places – Trafalgar Square, St Paul's, Piccadilly, Park Lane etc.

On July 13th, I started a gunnery course. It consisted mainly of revision of what we had learnt at the training regiment. After gunnery classes, several of us used to go swimming in a large, natural pool behind the camp and we had some great times there. On July 31st, after three weeks of gunnery, we moved by rail, *via* Kings Cross to the armoured fighting vehicle (AFV) ranges at Warcon, near Appleby, Westmoreland. *En route*, we actually stopped in Skipton Station. It was a very unpleasant sensation to see one's home in the twilight and yet be unable to visit it. At Appleby, we were under canvas and

---

1. The Gordon Services Club is a canteen of members of the armed forces. It was named after General Gordon.

the weather was none too clement. We fired almost every conceivable weapon, from pistols to six-pounder tank guns. The latter were fired into the side of a mountain at moving targets, giving the impression of a fun fair on a large scale. The family came to Ravonstondale to stay with Mrs Coates (a relative), but I was on duty and unable to see them.

Chapter 4
Training in the Lake District

On July 25th, we set out in troops on a four-days hardship march in the Lake District. The basis of this was that we had reporting centres twelve to fifteen miles apart where we were to sleep each night and we had to march to them during the day. Iron rations[1] were supplied, so we had to rely mainly on scrounging as much as we could. The first day, we trudged over the moors from Lake Ullswater to Hawes Water and, at night, we slept in a hostel originally built for the dam workers. An excellent meal was cooked by Jack Imeson. The farmer's wife gave us the use of her sitting room and Jock Baillie made the piano function. That evening Arthur Harratt drew the sketch of me shown *Figure 3.*

Figure 3

A sketch of the author by Trooper Arthur Harratt (Dated 18th August 1943).

1. Iron rations are basic survival rations.

Early next morning, we set off for Patterdale, on the shore of Lake Windermere. Here, we were lucky again because we were allowed to sleep on the floor of the village hall and use the kitchen range, on which Jack again performed cooking miracles. The third day was the longest march of all consisting of some fifteen miles from Patterdale to Ladgill over rough, open moorland. On this journey we had the remarkable experience of walking into the clouds at two thousand four hundred feet for three miles. It was a remarkable sensation, not being able to see more than five yards ahead and being blanketed by a thick damp, clammy mist. Rounding one corner, we met a gale head-on and it actually blew one fellow off his feet. When we eventually arrived at Ladgill, tired and hungry, we found that the rations and blankets hadn't arrived, so we slept in a barn, covering ourselves with sacks. In the morning, the farmer's wife provided us with porridge, sandwiches and tea for breakfast. Thus sustained, we walked on. Sergeant Morgan commandeered some Home Guard rations and we wrapped ourselves round them before returning to camp.

On August 24th, we returned to Crowborough on a special troop train. After two days stowing the tanks and generally striking camp, once again, we moved to Shakers Wood Camp, Brandon in Norfolk. This seemed to be our month for moves, as after only two days in Shakers Wood, we moved to troop camps. The most enjoyable thing about troop camps was that we were away from regimental discipline. Our particular camp was situated in a wood, not far from Swaffham, near the main road. Training consisted entirely of troop manoeuvres and troops were open to attack by other troops. Each morning at 8.00am, orders were received over the A-set (the wireless) from the Squadron Leader at Forward Headquarters (FHQ) camp about three miles away. One day, Corporal Wheatley and I constructed a sand table to demonstrate troop tactics.[1] We got quite settled down to the troop camp and in a way we were quite sorry to leave after three weeks.

After one night back in Shakers Wood, we moved again. This time it was to Squadron camp, near Thetford. Once again, this meant living under canvas, but the weather was good to us and it was quite enjoyable. There we did a week's gunnery revision course under Sergeant Lara, before taking our trade test back at camp. I gained a Class I pass and was appointed as a Class II wireless operator with nine pence a day increase in pay. This gave me one pound, eleven shillings and six pence per week clear. Of this, I drew one pound a week for myself, sent seven shillings home with four shillings and six pence remaining in credit. One night, Mossford and I visited an American Army canteen just down the road and we were amazed at the excellent food on

---

1. A sand table is a device used to demonstrate theatres of war, both historical and theoretical battles.

sale. It was far superior to ours. In fact, living conditions in general in the American Army are superior to ours. Perhaps that is why quite a few British Tommies have a dislike for the Yanks.

On September 18th we went on the Squadron's passion wagon to the St Ledger at Newmarket. The town of Thetford was only twenty minutes walk from the camp and we also spent several pleasant evenings there. On September 29th we struck camp and returned to Shakers Wood. October was occupied mainly by assisting the local farmers with the sugar beet harvest. Parties went out daily from the camp to the neighbouring farms and working hours were from 9.00am to 4.00pm. The sugar beet is picked two rows at a time. These are then placed in one row. Each alternate row faces the opposite way to facilitate chopping. The farmer pays the Government one shilling per hour per man and he usually gives us a little bonus as an incentive. This is generally about five shillings a day. Sugar beet picking was supposed to be a rest from training. It was a break all right, but there wasn't much rest attached to it.

Exercise Bridoon, a five-day scheme, started on October 31st. This was the biggest scheme since Exercise Spartan.[1] The whole of our Division was fighting the Canadian Armoured Division and we had to paint yellow crosses on all the tanks. We beat the Canadians easily and on November 4th, there came over the air those magic words 'Cease fire Bridoon'.

As the scheme finished before schedule, we went on home leave two days in advance and this is where my diary proper starts. But first of all, a few words about the lads in the Troop. At present, the Troop roll is as follows: Banfield, Baillie, Brown, Carrington, Dawson, Dewar, Harratt, Hide, Imeson, Jackson, Lowe, Slack, Symes, Taylor, Thomas, Tongrak and Watson and Lance-Corporals Probin and Sutcliffe. Banfield is a tall chap, an ex-lorry driver about eighteen, a volunteer and only a recent addition to the Troop. Jock Baillie is my greatest friend, a fellow of marvellous temperament who will do anyone a good turn. A more good-hearted person would be hard to find. An ex-butcher, he is about two months older than me and lives at 32 Elm Row, Leith Walk in Edinburgh. I first met him in Helmsley and we have been firm friends ever since. We were both in the Troop officer's tank. He was the gunner. Quiet and deliberate by nature, he does things in a slow, definitely Scottish manner and is very conscientious. Gunners of his calibre and efficiency are very rare. If there were more Jock Baillies, the world would be a far more pleasant place. Brown is a nineteen-year-old, ex-National Fire Service (NFS) despatch rider. He is rather boyish, but quite a witty and decent sort. Carrington is another volunteer and came to the Troop recently with Banfield. Dawson, an ex-engineering student, is yet another volunteer whose father was a captain in the

1. Exercise Spartan was the name given to the earlier exercise in the Lake District.

last war. Dave Dewar is another good one, a very sociable chap with a sensible outlook. Arthur Harratt was a commercial artist in civvy-street and, consequently, he does all the painting in the Troop. One of his pastimes is colouring photos which he does expertly. Hide is a good-looking fellow and, on the whole, he is a sensible, well-meaning sort. His Christian name is Garnet, but he always goes by the nickname 'Tropper'. This originated from the time he miss-spelt 'trooper' on his locker. The oldest member of the Troop is Imeson. He is twenty-nine, married and a father to be. A native of Bradford, Yorkshire, he was conscripted in 1940 and served with the Duke of Wellington's Infantry Regiment before being transferred here. He was one of the original troop tank drivers. In spite of his superior years, he is 'one of the lads'. Frank Jackson, ex-clerk, is another driver. His ambition seems always to be the last to be on parade, but he is not slow intellectually. Lowe is a fairly tall, moderately good-looking chap who is noted for his laziness and supposedly superior manner. He was the original wireless operator in the Troop and was rather annoyed when I became Troop officer's operator. He is now the Sergeant Major's operator and Hide is Corporal Wheatley's. Lance-Corporal Probin is the Troop officer's driver. He's aged about twenty-seven. A very likeable fellow in the Troop is jive fan, Ken Slack, of Warrington. Ken, 'Boogie' Watson and myself form the 'Jive Trio' of the 5th Troop. Every weekend we buy jive records between us and play them on Boogie's gramophone. He is very sociable and obliging and as good as they come. The other Lance-Corporal in the Troop is John Sutcliffe of Hebden Bridge in Yorkshire. He has kept a daily diary throughout his two and a half years army service. Single, aged twenty-eight, he is very methodical and works everything out logically and conscientiously. His unique characteristic is that he never says anything critical about the Army.[1] As Scottish as they make them is Andy Taylor. He still delights in the *Wizard* and *Rover* (comics). His trade is gunner mechanic. Taffy Thomas, needless to say, is a Welshman. Normally quiet, he gets really annoyed when he is roused, but that isn't often. He enjoys his pints, but very seldom gets really drunk and is comical at all times.[2] A fellow Yorkshire man in the Troop is Tom Tongrak of Hull who enlisted at Beverley. Boogie Watson is so-called because of his liking of jazz and 'boogie woogie'. An ex-milk man of 49 Arnott Road, Blackpool, he is a humorous fellow of twenty who is at present engrossed in the intricacies of swing. We have had some good times in record shops together.

That completes the troopers so let's have a go at the non-commissioned officers (NCOs). They number three: Sergeant Morgan, Corporal Wheatley and Corporal Hancock. Sergeant Morgan, aged about thirty, ex-sales accounts

---

1. The author later helps John Sutcliffe out of a tank when he is badly burnt. He also met up with him after the war.
2. Taffy Thomas later inadvertently saves the author's life at the cost of his own leg.

manager, is a very aristocratic looking fellow, very efficient and well mannered. Bill Wheatley, who had previously been a clerk in a Japanese bank, is a hefty piece of goods and at present he is after his third stripe. Corporal Hancock is a recent addition to the Troop and I daresay I shall have more to say about him later. Our Troop officer is Lieutenant Terence Goldsmith. He is twenty-one years old and joined us at Sledmere. A Canadian, educated at Cambridge, he is the very essence of conscientiousness. His eagerness is sometimes carried to the point of ridiculousness, but that is his only great fault. As his wireless operator, we get on well together and, although he is often called by the Troop, I think he is liked on the whole. His excessive use of smoke screens earned him the name of 'Smokey Joe'. He is rather scared of the Squadron Leader, but is efficient all the same. And, so you see, on the whole, we have got a very good Troop and are quite happy and contented together. Perhaps we shall go into action together. This diary will tell. For a photograph of A Squadron, 5th Troop some four months earlier, see *Figure 4*.

Figure 4

A photograph of 5th Troop, A Squadron. This photograph was taken in July 1943 and by October of that year many of these men had been transferred to other duties. At this distance in time the author cannot put a name to all the faces. Those he can remember are as follows: Front row: on the right, 'Tropper' Hide. Second row: second from left: Lance-Corporal Sutcliffe. On his right Sergeant Morgan. On his right Second Lieutenant Goldsmith. On his right Corporal Wheatley. Third row: first from left: Arthur Harrat. First from right: Jock Baillie. The author is first from the right on the back row.

Chapter 5
Home Sweet Home

Saturday 6th November
I arrived home unexpectedly at 7:15am on leave. After nearly breaking the bedroom window throwing little pebbles at it, father eventually let me in. Dorothy's face was a picture of blank amazement when she opened the door to my familiar knock that morning, as I was not expected until Monday. When she recovered, I cycled over to Carleton with her and returned to my first really good breakfast in four months. Harry Parry's 'Boogie Soul' and 'Saint Louis Blues' were my choice at Woods, a music shop. Then followed the first day on leave routine: 'What! You here again': that sort of business. The second house at the Regal and supper *chez moi* finish off an enjoyable day.

Sunday 7th November
What a simple pleasure to stay in bed until 10:30am after four months of reveille at 6.00am. A comfy bed is one of the best things about leave. One never appreciates these simple things until one has to do without them. And the Sunday dinner: what a change from army cooking. Oh the simple pleasures in life. After dinner and tea at our house we had supper in the witty company of the Mewies Family.[1] Marian is bearing up well after the news that John (Culshaw), her boyfriend, has been reported missing. I wonder how she stands it. She has great faith that he is still alive. 'Reported missing: believed dead in action' is a rather gruesome phrase, but we all still have hope of him being a prisoner-of-war or free in unoccupied territory. We are helpless in the matter and can only wait for further news. May God be kind to us.

Monday 8th November
Dorothy and I caught the 9:43am train to Leeds and arrived at 11.00am. Most of the morning was spent looking in shop windows and thinking about what we could buy if we had the coupons and the money. The Lonsdale Café served us a good dinner - roast duckling and apple-sauce. I paid twelve guineas cash at Lloyds Retailers Ltd of 10 Albion Place for a Pye portable radio that would be ready for collection on Friday. We kept the seats warm in the Tatler Cinema until teatime and, after another meal at the Lonsdale, we took up our two booked seats at the Empire to enjoy the jive of Oscar Rabin and his Band. The twenty-two mile return journey to Skipton took us two hours. Who said that this was the age of speed?

---

1. At the time the Mewies family consisted of Dorothy and Marian and their Father. His son Jack was in the Army and he was sent to Singapore just before it fell to the Japanese in February 1942. He was captured and spend three years as a prisoner-of-war.

Tuesday 9th November
Caught the 9.00am bus to Steeton to pay my usual visit to the Royal Ordnance Factory (ROF) where I was employed before I joined the Army. Mr Stanley Mason, the executive officer, tried to get me in through the side-gate, but to no avail. I had to go round to the main gate to sign the visitors' book. This usually happens on my visits, yet once inside, as an ex-employee, I am given the freedom of the factory. I always enjoy my visits to the ROF as there are some grand folks in the office and the year that I worked there was a very happy one. I sampled Miss Watson's canteen dinner and found it quite good. Returning for tea, I went to the second house of the Regal and then back to my precious bed again.

Wednesday 10th November
We had tea at Aunty Jessie's with Kenneth and Hannah who announced their intention of getting married on Dec 11th. 'Forever and a day' was the film at the Plaza and the day's entertainment was followed by supper *chez moi*.

Thursday 11th November
I went on the morning train to Leeds with Dorothy to see if my radio was ready. We travelled with Kenneth and Hannah who, I suspect, were going to choose the ring. Lloyds said the radio set would be ready on Monday, so I arranged to call for it then. Bought Dorothy a string of pearls as a twenty-first birthday present. Returning on the 3.00pm train, Dorothy cooked an excellent meal and I ate the Mewies' bacon ration for about a month to come.

Friday 12th November
It was a normal leave day. Finished up by playing Newmarket for four solid hours for the financial advantage of four pence.

Saturday 13th November
It's Dorothy's twenty-first birthday. Mother, father, Dennis and Sylvia gave her a pound, as did Aunty Jessie and Uncle John. We had tea at Hammonds Café at Keighley then saw 'Mission to Moscow' at the Ritz. My stepmother's brother, Norman, and his fiancée, Eileen, arrived and I met them on returning from supper at Dorothy's.

Sunday 14th November
Sunday morning in bed again. Perhaps this will be the last time for several months. But why think about that? There is another day of freedom yet. Get out and enjoy it. Such were my early morning thoughts. I eventually did get out and went to see Bob Horner.[1] We played through most of his swing

1. Bob Horner was an old school friend of the author and they had both been members of a dance band called 'The New Rythmists'.

records and he gave me 'Runnin Wild' and 'Honeysuckle Rose' by Joe Loss. Summing up: the last full day of leave was lazily enjoyable.

Monday 15th November

Leave is over and I have to report back to Brandon in Sussex by 11:59pm. It only seems a day or two since I came home, but I had 'had it' and there only remains time to bid my *au revoirs* and rush for the train. We say *tempus fugit*, but in reality it is not time that flies at all. It's our judgement of it that varies according to our environment and immediate circumstances. Time is an abstract, eternal thing and as such is unalterable. Indeed it has been theorised that time is non-existent, except in the human scientific measurement of it. But, however illogical it may seem, time has certainly flown this leave. Dorothy was at work, so after the informal farewells to the family and Norman and Eileen, I made my way to the station. I found it quite hard to leave Dennis and Sylvia. They are both at a very interesting age now, four and two respectively. I miss their silly little sayings and mischievous ways. Leaving home is not a pleasant job at any time, and although you get hardened to it after each leave, it still seems difficult.

I broke my return journey at Leeds to collect my radio-set, but it still wasn't ready so I arranged for it to be forwarded to me. John Sutcliffe joined me on the 1:10pm train to Peterborough. We travelled down together and had tea in a café in Peterborough, before going on to Brandon where lorries transported us back to camp. The feelings as we entered the barrack room are almost indescribable. They shrieked out at us: 'You've had it. You've had it' We cheered ourselves up with the happy thought that in another three months, we would be going on leave again.

Tuesday 16th November

It was back to earth with a bump. No more turning off the alarm clock and going back to sleep at 10:00am. Now, at 6:15am sharp, that terribly familiar voice bawling: 'Come on out of it'. I think that after leave, they should break us back into army life gradually. The sergeant could come round at about 9.00am the first morning and say: 'Come on Douggie, your breakfast is going cold'. The next day reveille would be at 8.00am and so on, until you were back in the full army routine, but somehow I don't think it would work. As it was, this was our first day back off leave and we had to go out at 7:45am and work on a farm all day. They certainly mean to let us know that we are back. Sugar beet. Sugar beet. Rows and rows of it and only two little hands that were clean off leave, to pull them with. The spirit is indeed willing, but the flesh is weak. Somehow, evening came and we fell asleep with cherished memories of our leave.

Wednesday 17th November

More sugar beet pulling on the same farm near Wisbech. The sugar beet is loosened by the plough and picked up two at a time. The two beets are bashed together in order to remove the dirt and then, it is laid out in rows. Next day, the tops are chopped off with a sickle and the beet put between the rows to be collected and sent to the nearest sugar extraction factory. Sugar beet was grown in this district before the war, but the output has increased considerably since the Government put a subsidy on it to keep up stocks of sugar in the country. Received a letter from my old school friend, Tommy Holden. He is now a leading radio mechanic on HMS Forth. See *Figure 5* for a photograph of his ship he included in his letter.

Figure 5

A postcard of Tom Holden's ship HMS Forth. He was an old school friend of the author.

Thursday 18th November

Once again, another uneventful day on the same farm, pulling sugar beet. In fact, the highlight of the day was receiving five shillings and six pence for my labours.

Friday 19th November

Even more pulling of sugar beet. There still seems to be miles and miles of it. Saw an Entertainments National Service Association (ENSA) show in the NAAFI. Not bad as far as ENSA shows go, but some of them don't go far enough away.

Chapter 6
Farming in Norfolk

Saturday 20th November
Ah! Eight hours of freedom. We jumped aboard the passion truck to Kings Lynn and tell the driver to 'gillo'.[1] We are actually going to see civilisation for eight solid hours. After a week cooped up in a wood away from everything, they suddenly let us loose on humanity. I wonder what the result will be? Some will get drunk; others just merry, some will chase women and some will catch them. Some, like myself, will just enjoy a quiet evening at the pictures and a meal at the YMCA. Yesterday, the Sergeant Major said that I ought to buy a violin, so I took the tip and got a haircut. Taffy Thomas and I finished up at the Majestic seeing 'Kings Row', an excellent film about a sadistic doctor.

Sunday 21st November
Today I turned navvy and helped on road construction until dinnertime. In the afternoon, the Army Sunday afternoon rule applied: in bed or out of barracks. There is no place to go out of barracks, so almost everyone took the other alternative. Even if there had been somewhere else to go, they would still have preferred to stay in. Actually, it isn't often that we get the chance to apply this rule and, on these unique occasions the camp is like a morgue. Deathly silence reigns and bodies lie on the two-tier beds down either side of the room. Some get up for tea: some don't. But we all get up for NAAFI supper. Then back to bed again.

Monday 22nd November
Exercise sugar beet again. The only good thing about it is being paid the five shillings and six pence at the end of the day. The Troop received a new Centaur Tank. It was christened 'Adonis'. We now have four Centaurs – Ariel, Adonis II, Achilles and Albatross.[2] Saw quite enough of them when on guard all night.

Tuesday 23rd November
Twas a clear and frosty morning when I set out on the nearby battle run as wireless operator in one of the 4th Troop tanks. The targets were tanks of our own Regiment and we fired live machine gun ammo at them. It sounds like rain outside the tank and like thunder inside it. The Squadron paraded at 7.00pm with bedding, arms and personal equipment, before setting off by lorry for Lichwell Ranges, near Brancaster on the Wash. On arriving there, we

1. The term 'gillo' was slang for get a move on.
2. All the names given to tanks began with the letter that was assigned to the Squadron.

dumped our kit and dashed of to the WVS canteen for a very welcome cup of char. When we returned to billets, we found that Sergeant Major 'Curly' Hague had put everyone who had gone to the canteen without permission on guard the following night. Thus, we did an extra guard for not asking if we could have a cup of tea. They'll be giving us 'chitties' for the WC next.

Wednesday 24th November
Preparation of AFV guns for firing. Tried the Besa and five rounds of the six-pounder (the main gun) on the battle run. AFV ranges have either got to have a huge mountain behind them or the sea. At Appleby we fired into a mountainside. Here, we fired into the sea and one could see the ricochets making tremendous splashes. We also practiced on targets that were moving at twenty mph. A Royal Army Medical Corps (RAMC) fellow is always in attendance 'just in case'. Cheerful thought.

Thursday 25th November
Three troop gunners fired the 75-mm gun. We returned to Shakers Wood about 6.00pm. Actually, I was very sorry to leave, as they were the best billets I have been in since I joined the Regiment. We are billeted in a huge country house with a maze of rooms and a labyrinth of corridors. True, we had to sleep on the floor, but even that is heaven if you are in 'civvy' billets near a town.

Friday 26th November
Great jubilation. We are informed that eighty percent of the Regiment will have Christmas leave. Not such a bad Regiment after all. There were many wisecracks, as we lined up to have our annual inoculation. Mossford suggested that the MO was a crack darts player and threw the syringe from the other side of the room. Someone else cheerfully proposed the theory that the needle was sharp to begin with, but by the time it got to our turn, it would be so blunt that it would bend before going into our arm. However, the actual prick is not bad, it's what follows that caused the bother. Your left arm literally gives you hell, you have a splitting headache and feel violently sick, but apart from that you feel perfectly well.

Saturday 27th November
We stayed in bed until 4.00pm today, but it took an inoculation to do it. It was grand to stay in bed and watch those who had not been inoculated stumble out into the cold black morning for roll call. Boogie brought me a cup of tea for breakfast. It was awfully decent of him. How the Army makes you appreciate sleep. Were it not for a gnawing hunger, I don't suppose I would have got up for tea either and I was back in bed again by 9:30pm.

Sunday 28th November
Breakfast 7:30am. Back in bed fifteen minutes later. It would be worth an inoculation every fortnight to get two days in bed. Or would it? On feeling my arm, perhaps not. This time, I managed to get up for dinner and write a letter. As I took it to the post, the camp reminded me of the famous scene from 'Gone with the Wind', a chaos of complete desolation, dead empty, the leafless trees gnawing at the sky and the stormy gale sweeping across as though it had taken some Epsoms and just found a penny. Finished off the evening by reading J.B Priestley's *Adam in Moonshine.*

Monday 29th November
It was a very different day from yesterday. Up at 6:15am and out by lorry to the farm where there were cries of: Whoopee! When the farmer said that he had no work for us. So we dashed back to the NAAFI at about sixty mph. The afternoon was spent de-greasing the 75-mm gun.

Tuesday 30th November
As we passed the aerodrome, on the way out to the farm in the morning, my old longing to be in aircrew returned. Since the prospect of service became inevitable, I always had a yearning for aircrew and in January 1942, I volunteered for it, both at Leeds and Bradford, but although otherwise perfectly fit, I was let down by my eyesight. There are many reasons why aircrew is preferable, mainly because you do at least prove that you can do something worthwhile. It takes years in the Army to become a sergeant, but in the RAF all three strips come at once after a year. Everything in the Army seems unfair compared with the RAF, especially the pay.

The ground round here in Norfolk is very flat and specially suited to aerodromes. Some time ago, I was elected entertainment representative for 5th Troop and tonight I attended my first entertainment meeting. A discussion on 'Jazz versus the Classics' was my suggestion, but the absence of a radiogram made this impossible.

Wednesday 1st December
Rain suspended work at the farm and after dinner we hitchhiked back to camp. Someone must think I am the intellectual type because tonight I was guest on the Squadron's Brains Trust. Perhaps they wanted the 'man in the street's' opinion.

Thursday 2nd December
Nine of us were sent threshing on a farm near Wissington. When I saw the threshing machine with all its gears, moving escalators and lots of string, looking for all the world like a Heath Robinson invention, I was convinced that all you had to do was switch on and watch it work, pressing Button A for

dinner time. But I was to be sadly disillusioned. We became slaves to the hungry monster. It could eat wheat as fast as we could provide it, disgorging the straw at the top of the escalator on to the ever-growing haystack. I never knew until now how tricky a business it was making a haystack. We certainly had to work fast, but it was a glorious day and we enjoyed it.

Friday 3rd December

More threshing. Since I joined the Army I have been gardener, tailor, road-maker, cook, window cleaner, builder, driver, wireless-operator, potato-peeler, floor-scrubber, coal-heaver, washer, painter, handyman and a host of other things, but now they are teaching me hay stacking. The Army at least makes you see the other side of things; what other people's work is like. The farmer paid for our dinners at the nearby sugar beet factory; a branch of the British Sugar Corporation Ltd. There, the beet is washed as it is unloaded, by using a high-pressure water jet, controlled from a gantry. It's then pulped and by several successive chemical operations, the sugar is extracted: about one ton to every three of beet. Wrote a couple of letters and went to bed.

Saturday 4th December

Went with the band to Swaffham to play at a dance. Saw 'Close Quarters': a very good film about an actual British submarine crew.

Chapter 7
One cannot live by cutting bread alone

Sunday 5th December
I suppose it had to come, sooner or later. I am on cookhouse fatigues for a whole week, which between you and me is a bit of a bind. All the cooking utensils have to be washed up and the mess rooms cleaned out after every meal. Then, in your spare time, you cut bread by hand. Using a knife too, of course. It's much easier with one. Bread: rows of it, all to be cut up. When I finish at night, my hand automatically goes backwards and forwards in a sawing motion. If the Regimental Sergeant Major (RSM) sees me, I shall perhaps get my discharge ticket.

Monday 6th December
Up before reveille to light mess-room fire. Bread. Bread. Bread. Bed.

Tuesday 7th December
It's the usual cookhouse routine. Wrote a letter to Dorothy about my post-war plans and hopes. My intentions are to get a Government Educational Grant to Leeds University or Technical College for approximately a year, to take the intermediate exam of the Institute of Cost and Works Accountants.[1] Then I want to do a year or more of practical work, if possible with two afternoons off a week to swot for my final exams by correspondence course. If I can't obtain a grant, I shall take up part-time employment and take both Inter and Final exams by correspondence course through the School of Accountancy, Glasgow. I wonder if I shall feel like swotting when I get out of the Army? The great temptation will be to be lazy and settle down in an easy job, but I don't think I shall have much difficulty in getting into swotting again because costing is immensely interesting to me. Let's hope I get a chance to show my interest.

Wednesday 8th December
More cookhouse fatigues.

Thursday 9th December
Still more cookhouse fatigues. They are broken only by the Duke of Gloucester's inspection. For a photograph of this particular inspection, see *Figure 6*.

---

1. The Institute of Cost and Works Accounts later became the Chartered Institute of Management Accountants.

Figure 6

The Duke of Gloucesters' Parade in which the author participated. (December 9th 1943).

Friday 10th December

Still more cookhouse fatigues. I was given half an hour's notice to play with the Divisional Dance Band at Divisional HQ. The combination was piano, two altos and drums and we received twelve shillings and six pence for our jiving.

Saturday 11th December

Jock Baillie relieved me in the cookhouse, so I spent a very enjoyable day in King's Lynn with Boogie Watson and Ken Slack. Bought 'Blue Lou' by the American all-star band. Saw the film 'The life and death of Colonel Blimp'.

Chapter 8
Christmas leave: a lucky break

Sunday 12th December

Woe is us. Christmas leave is temporarily cancelled as a move to Morpeth on Dec 27th is rumoured. The Regiment turned out *en masse* to watch the football match between our eleven and Division. Local spectators must have thought that we were a very enthusiastic crowd. Little did they realise that attendance was compulsory. The game was livened up a little by the fact that several people were knocked unconscious: all in the fun of the game.

Monday 13th December

We participated in a Squadron scheme acting as ants[1] to other Squadrons. Fire was represented by blanks. The King's Royal Rifles (KRR) Regiment is attached to us for the week and, today, they acted as the opposing infantry. As ants, we were static most of the time, so it was quite a cushy scheme.

Tuesday 14th December

Maintenance. Now it has finally been decided that eight men per troop can go on Christmas leave. In our troop, everything worked out all right, but in some cases, they had to toss for it. The suspense, of waiting for the coin to come down, must have been awful with Christmas leave in the balance. Still, I am one of the lucky eight, so why should I worry?

Wednesday 15th December

Left camp at 12.00-noon on Exercise Goose. After a successful attack, we harboured[2] in a wood at 7.00pm. In the dark, we carried out last parade maintenance, filled up with petrol, made our beds by the side of the tanks and erected the bivouac over them. We groped our way over to the cook's lorry and brought the hot meal back to eat by the turret lights. It is not exactly warm, sleeping out on a cold December evening. So Jock, Taffy, Boogie and I made a communal bed by overlapping the blankets and it proved to be quite warm. But so it should with twelve blankets and a greatcoat on top of us.

Thursday 16th December

It was still dark when we rose at 6:30am and stowed away the kit, in preparation for the day's 'battle'. Breakfast of boiled ham and fried potatoes, dished up in a nearby farm-shed and washed down with hot tea was very

1. The term 'ants' was army lingo for participants who played a minimal role in an exercise.
2. While the term harbour or harbouring has nautical origins, the land-based use of the term is perhaps best understood as a temporary collective haven.

welcome, even in dirty mess tins. At 8.00am, we checked the regimental net[1] and moved off in the murky light at 8:15am. The KRR's put in an infantry attack on the village of Little Cressingham, while we gave them fire support. Finally, the umpires decided that we had won the day and the order came over the air to collect our 'army' and return to camp. This we did willingly.

Friday 17th December

After a night's sleep in camp, we set out after dinner on another scheme: 'Exercise Anthony'. This time we went straight to harbour, north of Swaffham, and got settled down in record time. Our own troop officer, Mr Goldsmith, had gone on a religious weekend of some description, although I cannot imagine why, unless it was to get out of the scheme, and a new Second Lieutenant, Mr Van Greisen, took charge of the Troop for this scheme. Briggs was driving and my old pal, Jock, was gunner, so we made a snug three-piece bed. Mr Van Griesen slept with the officers and, in his absence I was put in charge of the tank. As we lay there in bed at 7:30pm, with the wind, whistling round the tank, it was hard to believe that it was only a week to go until Christmas Eve. I went to sleep with the very pleasant thought that next week at this time, I would not be sleeping outside a dirty old tank, but would probably be lounging on the settee at home in front of a roaring fire, thinking of all the poor suckers who were not so blessed.

Saturday 18th December

Reveille was at 7.00am. Breakfast. Checked the regimental wireless-network at 7:45am. Moved off at 8:15am through imaginary minefields, which the sappers had been clearing for us overnight. After one or two minor skirmishes in which we exchanged blanks with the 'enemy', we entered the battle area to fire our machine guns. Just as we did so, my wireless went 'dis'[2] and the troop officer had to transfer to another tank. There was no power meter drive reading and the set would not transmit on A, but reception was okay. As we were on the move and needed IC and B[3], I hadn't a chance to do running repairs. It was getting dark and beginning to rain when we finished firing on the battle course and it was 6:30pm when we arrived back in camp. By then it was pouring down and pitch black and everyone was cheesed off to hell. These schemes are made very realistic, which is all very well and necessary training, but sometimes they are carried a bit too far and when we complain about it, we are told that we will have it to do in action. The point is that, as yet, we are not in action, and if we were, we wouldn't mind doing it. I have never particularly liked Shaker's Wood, but it was grand to get back to it tonight.

---

1. The term 'net' was an abbreviation for radio network. The different units of the Regiment operated on different frequencies.
2. The term 'dis' was an abbrevation for dysfunctional. In other words: 'out of action'.
3. A, B and IC were channel frequencies. A-channel was for communication with the Regiment, B was for inter-troop communication and IC was for internal communication in the tank.

Sunday 19th December
Maintenance. The fact that there was no drive reading on the radio set was due to a faulty setting on the 4A valve. It was a normal lazy Sunday.

Monday 20th December
More maintenance, so I washed all the wireless headset ear-cushions and mouthpieces. Three smart members of 5th Troop presented themselves on guard: Boogie, Tropper Hide and myself. The officers were having a party out of camp, so we had a quiet night.

Tuesday 21st December
It's Sahugun Day, declared in honour of the famous Battle of Sahugun won by the Regiment in Spain in 1808.[1] Normally, I don't hold with tradition, but I am all for it when it gives me a day off. Sports were held at Regimental Headquarters (RHQ) in the morning, but the main event of the day was dinner in the NAAFI. We had roast turkey, goose, roast potatoes, stuffing etc., and beer at the Army's expense. Cheers for the cavalrymen who won the Battle of Sahugun. Why didn't they win a few more battles, so that we could celebrate them by having a day off and a feed more often? I took advantage of the afternoon off to 'blanco' my kit, ready for going home tomorrow. What a jubilant thought. Or perhaps it is me who is jubilant. If I had been ordered to blanco, I would have detested the job and said many rude things about it, but it's different when you are doing it to go on leave. There was a Squadron jerger.[2] I didn't go because they usually turn into organised drinking parties.

Wednesday 22nd December
Today I was up before reveille. The man's mad. No, he's not because he's going on leave today - ten whole days of it. Yes, actually going on leave and Christmas leave at that. I shall believe it when I get on the train. The fellows who are not going on leave dreamily tumble out for roll-call, while we dash hurriedly hither and thither, packing kit and getting ready to go home. To add to the confusion we have to leave the rest of our kit packed, ready to be moved to Whitby, as we have to report back there. The truck goes to Brandon Station at 7:30am. It is now 7:15am and I am completely disorganised. I tie up my kit bag, only to find that I have left my boots out, so in they go and I tie it up again, only this time, more securely. I turn the air blue when I notice I have left my denim overalls out and the knot has to be untied again. Eventually I get my kit miraculously packed, sling my respirator (gas mask) over one shoulder and put my pack on my back. It contains toys for Dennis and Sylvia and I rush out to catch the wagon.

---

1. The Battle of Sahugun took place on 21st December 1808. It was fought between the 15th Hussars and two French regiments and was part of the Peninsular War.
2. A 'jerger' is a tribal gathering, but in the above context it came to mean a party.

The train is late at Brandon and we arrive in Peterborough at 10:20am. This is the last day that HM Forces are allowed to travel on Christmas leave and, consequently, the trains are absolutely packed with service men and women. Somehow, we boarded the 11:10am to Leeds. I spent my waiting time in Leeds at Lloyds, enquiring about my radio. I found out that it would be ready for collection this coming Friday.

It was grand to see good old Skipton again; feel the bracing home air as you step off the station, see dirty, but dear old, Dewhirst's Mill saying: 'Welcome Home' and walking up familiar streets and seeing familiar faces. Then, the few quivering, exhilarating moments as you nervously turn the front door-knob and step inside, the only place in the world that you never get tired of coming back to: to behold all there you love and hold dear to you. This is what you are fighting for. You wonder if they have changed and if they think you have. These are joyous sensations that only those who have spent long periods away from home can fully appreciate. Everything was as I expected it would be and after a terrific tea, Dorothy and I adjourned to the pictures and then rushed back to an excellent supper.

Thursday 23rd December
I might as well make use of my uniform so I decided to wear it to hitchhike down to Steeton. This time I got into the ROF fairly easily and was led to Mr Mason's office. He has been promoted and is to take up his position as Senior Accountant at an ROF near Liverpool. Most of the offices have been decorated and the factory has its usual lavish display. Until now, the festive spirit hadn't been apparent, but only the Wages Department seems to be doing any work. Statistical records can wait a day of two, but hard-up workers can't. After a canteen dinner, and a visit to the administration departments in which I was given a hearty welcome, I returned to Skipton on army transport, then once again, to the pictures.

Friday 24th December
Feeling more civilized inside my blue suit, I called for Dorothy and we caught the 11:14am train to Leeds. It's grand to have the good old 'civvies' on again, to walk down the street with one hand in a pocket, and turn your nose up at officers. They give a peculiar feeling of freedom and a devil-may-care attitude, after the drab solemnity of khaki uniforms. On the station, we met Eva and Betty (distant relatives) going down to Doncaster to spend Christmas with Betty's husband, Bill, so we travelled with them. On calling at Lloyds, we were informed that the set had been sent for repair. I demanded a cash refund and it was agreed that it would be sent on. After the usual lunch at the Lonsdale, we spent most of the afternoon chasing gramophone records. I bought Tchaikovsky's Piano Concerto No. 1: opus 23 by Arthur Sandford and

Orchestra. I just had time to buy Dorothy a dress as a Christmas present, before we caught the return train. Finished off the day with supper *chez moi.* It is still difficult to realise that it's Christmas.

Chapter 9
Christmas 1943

Saturday 25th December

Christmas Day. Dennis and Sylvia came dashing into my bedroom to tell me what Santa had brought them. They are both thrilled about it all and Dennis describes all that he has got in minute detail, including an odd ginger biscuit that slipped in somewhere. I am forced to smile. We wouldn't be without them for the world. Last night, or rather early this morning, Dorothy and I had the first slice out of the Christmas cake and Dennis is firmly convinced that it was Father Christmas who helped himself. So this is Christmas Day 1943: the anniversary of the birth of Christ, bringing peace on earth and goodwill to all men. How ironic that sounds now when man is fighting for his very existence. Following the news that several thousand men have been slaughtered by the Nazis and that many more thousands are giving their lives heroically for their country in Italy and Russia, in other words, being slaughtered, comes the grand, joyful, exhilarating news - according to the preacher - that Christ brought peace and goodwill to earth. I cannot see it, but perhaps some day we shall see that there is some higher motive behind it all. We sit feeding ourselves, thanking the Lord for giving us Christ and bringing friendship to mankind, whilst men are blowing one another to eternity. What madness war is. Yet, there comes into our minds the thought that we are fighting for something worthwhile: freedom of thought, decency and honesty. Let's hope that we stick by these ideals when the battle has been won.

The question is on everyone's lips: 'Will this be our last war-time Christmas?' God grant it. In spite of rationing, we have a terrific Christmas dinner of chicken, duck and pork. Boy, oh boy, was it good. So was the tea we had at Dorothy's. Again, off we go to the inevitable pictures.

Sunday 26th December

Oblivion. What lovely sweet oblivion. Then I hear the gate click and casually look at my watch. It's 11.00am. Good grief! I promised to meet Dorothy at 10:45am. I leap out of bed as if I had been stung in a very tender spot by a huge wasp. The occasion calls for a *blitzkrieg* wash and shave and I am downstairs within twenty minutes. Grandma is just getting up when we visit her at Burnside Avenue. A huge dinner at home puts us out of action for the afternoon. When Dorothy's father and sister, Marian, arrive we turn the front room into a gambling den and feverishly play Newmarket for the huge stakes of a penny a time.

Monday 27th December
Cinema matinee, followed by tea at Aunty Jessie's with my family and my Aunty Madge, Uncle Cecil and cousin Brian. Then, it's off to the pictures again. I always did like film shows, but we often go for want of anything better to do. My father, a voluntary fireman, was on duty at the fire station, so Dorothy and I kept the home fires burning.

Tuesday 28th December
Dorothy is back at work. I was very fortunate to get hold of a radiogram attachment at Woods for six pounds, nineteen shillings and six pence. In the afternoon, I visited my fellow jive fanatic and guitarist, Bob Horner, at 34 Princess Drive and we had a record jive session, playing nothing but real solid stuff. Dorothy and I had seen all the pictures in Skipton so we solved the problem by going to Keighley.

Wednesday 29th December
Today was one of those days when I did many interesting things, but none of them are worthy of note. Nevertheless, it was an exceedingly enjoyable day.

Thursday 30th December
Eric Wiggan,[1] on leave from the RAF, called after dinner and we had a very pleasant afternoon reminiscing. We recalled the old jive days of the 'New Rhythmists' and what the various members of the group were doing now. Harold Mounteer is on radio-location work in the Army, Arthur Dransfield is a Flight Mechanic in the RAF, Bob Horner is 'reserved' as a student attending Bradford Tech, Bob Chapman is exempt because of his gammy arm, Donald Nicholson has just joined up and Eric is a cadet in the RAF. Of course, I am a wireless operator in the Army. Perhaps we shall jive together after the war. Duck for tea. Dorothy and I stayed in, so that mother and father could go to the pictures.

Friday 31st December
No one would have thought that Dorothy was violently ill as we walked to the station to catch the 11:14am to Bradford. But she was, or so her boss at work thought. After a moderate lunch at Collinson's, we looked round unsuccessfully for a portable radio, then after tea at the Co-op Café, I bought Dorothy a maroon coloured dress and we returned to catch the second house at the Regal Cinema.

---

1. Eric Wiggan was a friend of the author's at Ermysted's Grammar School. He was also a star member of their dance band: 'The New Rythmists'.

Chapter 10
A fortnight in Whitby

Saturday January 1st 1944

The clock strikes midnight, chasing away the old year. 1943 is a thing of the past. It is now 1944. As Dorothy and I sat there in front of a roaring fire, our thoughts turned, as no doubt did the thoughts of many others, to whether this New Year would bring peace and the return of our loved ones - Jack and John and the others. I don't suppose this year will see me out of the Army, but it should at least see the collapse of Germany, if not Japan. Who can tell what this newborn year will bring? In everyone's breast, the hope that the war will be over this year springs eternal. We had those same hopes last year and the year before that, but this year, things look far more promising. With the recent sinking of two of Germany's largest battleships, the continual bombing by the RAF and German losses as the Russians steadily advance, Germany, in my opinion, cannot hold out longer than November at the latest.

The New Year has barely been born two hours, yet Dorothy and I have to part for goodness knows how long and, believe me, this is not a good way to start a New Year. I have to report to Whitby by 2.00pm. This necessitates catching the 7:26am train from Skipton, so mother got up to make me a splendid farewell breakfast of the good old ham and eggs. It is not exactly easy saying goodbye to Dennis and Sylvia when they have just got up, but I managed it and very reluctantly dragged myself to the station. There I met Sergeant Major Bill Kavanagh of my own Regiment and we travelled down together. The journey back was very boring, as all journeys are when returning from leave.

We arrived in Whitby at 1:10pm and were shown our billets and they exceeded our expectations. 5th Troop is actually billeted in the top two floors of the Station Hotel in the main street. Boogie and I jubilantly claimed a room and got settled down. It certainly is a trooper's paradise, with a cinema next door, a church opposite, a YMCA and a NAAFI just up the road and a bar downstairs. All we need now is a featherbed and a chambermaid. Whitby itself is an ideal place to be billeted with the NAAFI and other service canteens, dodgems, amusement parks, cafes etc., on the sea front. It is the best billet I have had since I joined the Army sixteen months ago. It has hot and cold water in every bedroom. Boy oh boy! Am I going to like this place. On our inspection tour, Boogie and I spent fifteen shillings each on scoff, dodgems, penny in the slot machines and other amusement park impedimenta. We ought to have known better.

Sunday 2nd January

As a very nice welcome back from leave, we stay in bed until 8.00am. Sergeant 'Pop' Eddison has been bashing on the hotel door since 7.00am, but Boogie and I are heavy sleepers or, so we told him when he did get in, eventually. We had to forfeit our breakfast, but it was worth it. We spent a very pleasant afternoon walking on the cliffs and then returned for tea and the pictures.

Monday 3rd January

This billet is certainly 'the goods'. I could stay here nicely for the duration. No tanks have arrived yet, so we spent the day hard at work doing nothing. Went to see 'Hangmen also die', a rather gruesome, but good, propaganda film about the killer of Heydrich.[1]

Tuesday 4th January

Once again, no one could get in to waken us, so we slept through until 8.00am and missed breakfast. This is all very well, but you feel damned hungry about 9:30am. The trouble is that the cookhouse is a mile away and the walk back gives you an appetite and makes you hungry again. The first half of A Squadron's tanks have arrived and I was on the unshackling party. The tanks can only be brought from Malton to Whitby five at a time, owing to the stiff gradient. De-training[2] tanks is quite a tricky business, but we have done it so often that it's all in a days work. The shackles at the front and rear of the tanks are loosened and removed, then the tank is driven slightly forward to remove the rear sleeper and reversed to remove the front one. The sleepers are placed on the gaps between the buffers and the tanks are driven off slowly in first or reverse gear. Although at first it seems a momentous task, with practice, five tanks can be unloaded comfortably in forty-five minutes.

I was going to stay in tonight, but when I walked round the Squadron billet, I found there wasn't a single person in or, indeed, a married one either, so I too went out. Some time after I got back, Boogie arrived with lipstick smeared all over his face. He said that he'd been talking to a nice hulk of femininity. It is surprising how many of these women are dumb.

Wednesday 5th January

The remainder of A Squadron tanks arrived, but I was on fatiguing fatigues in the Sergeants' mess. Ken Slack arrived on the tank train and he, Boogie and myself went to see 'The Black Swan' a film in which there is quite a good duel between Tyrone Power and George Sanders.

---

1. Reinhard Heydrich was the chief of the Reich Main Security Office, the acting Protector of Bohemia and Moravia and a chief planner of the Final Solution the Nazi program for the genocide of the Jews of Europe. He was assassinated in a joint Czechoslovak-British operation.
2. The term 'detraining' simply meant unloading tanks from a train.

Thursday 6th January

The officers have found out that a two mile walk to the tank park twice a day is much too much work, so today, we moved the tanks to a Squadron tank park on the quay side, just opposite the hotel. They look quite picturesque, if tanks can ever look picturesque, silhouetted against the harbour in strange contrast to the dainty little fishing smacks. The inhabitants of Whitby are already whispering to one another that we are here for the invasion. I don't think that they would be at all surprised if some cruisers sailed into the harbour and we drove our tanks onto them and disappeared into the blue. For some months now, I have been chasing the jive film 'Reveille with Beverly' and tonight my chase ended when I saw it at the cinema next door. It features Count Basie, Duke Ellington, Freddie Slack, the Mills Brothers and Bob Crosby and boy, are they solid senders.[1]

Friday 7th January

Maintenance. After much debating whether my financial position could stand it, I eventually invested a penny and got weighed. Weight in battledress - 11 stones 4 lbs. Skipton seems to be putting itself on the map with the present by-election, caused by the sudden death of the Conservative MP, Mr Rickards. It isn't often that such a small town gets a column in a national newspaper. Skiptonians, at long last, are beginning to realise that politics is not a rich man's game, but something that vitally concerns their welfare. The election is made much more important by the introduction of a new party – The Common Wealth Party. There are three candidates. The *Daily Mail* provides a sketch of the candidates. See *Figure 7*.

---

1. 'Solid senders' was a collequial/fashionable expression of the day that was used to characterise popular music with which one strongly identified.

SKIPTON DECIDES TO-DAY

Last 'Round-up'

Candidates.—Mr. Harry Riddiough (Con.), Alderman J. Toole (Ind.), Lieutenant H. D. Lawson (Common Wealth). Polling: To-day.

By Daily Mail Reporter

SKIPTON polls to-day and the result is expected at noon to-morrow. Last night the three candidates had a final "round-up."

Mr. Riddiough and Lieutenan
awson followed each other a
neetings at the town hall—one
aking 90 minutes and then giving
vay for the other.

Typically, Alderman Toole went
ut alone to make his last appeal
mong the industrial workers.

Then the electors sat back to
lebate among themselves an elec-
ion which may be typical of those

Figure 7

A report on the Skipton by-election.
(*Daily Mail* Jan 7th 1944).

It seems to me that Alderman Toole doesn't stand a chance, as he is a Lancashire man and Yorkshire people are by nature prejudiced against them. That leaves us with Riddiough and Lawson. To those who know anything at all about politics, it is fairly obvious that Lawson is the man to put in, if only for his youth, enthusiasm and sound policy. But there are still many people in Skipton who vote for a certain party because their fathers and fathers before them voted for it and: 'what is good enough for my father, is good enough for me' - a ridiculous approach. 'We have managed all right under the old system' they say, 'so why should we change?' This is one of the attitudes that the Common Wealth Party will have to fight. After reading their manifesto in the barbers the other day, I sincerely hope that Lieutenant Lawson gets in because I agree fully with his party's policies and ideals. It is revolutionary, but it needs to be if we want a better world after the war.

Saturday 8th January

Drill parade on the seafront, followed by vehicle maintenance occupied the morning. The latest disciplinary idea instituted by the RSM is to have a roving town picket of a sergeant and two men - seemingly, sergeants aren't classed as men - patrolling the streets to maintain discipline. It fell to my lot, as a man, to perform the uncongenial task this evening. Needless to say, I did not check anyone. In a way, it's rather boring standing round streets looking for someone looking for trouble or some unfortunate individual with his coat collar turned up or his beret a few degrees too much to the right, but it does at least give one the chance to survey a cross-section of life at night. As an auxiliary military policeman (MP), you are apart from everything, standing aloof, not being able to take part in social activities, just silently observing the maelstrom of humanity flowing past. If I were a psychologist, I might append some very interesting character studies. The old part of Whitby is quite a den of iniquity. On a Saturday night, at 10.00pm, it seems to consist entirely of pubs and fish and chip shops. Girls of no more than fifteen, daubed-up with lipstick, roam the streets, hoping to be 'picked up'. This war has certainly brought with it a great lowering of morals. At 11:15pm we meandered round the streets to ensure that everyone is in their billets, then we turned in ourselves.

Sunday 9th January

Day guard does at least give one time to contemplate and spend time just watching. So it was today. It was early morning when I went across to the tank park and dawn was just beginning to show its young tendrils on the horizon. Slowly but surely, they crept over the sky in a beautiful array of colours that it would be impossible for me to describe. Now I see what inspired the rising sun on the Japanese flag. A lone gull hovers high in the air as though held up by one of those splendid rays. Oh if only I had wings and I could fly. Would I hover up there glorying in nature? Would I the deuce! I'd sell the patent and settle down in comfort on mother earth.

12,222

Voted For

Here is Lieutenant Hugh McDowall Lawson, Common Wealth candidate, returned at the top of the poll yesterday with a 221 majority over Mr. Harry Riddiough, the official Conservative candidate (who polled 12,001) in the Skipton by-election. Alderman J. Toole (Independent) forfeited his deposit with 3,029 votes. Lieutenant Lawson is the second Common Wealth candidate to

Monday 10th January

Hurrah! I see from the Sunday papers that Mr Lawson and the Common Wealth Party got in at the by-election. Two hundred and twenty-one votes is a narrow margin but it's quite enough. Mr Riddiough was favoured by all the farmers and had the present government's backing, including a telegram from Mr Churchill, but it didn't do him any good. He ordered a recount of the votes and paid the regulation twenty-five pounds for it, only to find out that another hundred votes were against him. Let's hope that this election of a Common Wealth MP is a symbol of the sweeping away of the old order that fosters want in the midst of plenty and the bringing in of a new government that is truly 'for the people by the people'. Coverage of the election result appeared in the *Sunday Despatch*. See *Figure 8*. Spent the evening wandering round the tanks like a silly fool.

Figure 8

The Skipton by-election result

Sunday Despatch Jan 9th 1944.

Tuesday 11th January

This morning found me wrapped round the base of the tank with one leg round the six-pounder and the other in the driver's compartment, trying to clean the turret floor. These tanks certainly weren't built for comfort. One has to be a contortionist to do any maintenance in the turret. Saw Will Hey in 'My Learned Friend'.

Wednesday 12th January

More maintenance. Had a terrific argument with Boogie and others about 'Fate'. Their belief is that fate controls everything and, therefore, whatever happens had to happen. If a child of four gets run over then it is no use moaning because fate wished that it should happen that way. It's the old fallacy that, if your number is on a bullet, then you will get it, whatever you do. Fate decides on exactly what date you die 'say the fatalists' and, whatever you do, you cannot alter it. As I pointed out, in that case, even if the police knew who had killed a certain person, they needn't bother trying to catch him, because whatever they did, he would die on the day that fate had fixed for him. Also, they reasoned that fate decides which men will get on in life and, if you are fated not to, then no matter what you do, you will never manage it. From that reasoning, it follows that one needn't work oneself to death taking exams etc., because if fate wills that you become a success you will be, exams or no exams. This, of course, is utterly absurd. Obviously, a person who believes in fate must be an atheist. If he believes that fate controls everything including death, it leaves no room for God. Either you believe that there is a God who is alive and has feelings and who controls the world and the lives of the people in it or, you believe that unfeeling fate exercises the same control. You have to believe in one or the other. This, I think is the strongest argument against fate. Admittedly, it seems strange when under identical circumstances, something happens to one person and not to someone else. A favourite argument that is always brought up is the question why is it that there can be six people in a car crash and only one survives? Surely it was fated that one should live? Fated my eye! I venture to say that there was a definite logical reason for it. Probably the angle at which the car received the impact made the shock in his seat much less or he was farthest from the window. Whatever it is, there is a logical reason for it, not a supernatural purpose.

My theory is that the Deity controls life and death and that he works things out to a definite purpose. There is some plot behind it all, which is inconceivable to our inferior human minds. We are given free wills and, therefore, the destiny of the world and our own human welfare is in our own hands. We can make our own decisions; fate doesn't make them for us. We have the power to make this world a fit place to live in or otherwise. But we have to do it ourselves and not just wait for fate to make it happen. This question of fate is a very vital, fundamental one since upon it rests one's whole attitude to life and the sooner we get rid of all the old fashioned ideas about superstition and fate, the better for our community.

Thursday 13th January

Maintenance. Saw 'Man and his Mate', a film about prehistoric man. It reminded me somewhat of life in the Army. There were a lot of uncivilized, badly clothed, ravenously hungry creatures, fighting for their very existence. The world hasn't changed much since then; women, food and war are still man's three dominant passions. We still fight for our existence, but with more fiendishly destructive weapons and I would rather deal with a dinosaur than poison gas. After three thousand years, we have built up a civilization which is very little better than the original one. Won't man ever learn?

Friday 14th January

Maintenance.

Chapter 11
From Whitby to Morpeth

Saturday 15th January

Farewell to Whitby. Left the Station Hotel on the advance party at 10.00am. One man from each troop formed the advance party and we travelled by road in Timber Wood's lorry through Darlington, Durham, Newcastle and Morpeth to a little village called Weldon Bridge. This is to be C Squadron's camp and we are moving on to A Squadron camp, a few miles away, as soon as the regiment presently occupying it clears out. Meantime, there is very little to do until we arrive there, so we ran a passion truck into Morpeth. Needless to say, I was more than sorry when we left Whitby because it was the best billet I have had since I joined the Army. There was always plenty to do and the stay was all too short.

Sunday 16th January

Why the devil does the cookhouse have so many tins to wash up? I only just finished them in time to catch the truck to Morpeth where, after char and wads,[1] Taffy Lewis and I adjourned to the pictures. The majority of cinemas are open on Sundays, although this is not yet the case in Skipton. Now there is the war on, the MPs haven't quite so much time to bicker about their favourite subject; should cinemas open on Sundays. I cannot see why all the cinemas shouldn't be allowed to open on Sundays. Keeping them closed on moral or religious grounds is ridiculous because people will stay away from church whether there are pictures or not. Almost every religious leader advocates keeping cinemas closed on Sundays. But surely that only goes to show the weakness of the church? If they can stand up to opposition and say: 'Come what may, the Church will remain steadfast', they would gain much more respect.

Monday 17th January

Trip to Rothbury RASC dump with SQMS Price to collect rations. Rothbury is a small town with one long main street, sporting a village hall, which is a dance hall-cum-cinema. When they have a dance, there is no cinema and *vice versa*. I noticed several inoffensive Italian prisoners walking round without any guard. They are having a much easier time than us. When we were fighting them they were nasty despicable people, but two days after we had beaten them, they were poor pitiable fellows. Why should this be so? No doubt we will think the same about the Germans after the war and let them off lightly as we did last time. I hope not. Not long ago, Professor Low started a terrific

---

1. 'Char and wads' was slang for tea and sandwiches.

argument on the theory that if by pressing a button you could exterminate the whole German race and thereby, end the war, would you press it? I certainly would. In my opinion the German people as a whole have been instilled with Nazism to such an extent as to be incurable. Individual cases could be cured, but not a whole nation. Admittedly, some great artists and scientists have been produced by Germany, but so have many inhuman fiends. The younger Nazis who have had Nazi methods driven into them since the age of three, cannot be convinced that their ideals are wrong. There is not enough time or space to deal with the question fully here, but I would certainly press the button.

Tuesday 18th January

Spent a very busy day doing nothing, while SQMS Price oversaw the take-over of the new camp. After tea, travelled by road to A Squadron's camp at Swarland. We arrived just as it was growing dark, so we merely settled in for the night. Corporal Cranley, the Intelligence Corporal, was with us, and he recounted some of his experiences in nudist camps.

Wednesday 19th January

It was an uneventful day moving stores and generally getting ready for when the Regiment arrives. The huts have to be swept out and made habitable and a nearby country house that once belonged to Lady Hamilton has to be made into a gunnery wing. Tonight I'm in the barrack room by myself. I went to bed about 8.00pm.

Thursday 20th January

I am very partial to my bed, but after erecting dozens of them today, I was cheesed off with them. After tea, I spent almost an hour collecting wood and coke and getting a good fire going. I had a wash and shave, made my bed, and settled down to write a few letters and read a good book by the fire. But my hopes for a pleasant, quiet evening were to be dashed to the ground. At 5:55pm, a corporal smashed into the room, said four words and barged out again. Those four words: 'guard in five minutes', ruined my whole evening. It was not exactly warm out there and thoughts of the ghost of Lady Hamilton stalking around, combined with the rattling of the doors in the courtyard, which is now the vehicle park, didn't help things.

Friday 21st January

After scraping boilers in the cookhouse and, for all the world, looking like a miner who had been down the pit for ten years without a break, a bath at the mill was very much appreciated. The so-called baths are three huge dye vats, ten feet by three feet and four feet deep. They are available to the Regiment on odd days. One has to clamber in as best as one can. Actually, they make quite good baths and the water is usually very warm. The only trouble is that if you lose your soap, you have to dive under the water for it.

Saturday 22nd January
Finished cookhouse fatigues early and caught the passion truck to Morpeth where Taffy Lewis and I saw the film: 'Escape from Danger'.

Sunday 23rd January
The roar of tanks announced to me that the Troop was arriving, so I went out to meet them and show them to the hut. They appreciated the fire and warm water which I had ready for them. After a week in a Nissen hut by myself, it was great to have their company again. Lance-Corporal Howard was taking a truck into Morpeth, so Boogie and I went with him and spent a very pleasant evening at a total cost of two shillings. The cinema cost us six pence; standing room only, but we soon got a seat. Supper cost us one shilling and six pence. The film 'I walked with a Zombie' was very interesting in its way and quite thrilling.

Monday 24th January
Goodness knows why the Regiment has to carry all this kit around. Today we were on fatigues, loading stores on to wagons from the baggage train at Alnwick Station. There were gas capes by the dozen and literally tons of ammunition. Whether we hold it in case of emergency or not, I don't know, but, in my opinion, we ought to fire the lot off and save carrying it all over the country every three or four weeks.

Tuesday 25th January
This morning I was chosen to represent the Troop at a lecture in Morpeth. We arrived early and had a spare half hour. Jack Imeson is going on a course on Thursday and is taking his wireless with him, so I take the opportunity to looked round Morpeth to see if I can buy one. I have been looking for one for some time now, but without success. Therefore, I was rather surprised when the shop had the model I was after –'a K.B. (all mains, 195 to 255v) superhet receiver'. I had a good look at it and tuned into several stations before eventually paying eight pounds and ten shillings cash for it.

The lecture was entitled 'In the event of capture' and was delivered in a very secret way, as if we were going abroad any time now. Our pay books had to be shown as we went in. The lecture was very interesting and vital material was put over in a very interesting way. We were told several ways of making our escape and what and what not to do in the first few hours of capture. The first few hours or days of capture are always the easiest period in which to effect an escape. There is a tendency to become overwhelmed by the situation and make no attempt to escape at this time, but one rues the lost opportunities. A very great advantage in our favour is that we will be fighting in occupied countries where people are only too glad to shelter escaped allied servicemen. We were warned to keep off the French coast at all costs and to make for the Norwegian coast. When crossing a neutral border, always throw away your arms, then you are classified as a non-combatant and you can demand to see the British Consul and, eventually, be returned to England. If you are carrying arms, however, you can be interned as an alien.

Wednesday 26th January
Maintenance in preparation for the forthcoming AFV inspection. In the afternoon the Troop went for baths in the dye vats at the mill. We clambered into the vats, six at a time, and splashed away to our hearts content. We made quite a funny sight, stood in a circle, washing each other's backs. The bath ended up in a free fight, seeing who could be ducked the most.

Thursday 27th January
Gosh! What a gale. Northumberland seems to abound in them: not just odd days but every day. The tanks have to be chained down to keep them from blowing away and each man is issued with two one-ton weights to shackle each ankle. Even then, every so often, a man is whisked off into the unknown by the wind. The others cling grimly to boulders and pity old Smith. He was a light sort of fellow. Every morning men are detailed to retrieve Nissen huts from neighbouring fields. It is not really as bad as all that, but Northumberland weather never is very clement. In today's paper there's a story on Army pay See *Figure 9.*

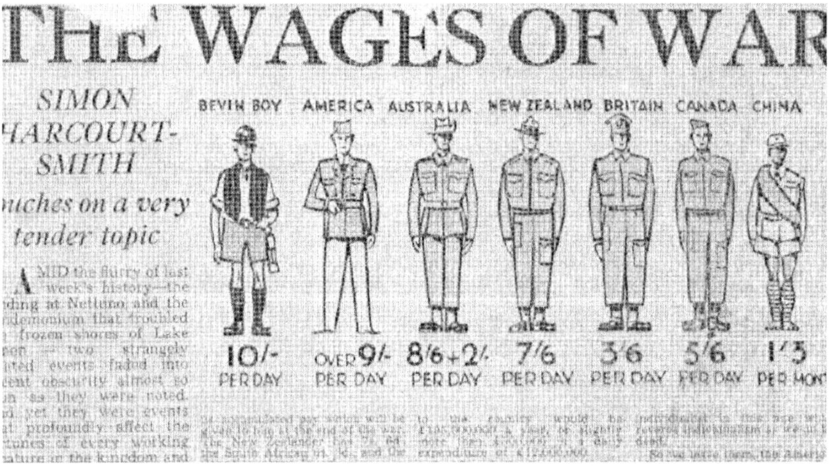

Figure 9
A newspaper article on the respective pay of the armed forces of different nations. (Source not known).

It's about time that someone took up this question of Army pay, not only in the various armies, but RAF pay as compared to Army pay, especially that of the Tank Corps. An RAF fitter gets about seven shillings and six pence per day, whilst a tank fitter receives only five shillings and a tank is as intricate as a plane, if not more so. One has to be in the Army for a year to earn four shillings a day, whereas, for the same period in the RAF, one becomes a leading aircraftsman on seven shillings and three pence a day. Also, the RAF has a better uniform, and they usually get much better billets. It all seems so unfair, especially when there are fellows in the Army who could easily do harder jobs. Had I been a wireless operator in the RAF instead of the Army, I would have been doing almost the same job, yet receiving much more pay for it and probably living in better billets.

The low rate of pay in the Army tends to make the Army appear as the scum of all the services. Soldiers are to be pitied; comfort funds are organised for them and cakes sold cheaply to them. It's no wonder that American soldiers are popular with UK girls. They can afford to be on nine shillings a day. Why should Australians get ten shillings and six a day and us a basic three shillings and six pence? After all, we cannot choose which country to be born in. I suggest that all Army pay should be nationalized and the armies of each country should receive equal pay. There should not be three services, but one large fighting force, with three branches on equal pay, and the walking out uniforms should be similar; all with a collar and tie.

Friday 28th January

It was a very quiet day as room orderly. Something on the radio today reminded me of John, Dorothy's sister Marian's boyfriend in the RAF, who has been reported missing. As I thought back over Tuesday's lecture, I realized that there is a very good chance that he was still alive. One can hardly tabulate one's thoughts on such a subject, but one can at least work things out logically, as far as possible, and then base one's opinion on them. As I see it, this is the situation. John is reported missing, believed killed, yet there are no details regarding his service number or burial ground. His Squadron Leader says that their radio went 'dis' twenty minutes after leaving the base, so it looks very much as though they were shot down over occupied coastal territory. The chances of remaining in hiding in an occupied country are fairly good, and many airmen escape to neutral countries. The rest, one can only theorise.

Saturday 29th January

It's a full day's maintenance, because of the AFV inspection on Monday morning. Of course, there was the usual tick (complaint) about having to work on Saturday afternoon, but it doesn't do much good, as we have to work all the same. However, we managed to catch a truck to Ashington at 6.00pm. Tropper Hide, Ken Slack and I spent the evening scoffing and going to the pictures.

Sunday 30th January

Thank goodness the AFV inspection is tomorrow. Everyone, including myself, is cheesed off with the maintenance, which consists mainly of beezing[1] the tanks up. Working this afternoon did not go down so well either. Lance-Corporal Probin was transferred to the 3rd Troop. We are all sorry to lose Eric as he's a likeable fellow and very good at his job. Bill Briggs and Andy Taylor were also transferred to the new Reconnaisance (Recce) Squadron, attached to the HQ, and Trooper Lowe leaves the Troop to work in the pay office. Thus, today, 5th Troop has changed considerably. One gets used to these changes in the Army and soon makes new friends.

Monday 31st January

Big scrounge (easy duties) in the officers' mess. One of the servants is on leave, so I am taking his place for a few days. I certainly had my eyes opened today. The officers certainly do live with a capital 'L'. They get up at 8:30am, their brasses and boots having already been cleaned for them by their batmen and they leave their bed and room just as it is. Rolling into the mess at about 8:40am, their breakfast is brought to them on dainty warm plates. And when I say breakfast, I mean breakfast, not the stuff we get. They finish off their marmalade, toast and coffee and just manage to get to Squadron Parade at 9.00am. The trouble is that the officers get so much done for them that they forget that the troopers have to do it all for themselves. Most of them haven't the faintest idea how long it takes to blanco a full kit, fold blankets and polish brasses. Mac Balmain, the Squadron Leader, goes out riding every morning after breakfast.

At lunch at 12:30pm, the officers invariably have beer or gin, but this comes out of their mess fees. Being an ex-cavalry regiment, most of our officers are country gentlemen who think mainly of guns, horse and hounds. Recently, however, our complement has been made up of second lieutenants straight from the OCTU: Goldsmith, Eggerton, Fellows, Van Greisen and Gent etc. These are all young fellows of about twenty-one, and most of them have never been employed. They went straight from university into OCTU. Their main fault is that they are too wary of the Squadron Leader. The politicians tell us that we are fighting for freedom, equality and a true democracy, yet we are fighting for it with an army which is the extreme opposite of democracy. Officers wear collar and tie to give us a feeling of inferiority. Mixing with the troopers is considered degrading. The corporals sleep in separate huts and even the sergeant majors are segregated. There is more class distinction in the

1. Beezing or beeze was slang for spit and polish or cleaning and shinning.

Army than anywhere else. The whole principle of the Army is aristocratic and ruined by tradition. Lance-corporals do orderly corporal, full corporals do orderly sergeant, sergeants do orderly sergeant majors and sergeant majors do orderly officers: all so that the officers don't have to do orderly officers so often. I agree that small menial tasks should not be done by officers to give them more time for the responsible job of leadership, but not to the extent where they do nothing for themselves. A very unfair ruling is that in outlandish places, and we are in them most of the time, officers who use their own blankets and camp bed receive a hardship allowance of three shillings per day. The troopers have to use awkward double-tier beds and receive no hardship allowance. Let's hope that when we have won the fight for democracy, we will start by making the Army democratic.

Chapter 12
Physical jerks and a spot of leave

Tuesday 1st February

This morning, at 9.00am, the people of Swarland rubbed their disbelieving eyes and gazed in astonishment and wonder at the peculiar spectacle on their football field. The Squadron was out there, doing physical training for the first time in months. I am sure the local inhabitants thought it was time we were pensioned off. After several months stagnating, half an hours PT was quite an effort, especially for the older blokes, who were wheezing and coughing after the first five minutes. We must have made a funny sight out there in slacks and shirts, waving our arms and legs in a half-dead manner. Actually, I welcome this PT, as we were getting rather slack and it will do us good. The rest of the day was spent scrounging in the officers' mess.

Wednesday 2nd February

PT this morning took the form of a four-mile run. The first three miles were pretty rough, but after that, we got broken-in and it wasn't too bad. I have got these officers' mess fatigues fully organised now. This is my programme: PT 9.00am to 9:30am. Leisurely towel down and dress; eventually arrive at officers' mess at 10.00am. One hour of fatigues followed by a tea break from 11.00am to 12.00-noon, then more fatigues and luncheon duties from 12.00 until 3.00pm. Not such a bad scrounge.

Thursday 3rd February

I thought these officers' mess fatigues were too good to last. This morning, I returned to duty and was made telephone orderly for the day. The idea is to relieve the clerk for meals and deliver messages to people in the camp, thus ensuring that there is always someone in the office to answer the telephone. Most of the day, there is nothing to do but sit around and pick up scraps of information about future training.

Friday 4th February

Today was quite a hectic, eventful day. The morning's ammunition fatigues went fairly quickly with the thought that in a few hours time, I should be on a train with my back to it all, heading for home-sweet-home, which is a very pleasant prospect, even if it's only for forty-eight hours. Sergeant Major Bill Kavanagh is also going home to Skipton this weekend, so he arranged for me to go early. I got ready in time and was paid early. We were just about to board the truck to take us to Morpeth when Captain Heathcote came dashing out of the office to say that he had had a phone call from the adjutant and all leave was cancelled as there was a draft[1] going from the Regiment over the weekend; with the obvious result - chaos. We have visions of North Africa or Italy. 'Boogie' argues that we won't go abroad until we get new tanks. For an hour, it was, literally, a toss-up between home and abroad. At 3.00pm, all those on the draft were waved off. I heaved a huge sigh of relief when I was not on it and dashed of to the truck with my pass. It was 6.00pm when I arrived in Newcastle. I decided to go to Skipton *via* Carlisle and not the recognised route *via* Leeds, as there was no connection from Leeds to Skipton until 2:37am on Saturday. However, my return journey will be *via* Leeds. The requisite leave pass is shown in *Figure 10.*

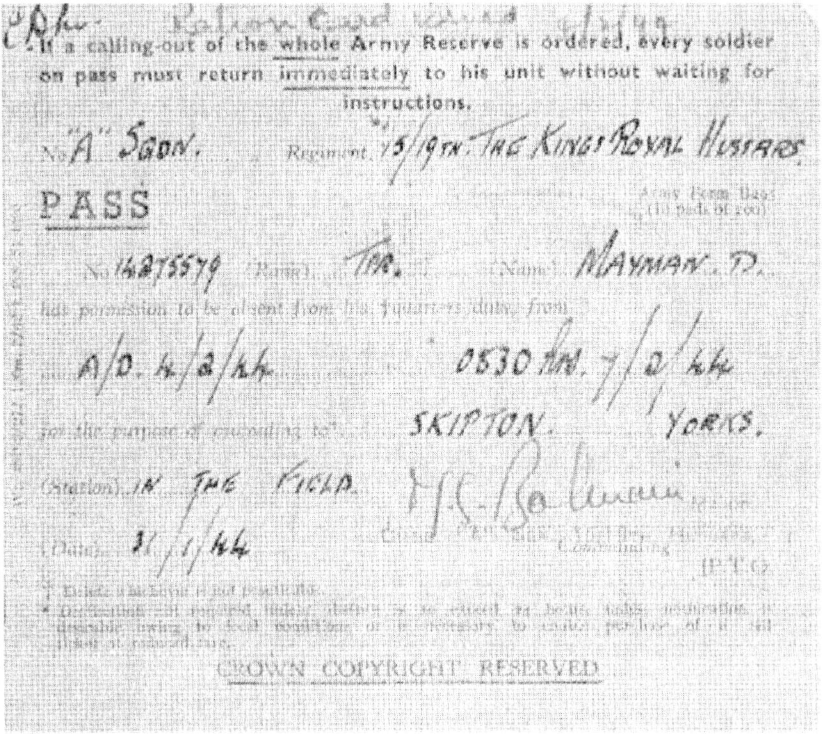
If a calling-out of the whole Army Reserve is ordered, every soldier on pass must return immediately to his unit without waiting for instructions.

No. "A" SQDN. Regiment 15/19TH. THE KING'S ROYAL HUSSARS

PASS

No. 14875579 Rank TPR. Name MAYMAN. D.

has permission to be absent from his quarters duty, from

A/O. 4/2/44 to 0530 HRS. 7/2/44

for the purpose of proceeding to SKIPTON. YORKS.

(Station) IN THE FIELD.

Date 31/1/44

Commanding

CROWN COPYRIGHT RESERVED

Figure 10

The leave pass that granted the author permission to go on leave to Skipton.

1. A draft is a movement or transfer of selected soldiers.

Gus Searle was going to see his girl friend in Appleby, so we had supper at the YMCA in Newcastle and both of us caught the 8:20pm to Carlisle. On arriving in Carlisle, we found Gus a place to bed down for the night and I bid my *adieus* and caught the 12:13am express to Skipton.

Saturday 5th February

When I arrived on schedule at 2:20am at Skipton Station, a RAF pilot officer happened to be going through the barrier before me. We exchanged a few words about the weather and the railway service, before we recognised each other. Then it came in a flash: 'Eric!' 'Douglas!' Yes it was none other than my old friend Eric Astin. He had just returned from Canada where he had been trained and commissioned as a navigator. It was a very pleasant surprise, indeed, and I was very glad to see him. You can imagine our feelings as we walked into Skipton from the station. We had so much to talk about, yet the tingling, elevating feeling of being at home after so long, made us lapse into silence for the first few minutes. I eventually got to bed at 3.00am. Rising about 9.00am, I rang Dorothy to let her know that I had arrived. Then, I paid a visit to my barber. In the evening, we saw the film: 'Watch on the Rhine' with Bette Davis and Paul Lukas and 'Something to shout about' with Jack Oakie. Father was on NFS duty and Dorothy and I kept our front room fire company until… I had better not put what time.

Sunday 6th February

After a terrific dinner at home, the family went out for their usual Sunday afternoon walk and Dorothy and I were left in to get the tea ready, but somehow it didn't get done. Visiting Mr Mewies after tea, we finished off the bottle of port. Sunday supper was quite a social event. Bill Kavanagh and his fiancé, Shirley Campbell, came at my invitation, so that we could all go to the station together. Eric Astin called, so we had a very pleasant couple of hours. Travelling is not quite so boring when one has a friend to travel with. There are only two 15th/19th Hussars from Skipton and it seems queer that both our betrotheds work in the same office. Our farewell supper was very pleasant, but, as usual the actual farewell wasn't, especially the last few minutes. Parting is not so good when there is always the possibility of going abroad, without embarkation leave, and the possibility that every parting may be the last. Bill and I consoled one another as best as we could on the train. Arriving in Leeds at just after 10:30pm, we caught the 10:45pm to York, had a short stay there, having a snack, and then caught the next train to Newcastle.

Monday 7th February

Station waiting room floors are never very soft and the one at Morpeth is no exception. In spite of that, we slept quite soundly until 8.00am, when the lorry arrived. It is surprising what a difference uniform makes. In civvies one wouldn't dream of going to sleep in a waiting room, much less on the floor, but in uniform it's one of those things that's done. In almost every waiting room, between 8.00pm and 8.00am, bodies can be seen, laid out on the forms, like a morgue, except that the bodies are clad in khaki, blue and black. The stench is always pretty bad and there is always one of the assembled-company that snores fairly loudly. It is a miserable sight indeed, and a disgrace to the community. Railway companies ought to be boycotted after the war. It is fairly obvious that railway reform is very badly needed. One has learned not to be annoyed if one's train is less than two hours late and it is not unusual for someone to enquire if the 2:25 from a certain place will arrive in time to catch a train two days later from a place two or three miles away. The question: 'what time does the 5:20 train leave? Is no longer a joke, but an annoying reality.

My first concern on arriving back at camp was to find who had gone on the draft. Eighty-six untrained men were posted from the Regiment to the 5th Royal Tank Regiment and 4th County of London Yoemanry. Twenty-five went from A Squadron, including Symes and Dawson from 5th Troop. At first, trained men were put on the draft, then, they were changed to untrained. If more untrained men are drafted from the Regiment, then we shall be turned into a fighting Regiment of experienced men only. If trained men are drafted, then we are merely an advanced training regiment that will be drawn upon to replace wounded men in fighting regiments. At present, we are an operational division. But I cannot see us going into action with less than a month's notice.

Tuesday 8th February

The NAAFI here has only twenty-two cups at present, so my job today as NAAFI orderly was fairly easy. I found quite an easy way to light a fire. No paper, a bundle of twigs, two logs, one cup of oil and one of petrol, a supply of coke, then pour the oil and petrol over the whole lot and ignite, preferably from a distance of approximately a hundred yards. When you have replaced the Nissen hut, the fire should go quite well.

Wednesday 9th February

Another day in the Squadron Office as telephone orderly, gleaning information about the forthcoming 'Exercise Eagle'. I shall be able to provide more details about it during the actual scheme. As soon as the Squadron clerk goes out, I dash round all the papers to satisfy my inquisitive mind about the military future. The tanks Ariel and Achilles[1] were handed over to the newly formed Reconnaissance Squadron. Our Troop is thoroughly disorganised at present with tanks going in and out and drafts and promotions taking place. In the past week, two troopers have left the Troop, one Lance-Corporal has been

1. Tanks were given names for reference purposes. These names were also useful as radio code names.

transferred to 3rd Troop, a trooper from FHQ has been brought into the Troop as a lance-corporal and two tanks have gone to the 'Recce' Squadron. Let's see what tomorrow brings.

Thursday 10th February

Tomorrow has brought plenty. Eric Probin, transferred to 3rd Troop, has been made up to full corporal, and two tanks have been brought into the Troop; one named 'April the Fifth' from 2nd Troop and the other, 'AP' from FHQ. They are both in a pretty disgusting state. I was sorry to lose 'Ariel' as I have been the operator on it ever since it came to the Regiment from the factory and Jock and I had got the turret in really ship-shape condition. Still, with a bit of luck, we should get a brand new tank soon.

It is now 10.30pm. Looking round the barrack-room, a varied scene presents itself. Several fellows are sitting round the stove, with me reading and the others writing letters or arguing about sex. A few are in bed reading and one or two are peacefully snoring and away from the Army for a few brief hours. One chap is conscientiously 'blancoing' a lanyard, whilst next to him, is another chap shaving in the same water; not at all unusual sight. The contents of someone's kit bag lie scattered all over the floor, and the owner is hastily repacking them. Most of the fellows think it is about time to retire and there is a display of underpants and hairy male bodies. Above all this, the gramophone blares out 'Saint Louis Blues' and, I too, think it's time to retire.

Chapter 13
Exercise Eagle

Friday 11th February

There is a roar of tanks as we move out in single file on Exercise Eaglet.[1] This amounts to merely a fifty-mile circuitous road move to ensure that the tanks, wireless etc., are in good working order for Exercise Eagle. 5th Troop had only two tanks on the scheme and both wirelesses went 'dis'. Mine blew four fuses in succession, so I switched the damn thing off and fell to slicing-up bread for jam sandwiches. This proved quite an enjoyable occupation for the rest of the scheme.

Returning to camp at 4.00pm, I was detailed for guard tomorrow night, but Arthur Harrat said he would do mine, if I did his tonight. Consequently, here I am in the guardroom with Ken Slack. We have just come in off first relief. It is quite cold out there, but we passed the time discussing jive and drawing up plans for how we would like the Army run. Needless to say, these included no guard duty. Four of us, and the guard corporal, are now sitting around the stove of the guardroom in equipment, with Sten guns. We have live ammunition, but never get chance to fire it. Not that we would be any good if the camp were attacked, although most of us wouldn't mind murdering one or two Jerries at the moment. If it weren't for them, we wouldn't be on guard tonight.

Saturday 12th February

Ken Slack, Tom Tongrak and myself decided to hitchhike to Morpeth. After a two miles route march, we were eventually picked-up by a civvy lorry. The YMCA provided a fairly decent tea and then we relaxed in the luxurious 'ten-pennies' at the Playhouse. The film was Robert Taylor in 'Bataan'.

Sunday 13th February

This morning I was not feeling so good, so I stayed in bed until 11.00am, while the lads were working on the tanks. The day's news contains more reports of Japanese atrocities against allied prisoners. If these reports are true, and they must have come from reliable sources, every bloody Jap ought to be exterminated. The Japs never were clean fighters and we can only fight them with their own methods. We ought to mercilessly 'wipe out' every filthy Jap that dares to fight under the Rising Sun. Germans are bestial, but the Japanese are even more so. I should derive quite a lot of pleasure from having a whole row of Japs in front of my tank and mowing them down with my BESA. Not a pleasant thought for a Sunday, but during a war, Sunday is entirely disregarded. After all, one can hardly slaughter six days of the week and, then, claim to know a God that is Love itself.

---

1. Exercise Eaglet was the preparatory exercise for Exercise Eagle.

Yet that is what we seem to be doing. Whether we believe it's for a righteous cause or not is a matter of personal opinion.

Monday 14th February

It's St Valentines Day. Not that it makes any difference. Exercise Eagle draws near and we spend the morning preparing the tanks for it. Boogie, Ken and I are in the same crew and, for the scheme we have collected one tin of spam, two tins of pork luncheon meat, one pound of jam, one pound of marmalade, a tin of OXO, six soups, one bottle of Bovril, one bottle of Marmite, two tins of grade three salmon and two sweet cakes. We certainly don't intend to starve. This afternoon, our Cromwell tanks were loaded onto war flats[1] at Alnwick Station. The Cromwell tanks are new and ready for action, so they are going by rail to save the wear and tear of a one hundred and forty mile journey. The Centaur tanks are going by road on Wednesday.

Tuesday 15th February

Received a present from home: a golden platinum stud-filling pen. Today is the last day of preparation for the scheme and the tank park was a scene of chaos. Men dash around the tanks, wildly lashing petrol filters and camouflage nets onto the tanks. We are to live in these tanks for a fortnight, so we try to make them as habitable as possible under the circumstances. Our new officer, Mr Gent, is as yet inexperienced in this type of AFV and, consequently, he leaves most of the preparation to us. Received the first letter that my brother Dennis has ever written to me. He will be five next month.

Wednesday 16th February

The weather was not at all promising as we assembled on the tank park at 9.00am this morning. There had been drizzle during the night and the atmosphere was still damp and clammy, but later on, the clouds rolled back and the rest of the day was quite sunny. After tuning into the Squadron and Regimental frequencies, we moved off in order; 1st Troop, 2nd Troop, FHQ, 3rd, 4th and 5th Troops, on the hundred-mile road march to the concentration area for Exercise Eagle. We met up with the rest of the Regiment, not far from Swarland, and moved in the order of A Squadron, RHQ, B and C Squadrons.

The move is to be split-up over two days and we are harbouring just south of Stockton. The journey down was, as far as possible, interesting. We passed through Morpeth at 11.00am and my lucky mascot panda, tied on my aerial, caused quite a commotion. Outside Newcastle we closed up into block formation to go through the town, with approximately three yards between the tanks. Seventy-odd tanks moving through the main thoroughfare of Newcastle is quite an event. The people of Newcastle turned out in full force to watch us

---

1. War flats are railway wagons for tanks.

pass through. No doubt, many of them thought that the Second Front had opened, as it isn't every day that a whole armoured brigade rattles down their main street. I must say we must have looked quite an impressive sight: a mass of tanks, stretching from the Odeon Cinema right across the Tyne Bridge. On through Newcastle, the next town we passed through was Durham. Just south of Newcastle we passed a terrific long line of brand new army lorries. There were at least a thousand of them. As far as the eye could see, there was one long row of lorries at right angles to the road, their windscreens glinting in the sun. A German, seeing this terrific army of vehicles, would have realised that Britain certainly isn't short of war materials. Leaving Durham Cathedral on our left, we forked left to Stockton. About four miles south of Stockton we halted on the roadside for the night. We had to sleep on the road behind the tank. After a big tossing-up era, it was decided that Ken was on guard.

Thursday 17th February

It wasn't at all good getting up this morning, in spite of the fact that the road wasn't too soft. The drizzle and semi-darkness didn't help either. Somehow we dragged ourselves out of the bivouac, folded the blankets and stowed the kit on the tank. Then came the Herculean task of cooking breakfast. Boogie mashed the char and I fried the liver. Surprisingly enough, we had quite a good breakfast of corn flakes, fried liver, bread and butter and hot tea. It was very welcome in the biting cold of the morning. After breakfast came a wash and shave in the open by the side of the tank. Passers-by on a bus heading for Northallerton must have thought we were a queer crowd. At about 11.00am we moved off on the second half of our journey. This was fairly uneventful. As we crossed the range of hills between Stockton and Sledmere, we ran into heavy hailstorms, heralded by a thick, heavy-laden grey sky. At 1:30pm we had a halt for dinner and somehow managed to thaw our numb hands out enough to cut a few slices of bread and open a tin of herrings. We eventually reached our destination and harboured in a wood about half a mile from the village of Rillington. Up to here, today's diary has been written out in the open and it has been trying to snow. This accounts for the disgusting state of this page. Now, however, I am safely in the NAAFI. It is crowded with fellows out of the Brigade. All that is being served is tea and biscuits, but it's very welcome out here in the wilderness.

Friday 18th February

Reveille 7:30am. I always appreciate my bed, but schemes make one appreciate it even more. Second Lieutenant Gent has been posted to the 3rd Hussars. In the meantime, he is attached to this Regiment from OCTU until he can join his Regiment. He is in charge of the Troop for this scheme because Mr Goldsmith is at Bovington on a seven-weeks wireless course. He is only nineteen and very cushy (easy-going) indeed. Today we were on maintenance, but towards dinnertime it dwindled into sitting round a wood fire and having a general powwow. The only dope (information) about the scheme we have heard so far is that the battle is between the 8th Corps and the 9th Armoured Division. The Guards from the 8th Corps are attacking from the south and we have to hold a line running east and west through Sledmere. Our Division is to be the 'Jerries' and all our vehicles have been painted with yellow crosses. Actually, the fighting has been going on for several days now, but our Brigade has not been needed up to now. The enemy's objective is to cross the River Derwent and we have to prevent them at all costs. If the enemy crosses it, they have won the battle.

Saturday 19th February
It's been a very exhausting day spent laying mines. Three men per troop were required to assist the Royal Engineers (REs) in laying mines along a valley in order to delay the enemy. The strategy behind this operation is that the enemy will come along the valley, see the minefield on the left and infantry trenches and dummy tanks on the right and make for a ridge in the centre. Our armour will sit behind this ridge and shoot at them as they come over. The angle of the ridge is so steep that the enemy will be unable to depress their guns far enough to retaliate. Our mines were laid without much difficulty. The mines were actually half petrol tins flattened out and laid alternately, two and a half yards apart, on either side of a wire stretched across the field by the RE's. Rolls and rolls of barbed wire enclose the whole area. Returning to camp about 6.00pm, Boogie, Ken and I set too and had fried corned beef, chips, fried bread, toast and marmalade and hot OXO, before crawling into our communal bed by the side of the tank.

Sunday 20th February
A civilized Sunday in a civilized country and, yet, here we are crouched round a fire in the middle of a wood, a group of half starved, dirty cavemen, eating half cooked food ravenously. Sixty-five miles away is a nice warm, comfortable home, with delicately cooked food. But because some foreign individual took it into his head that he would like to rule the world and incited his already war-fond nation to follow his whim, we are sitting here like Stupidity himself. Sunday night and we are in bed by 8:30pm. Not because we are tired but because, in the blackout, it is impossible to do anything else.

Monday 21st February
Reveille 4:30am. I don't think that even the lark gets up this early. If he does, he is welcome to it. It was pitch black and hailing slightly when we struck camp and moved off this morning. The Bivvy (bivouac) and sheets had to be taken down and stowed way in the bins[1] and all the blankets folded and

---

1. Bins are storage units on the outside of tanks.

packed: all in the dark. It isn't a nice job first thing in a morning. After a six-mile road march, we camouflaged our tanks in a valley about two miles from the enemy's position. We are to remain in reserve here under six hours notice to move. At present, I am an air sentry, sitting on the crest of a hill that is more like a mountain when you come to walk up it. There is a glorious view from here, but the weather is too cold to fully appreciate it. From here I can see the valley below and the next valley beyond that. One can hardly say that the scenery rolls away to the horizon as only plains give the effect of rolling into infinity. Up here the horizon rests abruptly on the crest of a hill, not so very far away. It is pretty rugged countryside generally and I mean the word 'pretty' literally. I had just written the above sentence when the enemy spotted our hideout and we were given five minutes notice to move. Chaos ensued. Half cooked meals and half made beds were banged into bins in an orgy of disorder.

That evening once more the inevitable fried corned beef and beans for tea, before withdrawing under cover of darkness to a closed harbour for the night. My wireless went 'dis' and I had to change two valves.

Tuesday 22nd February
Up at 3.00am to do the last relief on guard, which was, as all guards are in this country, immensely boring. Using our great friend the darkness again, the Regiment took up fighting positions and awaited dawn and the enemy. The former came, but the latter didn't, so we cooked breakfast. About 11:30am we had our first skirmish with the enemy. It was like a game of 'chase me'. A-Squadron sat behind a ridge, while B Squadron went into full view of the enemy, tapped them on the shoulder and beat a hasty retreat over the ridge. By all logical rules of battle, the enemy should have come dashing over the ridge and we would have shot them up, before they had chance to do anything. The only snag was that they didn't. So C Squadron was sent to tap them on the shoulder again and it too did a gilty (quick) move back over the ridge. But the enemy still refused to play. So B Squadron was sent out again. This time the enemy got really mad and charged over the ridge at full force. For ten glorious minutes there was a veritable chaos of Centaurs and Shermans. At which point the umpires called a halt and dashed hither and thither, wildly gesticulating. Goodness knows what the umpires' decision was, but I would guess it was in our favour, with several tanks being theoretically lost on both sides. The reader will have to excuse the dirty state of the diary while on this scheme, but considering that I haven't washed or shaved for three days, it isn't bad. Also, I am writing this inside the tank, as we sit waiting for the enemy to appear.

The enemy did appear later and we made another strategic withdrawal under cover of darkness to a position about ten miles away on the east flank of the enemy. At 10.00pm, on a very steep hill, two of our tanks broke down and blocked the road. Consequently, we had to halt there for the night. It was pitch black and raining, we were already soaked and hadn't eaten since breakfast. On top of this, we somehow had to make a bed in the rain and darkness, keeping the blankets as dry as possible. It is not an easy job and we all thought that we would get something new without coupons - (new) monia. Somehow we folded the blankets into the shape of a bed, erected the bivouacs over them and draped in misery we crawled into them.

Wednesday 23rd February

It was still raining and dark when we got up at 4:45am. We carried on with the second part of our journey. A few miles along the route we met the petrol lorry and halted to fill up. We had to walk about two hundred yards to the road, through almost a foot of wet slushy mud. If you stopped to get a fresh grip on the petrol cans, you were almost sucked under. Wading through mud in the rain on an empty stomach at 6.00am is not my idea of a picnic. When we eventually did arrive at our position, we did little actual fighting. We just sat behind hedges waiting for the enemy to appear. At 5.00pm we were issued with a rum ration. Needless to say, this went down with great gusto, in spite of having to drink it out of a pint pot. At 6.00pm we banged our heads on the roof of the tank jumping for joy when we heard that, as far as our Regiment was concerned, Exercise Eagle was over. We then proceeded to a regimental harbour on the side of the Helmsley-Scarborough road, about three miles from Scarborough.

Chapter 14
Nissen huts can be heaven

Thursday 24th February
Today reveille was not until 7:30am. Thank goodness. What is that round bright thing appearing in the sky that actually gives out heat? Crikey! It's the sun. Had we seen more of it during the last few days the scheme would not have been quite so cheesing. We remained by the side of the road all day, doing maintenance in preparation for the return journey to Swarland tomorrow. At 4.00pm we caught a truck into Scarborough and made the most of the occasion by having chops and fried potatoes in a café. It's Dennis' birthday tomorrow and I sent him some saving stamps. 'French without Tears' was very amusing. I like these English films about typically English people. And now back to home: a bed on the roadside by the side of a tank.

Friday 25th February
It's Dennis' birthday. It's hard to realise that it's five years since he was born. So many things have happened since then. This bloody war is one of them. Dennis is five now and has seen six months of peace. He cannot be fully conscious of the fact that we are at war, yet he will know in his subconscious mind that things are not as they should be. Child psychology is a very complex subject. Their minds are so simple, yet so hard to understand. I should say that Dennis' five years have been happy ones.

After dinner we set out on the first half of our return journey. We made good time and harboured just north of Sedgefield for the night. As there was no room by the side of the tank, we made our bed by the side of a nearby haystack.

Saturday 26th February
We were up at 6.00am. Cooked the inevitable bully beef in the dark. Move off at 7:40am. Near Newcastle we ran into a terrific snow blizzard. I closed the turret flaps down and got settled under a couple of blankets. It must have been hell in front for the driver. Because of the inclement weather, we had no halts at all and arrived in Swarland at 12.00 noon. What a welcome sight it was, in spite of the thick covering of snow. Even the stone-paved, cheerless Nissen huts are heaven after sleeping out for so long. We soon got our beds made and were quite content to enjoy the simple pleasures of life: heat, food and sleep.

Sunday 27th February
Thank goodness there is no work today. We need a full day to recuperate after the scheme. Boogie's pick-up (gramophone) is now working through my wireless and is blaring away. Today is the first information we have had on the new BBC

General Forces programme. News at odd hours of the day, read at dictation speed is one of it peculiarities. Too much time seems to be taken up by messages to and from overseas. After all, these are only really of interest to the very lucky few who send or receive them. They are an excellent idea, but I don't see why an entirely new programme - the Forces Overseas programme - couldn't be created for such items and leave the Home Forces programme free for entertainment only. This could easily be done, in spite of the shortage of staff, by having more recorded programmes. After all, a record of a top-line artist would be appreciated more than the personal appearance of a second rate one.

Monday 28th February

Not a very exciting day. We receive the war news as usual. Fierce fighting is still going on in Italy. The Russian Army has advanced another two miles. More Japanese atrocities; these include the murder of doctors and patients in a hospital. More RAF raids on German industrial towns. I don't think that the raids on London will become any heavier. Jerry has too many planes occupied on the Russian Front.

Chapter 15
Tragic news from home

Tuesday 29th February

Earlier in this diary, I described my first meeting with death when a motorcyclist crashed into one of our lorries. Today I heard about another death, but this one had fifteen times the effect on me. Today, I received a letter from Dorothy informing me that the Air Ministry have reported that our dear friend, John, has been killed in action. I cannot adequately express my feelings and thoughts. They are so difficult to marshal when my mind has been so numbed by such a shock. My thoughts are so numerous, yet incoherent. I do not think I fully realise yet that it is true. Something inside of me says: 'He cannot be'. Then the stark reality sets in, bringing with it a mood of morbid depression. Life has become such an established fact that death seems impossible. This room is full of boisterous men singing, full of life, and death seems so far away. Yet I have to face the fact that I shall never see John again: that we will never be able to finish our series of nocturnal discussions at the bottom of Bunker's Hill. And how much harder it must be for Marian who has known him so much more intimately.

The suspense of his being reported 'missing' is over now, but so is the faint ray of hope that went with it. Rather than bear the suspense, one tries to find out something definite and then when one does, one would rather have had the suspense with its tiny glimmer of hope. It is surprising what the human mind clings onto under these circumstances. None of us really gave up hope and it will take a long time to make us give it up even now. By 'we', I mean Marian, Dorothy, their father, John's aunt and all his friends. I find that one's reaction to the death of a friend is entirely opposite to what one sees on the films or reads in cheap novels. One doesn't sit down and say: 'It had to be' or go into a fit of weeping or feel like going out and getting drunk. Instead, one has to face a stark reality that numbs the mind because of its bluntness. True, one does not feel like eating, but the worst feeling is that of utter helplessness. Everything seems so useless, pointless and without reason. One's sense of values is changed entirely. One realises the eternal truth that life is the most valuable of all worldly possessions. Money, position, career and home: nothing else matters; these things become worthless. When I first joined the Army, I thought that I couldn't bring myself to kill any Germans, but now I am convinced that I could murder every German or Jap that I can lay my hands on. Perhaps someday, I shall get a chance to even the score with Jerry. I hope so. I would like to think of some fitting words of tribute for John, but I can't. His life is the greatest tribute. *Figure 11* reproduces an extract of a letter I received from Dorothy writing of the situation at home in the wake of John's reported death.

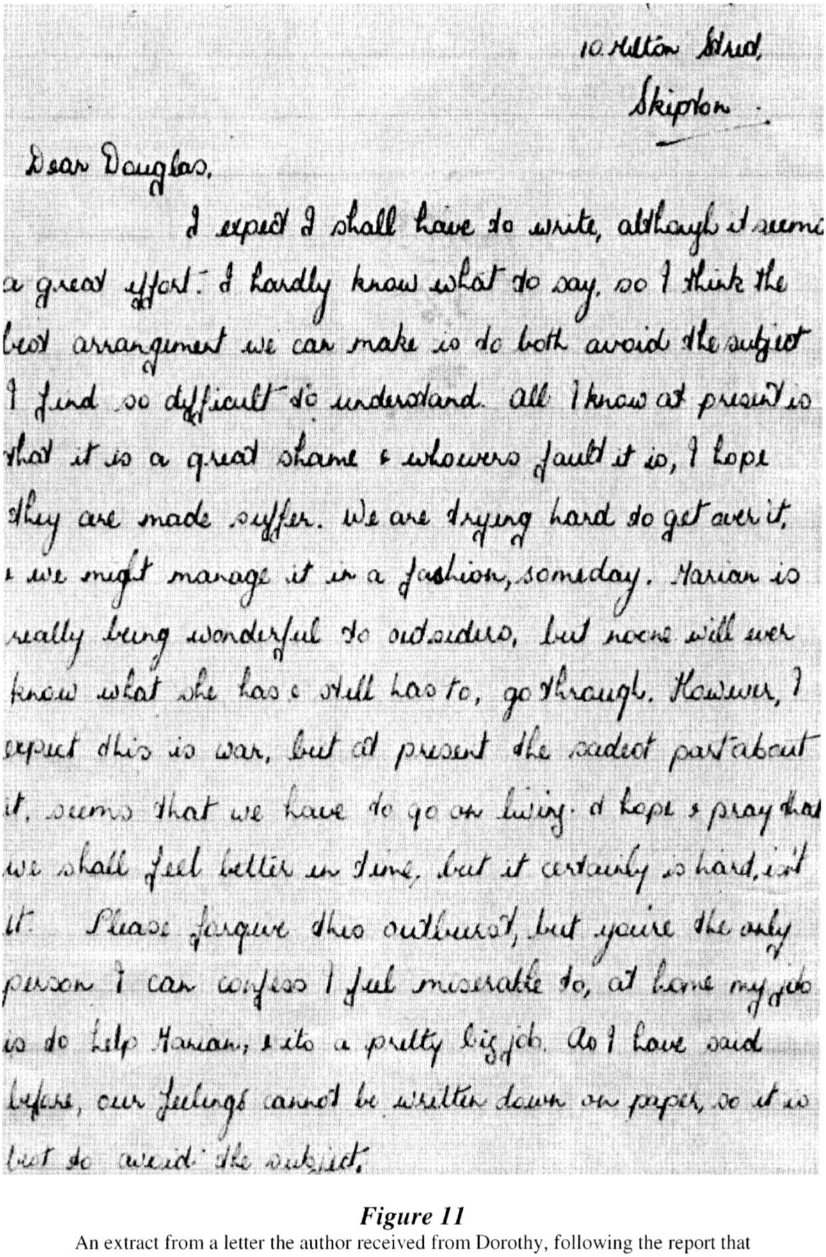

10 Hilton Street,
Skipton.

Dear Douglas,

I expect I shall have to write, although it seems a great effort. I hardly know what to say, so I think the best arrangement we can make is to both avoid the subject I find so difficult to understand. All I know at present is that it is a great shame & whoever's fault it is, I hope they are made suffer. We are trying hard to get over it, & we might manage it in a fashion, someday. Marian is really being wonderful to outsiders, but none will ever know what she has & still has to, go through. However, I expect this is war, but at present the saddest part about it, seems that we have to go on living. I hope & pray that we shall feel better in time, but it certainly is hard, isn't it. Please forgive this outburst, but you're the only person I can confess I feel miserable to, at home my job is to help Marian, & its a pretty big job. As I have said before, our feelings cannot be written down on paper, so it is best to avoid the subject.

Figure 11

An extract from a letter the author received from Dorothy, following the report that her sister Marion's 'boy-friend', John, had been killed in action.

Wednesday 1st March

I wonder how Marian is feeling today? Very bitter I suppose, although Dorothy says she is bearing up well. Most of the day was occupied by thoughts of John and I was not in the mood for taking in statistical details about the artillery methods used on the 75-mm gun. For the first time in my Army career I was issued with brand new blankets. It was not before time either, as my others were in a pretty filthy state. Before retiring, Joan Butler's humorous *Trouble Brewing* took my mind off the sad news of yesterday.

Chapter 16
An Interlude

Thursday 2nd March

There was a gale during the night and a foot of snow outside this morning. The Finns and the Russians are still negotiating peace. Tom Tongrack's wife is expecting and he has received a letter saying that she is going into hospital, so he's going on compassionate leave this weekend. There was an Army Bureau of Current Affairs (ABCA) lecture by Captain Heathcote.

Friday 3rd March

It isn't very often that one gets a chance of a trip home in a car from the camp right to one's front door, especially with a Sergeant Major chasing you to ask if you want to go. It's the sort of thing one dreams about, yet it happened to me today. Bill Kavanagh was taking a utility van to Skipton and returning on a Light Aid Detachment (LAD) van tomorrow afternoon. I naturally jumped at the opportunity and got ready, but I was doomed to be disappointed. There seems to be some gremlins at work trying to stop me from getting home on a short pass.[1] At noon today I was told to pack all my kit and stand by, under an hour's notice, to move because I was being attached to the Royal Marines in Wiltshire for an indefinite period. It is now 10.00pm, so we will not be going tonight and no one knows what time we're going tomorrow, if at all. No one knows why we're being sent, other than to do maintenance.

Saturday 4th March

I don't know how on earth I'll get all this kit packed. My personal wireless is the biggest problem. It doesn't look as though we are going until Monday now or even later. I could have been home and back quite easily by now. But I suppose this is war. Three new members to the troop arrived today: Weaver and Whithorn from the 52nd Training Regiment at Bovington and Everest from the 7th Hussars. The latter Regiment has recently returned from North Africa. I shall have more to say about the new arrivals later when I get to know them. First impression is that they are quite decent fellows. It was revealed today that the famous quads born a few days ago to the daughter of a miner, with all England acclaiming them, as a diversion from the usual war news, are illegitimate. Their father is a US staff sergeant and is waiting for a divorce from his wife, so that he can marry the mother of the quads, or now, triplets since one died yesterday. If the Press had known this, they would not have splattered it all over their front pages.

John Sutcliffe, Boogie Watson, Ken Slack and I missed the 2.00pm passion truck, so we hitchhiked to Ashington. We were very lucky and got a lift in a

---

1. A short pass was the clearance required for a short period of leave.

Service Corps wagon all the way. To see the queues at confectioners and cafes, one would really think that Britons were starving. We queued for half an hour at the Co-op café only to find that there was no food left, so we had to be content with the YMCA and cheese sandwiches. After seeing the first house of the pictures: Betty Grable in 'Sweet Rosie O'Grady', we dashed along to the second house of another cinema to see Lawrence Olivier and Penelope Ward in 'Demi Paradise'. This was really an excellent film about a Russian's perception of the English people. British films are certainly looking up.

Sunday 5th March

It was a very unusual Sunday in that we had the entire day free. I occupied the time writing letters and reading *Costs and Cost Accounts*. However, at 7.00pm, we ran short of coke for the stove and it went out. In a fit of crazy boredom I suggested to Boogie that we went out for a run. Strange to say, he took me seriously and we donned gym pants and running pumps and strode out into the cold, still evening air. The brisk three-mile run was very enjoyable although everyone who saw us thought we had fallen off our perch.

Monday 6th March

Firing the Sten gun on the range this morning, Trooper Scriven had a double feed and an explosion in the chamber. This forced the brass case of the second bullet into the third finger of his left hand.[1] At first we thought it had severed the bone, but it turned out to be only a very minor flesh wound. This was the only exciting incident of the day.

Tuesday 7th March

Cookhouse fatigues. Parliament is still bickering about the proposed rise in Service pay. It looks as though we will not get a rise in basic pay, but dependants-allowances will be increased.

Wednesday 8th March

A dismounted scheme (exercise on foot) this morning under Corporal Hancock turned out to be merely a stroll along the riverside and back. On this walk, I saw my first squirrel at close quarters. In the afternoon the Army taught me yet another trade – distempering. I slapped away to my heart's content and distempered the floor in the process. It didn't look much better when we had finished, but it passed the time. The evening was so clear and warm that it seemed a shame to waste it round the barrack room stove. Consequently I gathered two volunteers, Frank Jackson and Ken Slack, and we set out in PT shorts to run to Long Framlington, four and a half miles away. None of us thought we would manage it, but it proved surprisingly easy.

---

1. A double feed is a firing fault that occurs when two bullets enter the chamber simultaneously.

Thursday 9th March

This is the first really decent day since we came to Swarland. It reminds us that spring is on its way. The first spring lambs are playing poker (gambolling) in the fields. In spite of war, nature still unfolds her beauty in the usual way as though nothing had happened. The miner's strike over the Porter Wages Award has now spread to South Wales and seventy thousand miners are now on strike. *Figure 12* expresses my views on it exactly. For a solid hour and a half, we queued for the monthly exchange of kit. All I managed to exchange was a pair of gaiters and a shirt.

Whoever is to Blame—Now is Not the Time to Sit Down

Figure 12

A cartoon that is critical of the miners' strike in the context of the war effort.
(*Daily Sketch* March 9th 1944).

Friday 10th March

Since Mr Gent left the troop to join his Regiment, the 3rd Hussars, in Syria last Monday, a new lieutenant, W. R. McM.Winckley, is in temporary charge of the troop and, this morning, he took us for a cross-country run. Half way round, we stopped and did exercises, tree climbing and unarmed combat. When we returned, we were about all-in, but on the whole, it was enjoyable. In the afternoon, six men per troop were allowed to go to see training films at the Coliseum Cinema in Morpeth. There were two tank recognition films, one on

VD and a long film about the Russian campaign. I could do with training films every afternoon. The following notice met us at the door: 'Officers and NCOs use the dress circle: other ranks downstairs.' It's beyond comment.

Saturday 11th March

After a drill parade in the morning, the weekly passion truck deposited us in Ashington at 3.00pm. This time we did not intend to go without tea, so we queued up at the Co-op café at 3:30pm. Pie and chips were our reward. After queuing for an hour to see Bette Davis in 'Now Voyager', we reached the box office only to find that there were no seats or standing room left. Needless to say, we said: 'Oh dash and bother', but we managed to get into another cinema to see 'True to Life'. After which we did a hundred mph sprint or, that's what it seemed like, to the Regal Cinema at the far end of the town and saw Bob Hope in 'Let's face it'. Several milk shakes and OXOs in the snack bar finished off an enjoyable afternoon out. These weekly trips to civilization relieve the tension, yet make one long for the time when one can return to it permanently and not merely be privileged to visit it once a week. In other words, roll on civvy-street.

Sunday 12th March

A really juicy lemon: shall I eat it or send it home? I'll eat it. No, I'll send it home. But it looks good. I think I will eat it. No, it's only right that I send it home. They haven't seen a real lemon for years. Still, neither have I. Yes, I'll send it home. Too late, I've eaten it. Thus, ends the epic of the lemon. Church parade this morning only lasted three quarters of an hour. The address was very simple, yet I suppose effective. Personally, it didn't greatly inspire me, although I must admit it did perhaps give a tiny spark of reverence. Believe me, it's quite a change going from church parade into the atmosphere of the barrack room. Of the three new fellows in the troop we have found out that Kid Whithorn is eighteen, and must have a streak of insanity in the family. There must be, because I cannot think of any other reason why he would sign on for twelve years in the Army, with the last five years in the Reserves. Dave Everest is one of the few old soldiers who doesn't sling, (boast about), his service about, whilst Gordon Weaver is a reserved sort of fellow, interested in classical music. The boredom in this place gets so great that several of the fellows are in the old hall playing an advanced form of hide and seek. Time drags on. It's time we heard something about leave.

Monday 13th March

At last we have some definite news about leave. The first party is due to go on Friday March 17th and the second on April 4th. I, along with twenty-four others, go as a detachment to the Royal Marines on March 21st. This means we've 'had' leave on Friday. The present arrangements are that if we don't go on leave soon after we arrive at the Marines, the Regiment will send some men down to relieve us for ten days: the sooner the better.

Tuesday 14th March

Because of Eire's refusal to expel all Nazi agents, Britain has banned all travel to and from Ireland. This means that the Irishmen in the British Army can't go there on leave. This will be quite a hard blow to them, but it's time something was done about the Irish Nazi question. I can't see why we don't invade or forcefully take control over there. Parliament is discussing the suits that will be issued to servicemen when they are discharged. They promise us West End style and quality in seven different colours. We shall see if they keep their promise. This morning, I was troop officer-cum-troop sergeant-cum-troop corporal-cum-troop-lance-corporal-cum-troop. The rest of the Troop was on firing practice at a nearby range. On Squadron Parade, I came smartly to attention and reported the Troop: 'Present or on duty Sir'. Troop leaders were then told to carry on, so I marched myself back to the Troop hut and detailed myself off to do one or two odd jobs and have the rest of the day off.

Wednesday 15th March

I was up at 6.00am with Lance-Corporal Sutcliffe and troopers Harrat and Watson to take Albatross (tank) to Alnwick station. This tank is going into the Command Workshops at Catterick for a new engine and general reconditioning. We arrived at the station at 7:30am, much too early for the Railway Company. There were four tanks going to Command Workshops, one each from A, B and C Squadrons of the 15th /19th KRH and one from C Squadron of the Fife and Forfar Regiment. The first three tanks were loaded on easily enough with the usual red tape about the tanks being a quarter of an inch too much to the right or the left, but the C Squadron tank had to be towed on by a Royal Electrical and Mechanical Engineers (REME) Scamel[1] because it had no drive between gear box and engine. We loaded the tanks onto the train and had a well-deserved break at the YMCA, where they dished up some excellent coffee. Tonight, on guard, I rolled up with paillasse, (straw mattress), blankets and civvy pillow: a thing unheard of in guard circles, together with something even more unheard of. With the Sergeant's permission, I took my wireless as well. When the orderly officer came round we had to shout: 'Turnout the Guard', above the blare of the wireless, but he never said anything. Trooper Tate has joined the Troop.

Thursday 16th March

I woke Boogie Watson at 4:30am on second guard-relief, as he had to leave camp at 6.00am to proceed to Catterick with the other three drivers. He is in charge of the party. Sergeant's mess fatigues gave me chance to get some decent grub for a change. The Finns have refused the Russian's peace terms. Goodness knows why? This will lengthen the war by at least two months,

---

1. A 'Scamel' was a truck for transporting tanks or other heavy vehicles.

although it may not take the Russians long to break Finnish morale. It is hard to say what the final result of this clash will be.

Friday 17th March

It is not very pleasant sitting here, watching the other fellows go on leave. The thought that when they have had it we shall still have ours to come is little or no consolation. This afternoon, I watched a demonstration given by the REs. They use explosives as we use oil and even use 75-grenades for felling trees, instead of sawing them down. To remove barbed wire fences, they use a special torpedo, consisting of several 75-grenades, fused in series. These are merely placed under the barbed wire and ignited; the person doing the igniting then sprints for dear life. It is getting quite light at night now. Blackout time is 7:52pm.

Saturday 18th March

Quite a cushy day as telephone orderly. The only phone message I received ran something like this:

'Hello is that you?'

'Yes, is that you too?'

'Yes: B Squadron here. Have you a fellow called Mallineau in your Squadron? Oh, no you haven't. Goodbye'.

'Goodbye'.

Still, that is quite sensible for the Army. Catching a truck at 6.00pm, Ken and I spent a fairly enjoyable evening in Ashington.

Chapter 17
Helping the Marines to prepare for the Second Front

Sunday 19th March

Big packing gaff, ready for moving off to the Marines at 8.00am tomorrow. With all my luxuries such as civvy pillow, pullover, wireless etc., packing is quite a big job. I shall need one hand to carry my kitbag and the other for my radio, so it looks as though the only way to take my blankets will be to tie a rope round them and drag them on the floor behind me.

Heard the Valse and Entracte from Coppelia by Delibes, played by the Minneapolis Symphony Orchestra and the Entracte from Rosamunde by Shubert played by the San Francisco Symphony Orchestra. I shall try to get these two records next leave.

Monday 20th March

There was a slight drizzle as we left the guardroom at Swarland at 8.00am this morning on the four hundred and twenty-seven mile round journey to Corsham in Wiltshire. In peacetime this journey would have been a major event, but now we take it entirely as a matter of course. Our route was *via* Morpeth, Newcastle, Durham, Darlington, and then down the Great North Road, through Boroughbridge, Wetherby and Doncaster to Leicester. I must have ridden many thousand miles in the back of army lorries and this journey will add a good few more. It is quite interesting watching the scenery roll by, yet the soporific effect of the intermittent white line eternally disappearing into the distance causes one to doze occasionally. When the lorry stops the road appears to be moving forward slowly to the rear of the lorry, and stationary objects on it, appear to grow larger. This is a well-known optical illusion to back-of-lorry travellers. We stayed the night at Lutterworth Staging Camp, thirteen miles south of Leicester. Here the lorries were filled with petrol and we were given a hot meal and bed for the night. In the mess room I met Tom Mortlock, an ex-5th Troop member, now in the Service Corps. It's a small world after all.

Tuesday 21st March

We were up at 6:30am, washed and showered, had breakfast and on the road by 8:30am. Once again, the road rolls away beneath us. This time we passed through Rugby, Oxford, Banbury, had dinner in Swindon and then on through Chippenham to the marine camp. No one seems to know what we are down here for, but we might know something definite tomorrow. It is officially announced today that as from April 1st, the entire south coast and parts of the east coast are to be out of bounds for 'operational reasons'. This area extends for ten miles inland, all round the coast, and the only people allowed in are the inhabitants, MPs, soldiers on duty and civilians on compassionate grounds.

Wednesday 22nd March

Today in a secret lecture by our own officer who had received the dope directly from the Colonel of the Marines, the twenty-five members of our attachment were told the reason for our being here. The Marines have now got Centaur tanks with 95-mm howitzers. When the Second Front opens, these are to be run off the invasion barges onto the beaches, to give covering fire to the infantry. The original idea was to take the engines out of the tanks and lash the tanks on to the invasion barges, using the latter as pillboxes.[1] The engine space would be used to store more 95-mm ammunition. Monty[2] disagreed with this plan and insisted that the tanks had to be run ashore and moved forward, giving covering fire as the Infantry advances. Our job down here is to prepare the tanks for this operation and we may even be here to help load the tanks on the invasion barges. The Marines know very little about tanks and we have to teach them elementary maintenance. Of course, we don't need to teach them any tank tactics because they're only going to use the tanks as mobile guns and, therefore, they only require knowledge of artillery procedures. For a change, we're doing something that we know will be of some definite use. The lives of the marines who take the tanks over there are partly in our hands and so maintenance must be done thoroughly.

Tuesday 23rd March

We're slowly getting used to Marine terminology. The 'galley' is the cookhouse, the sick bay the 'MI Room' (Medical Inspection room). 'All hands on deck' means fall in outside and so on. A marine asked us if we were going ashore tonight and we thought to ourselves: 'ashore?' They are used to being at sea half of the time and are conversant with all the naval terms. Consequently, they say 'going ashore' as we would say 'going out'. If you go down to the village, you have 'gone ashore'. You are not reported 'absent' but 'adrift'. If you stay in camp at night, you are 'on board'. The only thing that surprised us was that they don't answer: 'Aye, Aye'.

We are billeted in a hostel that was originally built for munition workers employed at the large underground factory here. The rooms are steam heated, have two windows and electric light with real bed switches: besides which there are real washbasins, real baths and real hot water. These are great

1. A pillbox is a small round concrete emplacement. It can be used as a protected outlook post. It can also house a weapon.
2. 'Monty' was the affectionate abbreviation for Field Marshall Montgomery, the Commander-in-Chief of British Forces.

luxuries for the serving soldier. Wiltshire is noticeably warmer than Northumberland and it needs to be. Today we got to work removing fittings from the tanks to make more room for 95-mm ammunition. Later in the day I went out to the ranges to show some marines how to do last minute maintenance. This turned out to be a bit of a farce, but on the return journey, we were watching the people we passed and my thoughts turned to a soliloquy on faces. It seems to me that although one's face portrays one's character; more important still is how one's character forms one's face. No matter how handsome a hard-hearted girl tries to make herself, she will still have that thin, hard set mouth and so on. Thus, my theory is that while faces cannot be regarded as an absolute guide to character, in most cases, they can.

Friday 24th March

The newspapers have quite a bit of news this morning. There has been another large-scale raid on Berlin in which many thousands of tons of bombs, including the new twelve thousand-pounders were dropped. Simultaneously, there was an attack on London, but only on one tenth of the scale of the attack we inflicted on them. Germany has taken over complete control of Rumania and its Prime Minister, Antonescu, has been summoned to Hitler for a private conference. The Russians have crossed the old Polish frontier and the Japs are reported to be six miles inside India. In Italy, the struggle for Cassino still goes on. We tried to do maintenance on the tanks at the ranges this morning, but the Marines do not seem in any hurry. When we knock off for meals, they say: 'The Second Front will have to wait for an hour because we're hungry'.

Saturday 25th March

It's a gloriously fine day, even for March. This is the first touch of hot weather for several months. It warranted a visit to Bath, eight miles away. The first impression one gets of Bath is that it consists of a few houses, scattered in amongst several churches. It is not really a large place and only a city because of its cathedral. Returning to Corsham on the 10.00pm train was not a luxury journey. The platform was crowded with servicemen, mainly marines, and female munition workers. The crowd carried Brown, MacOwen and myself into a luggage van. Had there been a hole in the van, it would have been a second black hole of Calcutta. As it was, the air could be cut-up into chunks. There was a strong smell of sick and a heavy layer of smoke. Then followed a most revolting spectacle. Several marines, much the worse for drink, got together in the centre of that crowded and mixed community and sung the filthiest songs imaginable, entirely disregarding the respectable members of the opposite sex who were unavoidably jammed up against them. Goodness knows what civilization is coming to. I am extremely broad-minded and do not begrudge anyone an odd pint, but drunkenness I cannot stand. It decays the core of our civilization.

Sunday 26th March

It was a glorious and eventful day. Twenty-two of the attached personnel, including myself, left Chippenham station at 10:15am in order to bring eleven new tanks back from a Leicester factory. Arriving in Paddington Station at 12:45pm, we noticed the damage done by a bomb only a few nights ago. The railway track has already been repaired and the debris cleared away. After lunch in the Forces Canteen in the station, we were conveyed across London to Maryleborne Station in an open Service Corps wagon. An hour to spare at Maryleborne gave us the opportunity to get an eyeful of London's lovely luscious females, but I found myself more interested in going into a milk bar. It really is a marvellous day and quite hot for March. London already displays its spring clothes and I notice that most of its females are already stockingless. Not that I make a habit of noticing legs, but it passes time; quite pleasant too. London fascinates me somehow and I enjoyed the brief hour there. I have become quite a *Voyageur* recently: supper in Hawthorn on Thursday, in Corsham on Friday, tea in Bath on Saturday, lunch in London on Sunday and now supper in Lutterworth, near Leicester.

The Russian Army crossed the Rumanian frontier today. *Figure 13* provides a cartoonist's view of Hilter's advance and subsequent retreat.

Figure 13

A cartoon comparing Hitler's arrogant advance on Moscow with his ignominious retreat. (Source not known).

Parliament is still bickering about service pay and medals and promises us new houses: sometime. Churchill's speech at 9.00pm tonight was not very inspiring or solid, mainly a review of the war in general. The most hopeful factor is our air supremacy. It was such a marvellous night that I simply had to go for a walk and enjoy it. I drank in the cool soft, still, country air and let my thoughts wander at random. They wandered from the appreciation of the glorious sunset and the peace of the countryside to how I hope to plan my career after the war.

Perhaps I was a little hypersensitive, but the calm beauty of the evening, coming as it did, after many months of harsh winter, filled me with a simple ecstasy. So great was this feeling that I actually stood there in that great panorama of nature and offered up a tiny prayer. Goodness knows what came over me, but I am not ashamed to admit it. Yes, it really was a glorious day. Life certainly is worth living.

Monday 27th March
Catching the 7:40am from Lutterworth station, we arrived in Leicester somewhere around nine and made our way to the ordnance depot. There we took over eleven Sherman tanks and drove them out onto the road, awaiting the military police's permission to pass through Leicester. This permission did not come through until 4.00pm, so we spent the day basking in the sun on the grass by the side of the road. Once again we stayed the night at Lutterworth Camp, this time sleeping in the basement of a Methodist Chapel.

Tuesday 28th March
Leaving Lutterworth at 9.00am, we rumbled into Coventry about 11.00am. We had not been halted there more than five minutes when a lady brought us out two jugs of tea. That started it. We were bombarded with cups of tea; people appeared from every conceivable direction behind jugs of tea. Altogether, I had five cups of tea and one of Bovril. Then some kind old lady gave us a box of a hundred Players. It gave us all a good impression of Coventry people. The little we saw of Coventry was fairly battered by the air raids. We rumbled on. At one town, we were well looked after by the Yanks, who did short halt maintenance on our Shermans and offered cigarettes all round. I had a very interesting chat with one of their officers who told me that to make a long train journey in America now, one had to make a reservation several days in advance. Once again, we rumbled on and spent the night in Cirencester Staging Camp.

Wednesday 29th March
We were only supplied with two blankets and it was so cold overnight that we got up at 5.00am, lit the fire and sat round it. At 10.00am we moved off on the last stage of our journey. On the tanks were chalked such witticisms as: 'Any old iron', 'Washing done', 'HMS Never Budge', 'Wee Jock's Battle-Wagon', 'The Zombie's uncle' and, my own addition, 'Fragile, with great care'. A very good slogan in view of the present Parliamentary debate about service pay and the 'salute the soldier week' in London is: 'Don't salute us – pay us'. And, thus, we rattled into camp at 3.00pm. A hot bath got rid of the dust of one hundred and fifty miles.

Chapter 18
Still with the Marines

Thursday 30th March
It sure is time we heard something about leave. We just drift on and no one seems to worry about us.

Friday 31st March
We lost ninety-six bombers over Germany last night with Nuremburg being the main target. Approximately two hundred thousand tons of bombs were dropped. It must have been some raid. The Japs are now forty miles inside India.

Saturday 1st April
Three-pence tickets saw Jock Baillie, Bert Nowell and myself into Chippenham on the 2:37pm train. There we had tea in a TOC H[1] services canteen. We then reclined in luxurious cinema seats in the Astoria at the cost of one shilling and nine pence each. The film was 'Best Foot Forward', a musical starring Harry James and his band and it provided good entertainment.

Sunday 2nd April
Double summer time has begun and blackout time is now 8:58pm. I prefer double summer time to ordinary summer time and I hope that the practice will continue after the war. It's grandma's birthday today. I sent her a letter in lieu of a card and Dorothy is taking her a present from us both. The free afternoon was utilized in having a bath at my leisure, changing into clean serge and writing a few letters. *C'etait un bon soir* and I took full advantage of it by going for a walk through the village of Hawthorn and over the underground factory and round to Corsham. When a shift is coming off duty one sees a building that would seemingly not hold more than fifty people and out of it comes a steady stream of humanity: 'Fahsands ov em', as our London friends would say. It must be quite a strange sight to anyone who doesn't know that an underground factory is there.

Monday 3rd April
'The epic of the runaway tank' describes the only interesting incident today. The tank park is on a slope and we had been working there for half an hour before anyone noticed that there was one tank missing. The space where the tank should have been was found and behind it was a broken down fence and track marks down into a valley. Way down there, the tank reposed peacefully

---

1. TOC H is a Christian service club. It was founded in 1915 as a rest house in Belgium called Talbot House. Army lingo has translated this into Toc H.

in a shallow stream. While the driver would have left his brakes on and put the tank out of gear, in the night the hydraulic brakes must have lost pressure. The tank ran backwards down the hill, coming to rest when it struck the opposite bank of the stream. She came out under her own power. A game of chess with Jock Baillie provided the evening's entertainment.

Tuesday 4th April
Luck. Sheer luck, that's all. That the barrel of the 75-mm gun was pointing at mother earth when it went off this afternoon could have been nothing else. Everyone was working normally in the tank park when there was a terrific explosion and earth and bricks flew in all directions. Curiosity brought a crowd to the scene. Apparently, a REME gun-fitter had been testing the gun with a 'dummy' round from stores and the 'dummy' proved to be very much alive. I instructed a class of Marines on 'first and last parade maintenance'.

Wednesday 5th April
The Russians are pouring into Rumania. Charlie Chaplin has been found 'not guilty of immoral conduct' with Miss Joan Barry. Took my radio to a repair shop in Corsham. We are getting used to the life down here with the Marines. Lance-Corporal Jimmy Moorshead now shares a room with Trooper Scriven and myself and he's quite a decent sort.

Thursday 6th April
The day started badly with rumours that leave for all Services had been cancelled. This has not as yet been confirmed. The tanks have to be prepared for a very mysterious scheme that starts on Saturday. There are certain modifications that can't be done until midnight tonight for reasons of military secrecy, I suppose. Of course, there is a big tick (moan) amongst the drivers who have to take the tanks through the REME workshops after midnight because it all seems so pointless. As a wireless operator I was exempt from this and went to Corsham Cinema to see Barbara Stanwick in 'The Gay Sisters'. This is a very good film with a very unusual storyline.

Friday 7th April
Things are getting exciting here. 4th Troop is going on what is called a 'wading exercise'. It's very secret and no one knows where it is they're going. They have been issued with Mae Wests, hammocks, a new type respirator and they have to take full kit. They are even forbidden to write home. All the tanks are taking sixty-five rounds of 95-mm HE shells. It certainly looks ominous, especially as it is so secret, and we wouldn't be at all surprised if it turned out to be the real thing in the form of an attack on the Channel Islands – Jersey, Guernsey and Sark. Several of my friends are drivers on this stunt, but I remain behind with the other wireless operators.

Actually, the scheme is a mock invasion and the tanks are to go out to sea in invasion barges and then make a landing under fire further down the coast. And this is Good Friday; the day that Christ died in order to bring peace and human understanding to the world. It all seems to have been in vain. The padre conducted an open-air service this morning. The Marines stood bare headed with their rifles in their hands and when the service was over, they marched over to the tank park to beeze up their weapons of fiendish destruction; a very ironic sequence.

Saturday 8th April

On grounds of wishing to see the cup-tie between Aston Villa and Bath, we got the use of a fifteen-cwt truck and arrived in Bath about 2.00pm. It was a gloriously warm day and the ladies of Bath proudly displayed their new spring fashions. Tea in the Forum Cinema Café proved to be a very elite affair, with dainty cups and fancy cakes. Nevertheless, it was leisurely and enjoyable. We went to see 'Crazy House', a comedy film. In spite of its amusement facilities, somehow, I don't like Bath. There's something about the place that makes it seem so dead. Towns are like that. Either you like them after the first day or you don't like them at all.

Sunday 9th April

The great news of today is that the Russians have reached the Czech border. A headline announces: 'Invasion waiting for the order: "Go"'. It's estimated that eight thousand tanks are ready. I wonder if our tanks are part of this eight thousand?

Monday 10th April

Easter Monday. Not that I have noticed it. In fact, I have worked harder today than is normally the case. Taking links out of a Centaur's track is not a very enjoyable way of spending Easter Monday, but I can think of worse. Last Easter Monday, I was in York Military Hospital with an abscess on my right eye and Dorothy came to see me.

Spent the evening reading the April edition of Common Wealth Review and it's converted me entirely to their party. I agree entirely with the principles as laid down. See *Figure 14*.

Capitalism can only mean bad working and living conditions, unequal chances in life and unemployment. Let's sweep it away and substitute a way of living based on Christian principles where there are no rich or poor, but everything belongs to the community. The recent miner's strike would not have occurred if the miners had jointly owned the mines and shared the profits amongst themselves. Their main grouse was that they were slaving away and the profits were going into the already rich mine owner's pockets. Yes, there is some profound sense in the Common Wealth Political Party. We must give it our wholehearted support and, thus, make for ourselves the better world that we have been content to sit down and dream about so far.

Tuesday 11th April

It was a very uninteresting day, both for war news and local events. Some murder story by a nondescript writer passed the evening.

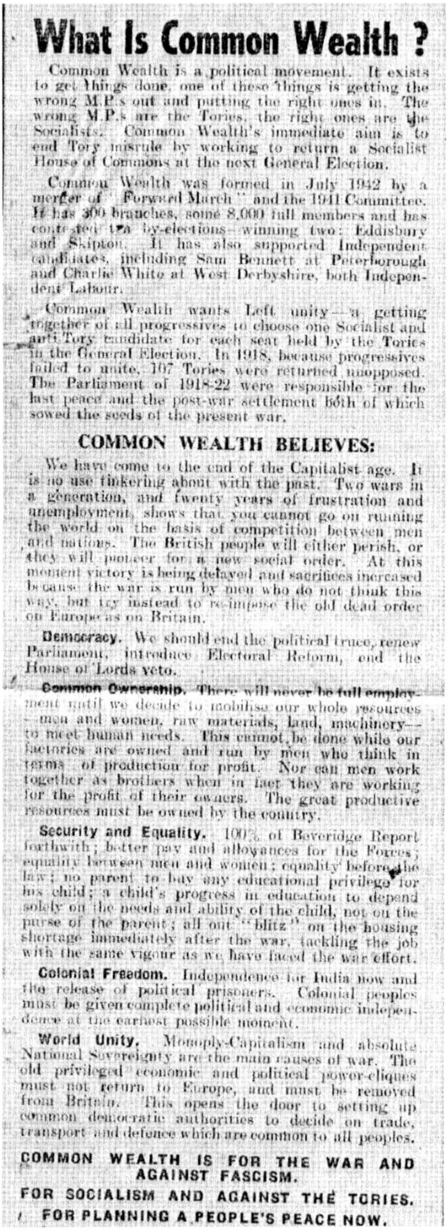

What Is Common Wealth ?

Common Wealth is a political movement. It exists to get things done, one of these things is getting the wrong M.P.s out and putting the right ones in. The wrong M.P.s are the Tories, the right ones are the Socialists. Common Wealth's immediate aim is to end Tory misrule by working to return a Socialist House of Commons at the next General Election.

Common Wealth was formed in July 1942 by a merger of "Forward March" and the 1941 Committee. It has 300 branches, some 8,000 full members and has contested ten by-elections winning two: Eddisbury and Skipton. It has also supported Independent candidates, including Sam Bennett at Peterborough and Charlie White at West Derbyshire, both Independent Labour.

Common Wealth wants Left unity—a getting together of all progressives to choose one Socialist and anti-Tory candidate for each seat held by the Tories in the General Election. In 1918, because progressives failed to unite, 107 Tories were returned unopposed. The Parliament of 1918-22 were responsible for the last peace and the post-war settlement both of which sowed the seeds of the present war.

COMMON WEALTH BELIEVES:

We have come to the end of the Capitalist age. It is no use tinkering about with the past. Two wars in a generation, and twenty years of frustration and unemployment, shows that you cannot go on running the world on the basis of competition between men and nations. The British people will either perish, or they will pioneer for a new social order. At this moment victory is being delayed and sacrifices increased because the war is run by men who do not think this way, but try instead to re-impose the old dead order on Europe as on Britain.

Democracy. We should end the political truce, renew Parliament, introduce Electoral Reform, end the House of Lords veto.

Common Ownership. There will never be full employment until we decide to mobilise our whole resources—men and women, raw materials, land, machinery—to meet human needs. This cannot be done while our factories are owned and run by men who think in terms of production for profit. Nor can men work together as brothers when in fact they are working for the profit of their owners. The great productive resources must be owned by the country.

Security and Equality. 100% of Beveridge Report forthwith; better pay and allowances for the Forces; equality between men and women; equality before the law; no parent to buy any educational privilege for his child; a child's progress in education to depend solely on the needs and ability of the child, not on the purse of the parent; all out "blitz" on the housing shortage immediately after the war, tackling the job with the same vigour as we have faced the war effort.

Colonial Freedom. Independence for India now and the release of political prisoners. Colonial peoples must be given complete political and economic independence at the earliest possible moment.

World Unity. Monoply-Capitalism and absolute National Sovereignty are the main causes of war. The old privileged economic and political power-cliques must not return to Europe, and must be removed from Britain. This opens the door to setting up common democratic authorities to decide on trade, transport and defence which are common to all peoples.

COMMON WEALTH IS FOR THE WAR AND AGAINST FASCISM.

FOR SOCIALISM AND AGAINST THE TORIES.

FOR PLANNING A PEOPLE'S PEACE NOW.

Figure 14

The principles of Common Wealth Party (*Common Wealth Review*, April 1944).

Wednesday 12th April

4th Battery is away on an invasion practice and most of 3rd Battery's tanks are on the ranges, so we had a very easy time today. I spent one of the most enjoyable evenings since I came here, at Corsham Community Centre Badminton Club. As a visitor, I was warmly welcomed and had several games. It feels great to have a game again, although I certainly need some practice. After tonight I vowed that one of the first things I would do on returning to 'civvy-street' would be to join a badminton club. I am going to need a deuce of a lot of money to do all the things I want to do. Goodness knows where it is going to come from. Met Anne, a very charming brunette in the Land Army, at the badminton club, but the attraction is purely platonic.

Thursday 13th April

Spent the morning tightening tracks. To take a link out of one of them we had to jack-up the front bogie-wheel[1] to get extra slack on the track. Saw Brian Donlevy in the film 'Gentlemen after Dark'. The London Philharmonic Orchestra is playing in Bath, but I cannot get to see them. Getting cheesed off with this 'no leave' business.

Friday 14th April

A school for the Pioneer Corps has been opened down here, the only one of its kind in the south of England. The students are tough grizzly old soldiers, most of them in their early forties and they are being taught to read and write. Yes, being taught to read and write in this year of scientific achievement - 1944. Standing outside the classroom one can hear the Army Education Corps (AEC) sergeant saying: 'PIG spells pig. Now you say it'. A grizzly old fellow stops chewing his tobacco twist and manages to spell PIG.

Last night, the RAF subjected the French and Belgium coasts to very heavy bombing. I don't think that the Second Front will be long now. Received a new pipe from Dorothy's father to replace the one that I lost in Bath last Saturday.

Saturday 15th April

Arriving at the badminton club early, Charles Edge and myself had a very exhausting game of singles. Returning to camp we were caught in a thunderstorm, but managed to dry out enough to go to the second house show at the cinema in Hawthorn. The seats are wooden ones, all on the same ground level. If I go there again tomorrow night, I will be able to finish my book entitled: 'A hundred different ways of sitting on hard cinema seats'. I would then have to compete with the fellow who walks up and down the cinema queue saying: 'Cushions for hire: sixpence per performance'.

---

1. A bogie-wheel, sometimes called an idler wheel, is at the front of the tank. It supports the track without driving it.

Sunday 16th April

Our jobs this morning were 'Inner Cleanliness' and 'Make and Mend'. I swept the room out and put one bachelor button[1] on my trousers and had the rest of the day free. Sutton Vane's *Outward Bound* proved to be a very interesting book on the age-old theme in fiction of what happens to the soul after death. He depicts the people going on a boat journey, acting normally and gradually realising that they are dead and the thought doesn't worry them. They arrive at a mysterious place, which is both heaven and hell, where life goes on more or less as normal. They don't have a fiery judgement, but their punishment is in having all their sins known in a community where honesty and decency are the only things that matter. It is not a spiritual state, but one where worldly pleasures are still available. In other words, life goes on much the same as on earth, only on a much higher moral plane. No wonder the play is such a sensation in London and almost every other country in the world. Leisurely walk finished a leisurely Sunday.

Monday 17th April

There is nothing of interest to report, except that Jock Baillie beat me at chess. The war plods on.

Tuesday 18th April

Took the afternoon off and went down to Corsham Post Office to post a parcel. Obviously, there isn't much work to do. An ENSA show in the Community Centre provided the evening's entertainment.

Wednesday 19th April

What next? Today's paper gives details of our new human torpedo. Radio-controlled torpedoes have not been very successful, so we go all naïve and try human controlled ones. It sounds ridiculously simple. Two men sit astride the torpedo and guide it to its destination. When they're sure that it will find its objective, they slide off and swim back to their ship. The amazing thing is that most of them get away with their lives.

Spent a very enjoyable evening at Corsham badminton club with Charles Edge. Within half an hour we were made members, elected to the General Committee and selected to play in a match next Wednesday.

Thursday 20th April

Received two ounces of Prince Albert, a brand of American tobacco, from Dorothy. It's jolly good stuff. War news as usual – Russians slowly advancing: fight for Cassino still goes on: Japs slowly being beaten back out of Burma. Wonder how and where Dorothy's brother, Jack, is?

---

1. A bachelor button is a button that doesn't require any sewing skills. It is attached by means of a press-stud.

Friday 21st April

Major Rankin's visit cleared up several points. He wants thirty volunteers to drive the Marine's tanks into action. They are to remain on the beaches for several days, then return to a RAC pool in this country. As a wireless operator, this doesn't affect me. The non-volunteer drivers, the gunners and wireless operators are to maintain the tanks right up to putting them on the barges. After which we return to our Regiment and go into action soon after the Second Front has got underway. There's to be no leave. At least, now we know where we stand.

Saturday 22nd April

It's four months today since I last went on leave and it looks as though it will be another four before I go again: woe is me.

Sunday 23rd April

For once I followed the principles of the Lord's Day Observance Society, my entertainment being a leisurely Christian bath and an innocent simple walk in the evening. Cannot deny that I enjoyed it.

Monday 24th April

Bristol was bombed last night and five enemy planes were shot down. According to the radio there was 'some damage and several casualties'. We heard the siren in the village and bombs dropping in the distance. The RAF is still systematically erasing the enemy's production centres.

Tuesday 25th April

Sir John Anderson (The Chancellor of the Exchequer) presents his annual budget. Very few taxes are raised. The tax on beer is to go up one penny a pint, but the brewers have to stand it: loud cheers in the House.

Wednesday 26th April

Charles Edge and I played for Corsham v Hawthorn at badminton. The result is a draw. Literally, we had a smashing time. After a prolonged Parliamentary debate, the increases in Service pay were announced today. The terrific sum of three-pence a day extra is to be given to non-tradesmen only, while marriage allowances are to go up by absolutely nil. And it has taken the Government almost two months to take this drastic step.

Thursday 27th April

3rd Battery is going to the south coast on a mock invasion, at least we hope it's a mock one. We followed them down in the fitter's truck, repairing the tanks as they fell out. ur route was *via* Devises, Salisbury and Ramsey to Southampton. e spent the night sleeping under the stars, just outside the banned area.

Friday 28th April
It's Sylvia's birthday. She is three today. We really thought that we had had it when the barbed wire barriers of the banned area closed behind us. 'Abandon hope all ye who enter here' seems to be the motto in this area. Anyone who says that there isn't going to be an invasion to open the Second Front ought to take a peep at the concentration area. Tanks of all descriptions, lorries, Bren carriers,[1] amphibious vehicles, troop transporters are all crammed together; in their thousands. The troops are all under canvas in the woods, just waiting. Our tanks are going on a scheme on invasion barges from Southampton and are to return there in about a week's time. I don't think that the first landings will be as big a massacre as is generally anticipated because the Navy and RAF will flatten the coast before anyone goes in. It was with relief that we left the banned area at 8.00pm and arrived, tired, but contented, in Corsham at 11.00pm.

Saturday 29th April
Colonel Knox, US Navy-Secretary, has died. Had a quiet evening at pictures with Jock Baillie.

Sunday 30th April
It was a gloriously hot day so I spent it accordingly.

Monday 1st May
The war drags on, with the Russians capturing the Ploesti oilfields in Rumania. The Italian Front remains in a state of checkmate, while heavy raids by the RAF and the USAAF continue to flatten German industrial towns. Two thousand planes were estimated to have taken part in last night's attacks on various nerve centres. On the Home Front, beer is to be stronger.

Tuesday 2nd May
I spent most of the day trouser pressing; it's a very fiddling, boring job in civvy-street, but one of the pleasures of Army life.

Wednesday 3rd May
The Germans are still making wild guesses as to when the invasion of Europe will start. They seem to be expecting it any minute and their guess is as good, if not better, than mine. It's estimated that the Germans have one hundred divisions and two million men in readiness on the Western Front. Even so, I don't think that the Second Front will be half as difficult to open as is generally imagined as we have several natural advantages. The first is that, being the attacking force, we can choose our time and place and we have quite an extensive front over which to make that choice. The parts of the coast to be

1. Bren carriers are small track vehicles that carry a mounted Bren gun.

landed on will be so flattened by navy shelling and RAF bombing that only reserve defences will be able to be used. Once inside the occupied countries, the oppressed peoples will give us aid. I cannot see this Second Front starting for at least another month yet.

Thursday 4th May

Our government has warned Portugal to cease exporting wolfram[1] to Germany. Meat has been withdrawn from the ration-list in the USA. The only items now on ration over there are butter and cheese and a few tinned goods. Saw my first jet-propelled plane screaming across the sky at a terrific speed.

Friday 5th May

Payday. Reviewed the financial situation. It's not so good. During past fortnight, expenditure has exceeded income, and I've been drawing on the Reserve Capital Account.

Saturday 6th May

There was a special 2.00pm parade to give us our orders for moving into the concentration area tomorrow. Result: big hurried packing effort.

1. Wolfram is tungsten ore that is used in the manufacture of steel.

Chapter 19
Into the Invasion Concentration Area

Sunday 7th May

Move by road on Marine lorries into invasion concentration area on the south coast. As far as I can gather, the camp is situated in the position shown by the cross in my sketched map. See *Figure 15*.

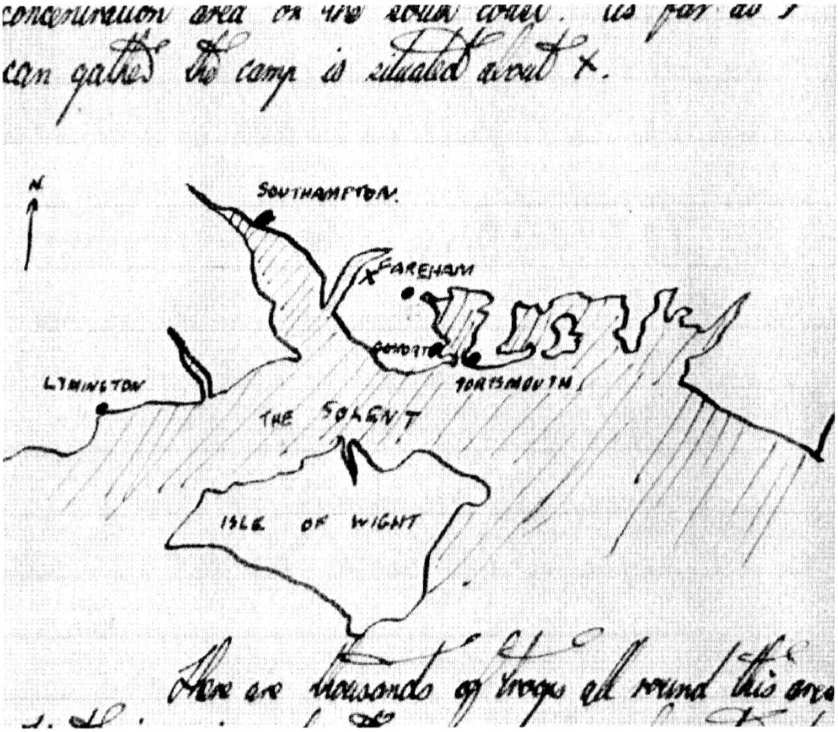

Figure 15

A sketch of part of the south coast of England drawn by the author.
The spot where he presumed the location of his of the camp is marked with a cross.

There are thousands of troops all round this area. First impression of the camp is of a conglomeration of tents, surrounded by miles and miles of barbed wire. At varying intervals around the camp, are loudspeakers that are controlled from the camp commandant's office. These are used to give out orders and to call people to the office. It's quite a good idea really. The great factor down here is obviously going to be the weather. One can tolerate life under canvas in warm weather. Our address is Camp A18, C/O Army Post Office, England and all mail is censored. In fact, security is a bye-word down here. The civilians peep pityingly through the barbed wire at us. It only needs the loudspeakers barking: 'Achtung!' every two or three minutes and we could call it Stalag XV.[1]

Monday 8th May

Awoke quite refreshed, after my first night for some time under canvas. Two alerts sounded during the night. Work begins in earnest, repairing damage done to tanks on the last invasion scheme. The grub here is excellent, far superior to Marines' cooking. The authorities certainly do not intend to have any weakening of morale, as there is entertainment of various sorts every evening. Psychological warfare is coming into it's own now. A REME major in Italy has captured one of the enemy's latest radio-controlled tanks. It has a crew of one. The driver gets it as near it's objective as possible, then dismounts and steers it the rest of the way by radio. When it reaches its objective, its cargo of explosives, fitted with a time fuse, is released by means of a radio signal, then, the tank is steered back to the driver.

Tuesday 9th May

The Rev H.G. Green, Vicar of St Nicholas Church, Ipswich is causing a stir by confirming the authenticity of a vision of the crucifixion that was claimed to have been seen in the sky during a recent air raid. See *Figure 16* for a newspaper account of these events.

1. Stalag is a German term for a prisoner-of-war camp. The camps were assigned numbers.

Crucifixion vision seen in raid was real, says vicar

From Our Own Correspondent

IPSWICH, Sunday.

THE REV. H. G. GREEN, vicar of St. Nicholas Church, Ipswich, announced at the evensong service tonight to a record congregation that after making his own inquiries he had completely satisfied himself of the authenticity of a vision of the crucifixion seen in the sky recently while an air-raid Alert was in progress.

The vicar, who said the spectacle had been witnessed by hundreds of people, interpreted it as a good omen for Britain.

"If only a dozen people had seen it instead of hundreds," he said, "I should still say it was God's call to this nation.

"I was brought into the matter by a sheer coincidence and I did not know what I was letting myself in for. My telephone has been ringing constantly ever since. People have called on me and bundles of letters have been thrust through my letter-box by every post."

Ships sunk on enemy "doorstep"

By the Naval Correspondent

THE daring adventures of a British submarine, which crept through mine-

Figure 16

A newspaper story that focused on a vicar's support for the claim that a vision of the crucifixion had been seen in the sky during an air-raid alert. (Source not known).

Wednesday 10th May

We had a strange night out. We were given an extended twenty-four hour pass from 5.00pm today to 11:59pm tomorrow. Jock Baillie and I hitchhiked to Fareham. We had a look round and decided to go on to Portsmouth for the night. Arriving there about 7.00pm, we dashed all over the place, looking for somewhere to sleep, but without success. We finally had a look round the town, had supper in the Royal Sailors Rest canteen and then returned to camp.

Pompey, as Portsmouth is nicknamed, is the most battered town I have yet seen. Almost every third house or shop has been damaged in some way or another by the raids. Yet the cinemas remain intact. However, most of them close about 9.00pm. Marines and sailors litter the place.

Thursday 11th May
It's Shirley Campbell and Bill Kavanagh's wedding today. Since I'm still on a twenty-four hour pass, I re-visited Portsmouth with Jock. Saw the films 'Madame Curie' and 'Gung Ho'.

Friday 12th May
The unknown day of the invasion is to be known as 'D-day'. Given the secrecy surrounding it, I'm surprised that all the papers are full of it. They also report how Allied HQ men, known as the G5 Army, plan to control beaten Germany. Everything seems fine, except for the minor point that we have to beat them first.

Saturday 13th May
It's the fourth birthday of the Home Guard, formerly the Local Defence Volunteers. They celebrate the occasion by doing main guard at Buckingham Palace.

Sunday 14th May
Four more fellows are now packed into our tent, making ten in all. Our beds, which are blankets wrapped round a straw mattress, are side by side, touching one another and there is no floor space at all to stand on. A sprinkling of tomato sauce or olive oil would complete the picture. It is a case of numbering off and odd numbers breathing in, while the even one's breathe out.

Monday 15th May
There was an excellent firework display last night. We were woken at about 2.00am by an air-raid siren. An air-raid alert is commonplace now in the fifth year of war, so we turn over and go back to sleep, but not for long. With a crash and a 'whoof', the barrage started. It was impossible to sleep through it. Flares came down as tracers went up. The rocket guns[1] with their unmistakable 'whoof' joined in with the Beaufors guns.[2] Altogether, the sky was a galaxy of flares, tracers, rockets and searchlights. The 8.00am news announced that fourteen enemy planes had been shot down in Southern England. The rest of the day was uneventful in comparison.

---

1. As the name implies a rocket gun launches a rocket that has its own propulsion as opposed to a shell that has to be fired.
2. A Beaufor gun is an anti-aircraft gun.

Tuesday 16th May

If last night's raid was enjoyable as a firework display, the one early this morning was an unpleasant vision of stark reality. I did not hear the alert, but was wakened at 1.00am by a terrifying crescendo of gunfire. When things got hot, we were ordered over the loudspeakers to take cover. But as we had no slit trench behind our tent and it was too cold to get out of bed, we merely donned our steel helmets and curled up in bed. There were guns to the left of us, guns to the right of us, guns behind us and guns in front of us. In fact, there were a lot of guns. As we lay there in bed, if you can call four blankets wrapped round a straw mattress a bed, our minds were not at all eased by contemplating Newton's theory that what goes up must come down. In other words, shrapnel was our main enemy and our hearts chilled as we heard it whistling down, unpleasantly close. We cracked jokes to pass the time and, as soon as the all clear blew, we dropped off to sleep. In the event, shrapnel hit no one; nor were any bombs dropped on the camp. The only war news of the day comes from Italy. The Allied armies have smashed through the Gustav Line,[1] except for its northern anchorage at Cassino, which they didn't attempt to attack.

Wednesday 17th May

Started waterproofing the tanks, both the Centaurs and Shermans. All bolts, joints and weldings have to be sealed with Bostik AA: a black paste that can be applied either with a brush or from a tube. The Shermans have to have exhaust extensions, which are blown off with Cordtex[2] after use. Every tiny hole has to be sealed.

Thursday 18th May

More waterproofing. We had come to regard our attachment to the Marines as permanent, so no-one would believe Arthur Galsworthy when he told us that we all had to pack ready to return to Corsham tomorrow, that is with the exception of troopers Scriven and Perkins. When this was found to be true, there was naturally great jubilation. Apparently, the reason for this sudden departure is because the camp is being sealed and only operational crews will remain there.

---

1. The Gustav Line was the main line of German fortification that ran across Italy from just north of the mouth of the Garigliano River in the west, through the Apennine Mountains to the mouth of the Sangro River in the east. It was centered on the monastery of Monte Cassino.
2. Cordtex is a type of detonating cord generally used in mining. It is comprised of an explosive core of pentaerythritol tetranitrate inside a plastic coating.

Chapter 20
Return to Corsham

Friday 19th May
We left Camp A18 in a three-ton lorry at 10:30am and arrived in Corsham 2:15pm. This adds another hundred miles to my travelling mileage in the back of army lorries.

Saturday 20th May
Our armies in Italy are now approaching the Hitler Line[1] and tanks have broken through in one or two places. Played badminton.

Sunday 21st May
An informal photograph of Chief Air Marshall Sir Arthur Harris fills the front page of today's *Sunday Graphic*. Therefore, one can easily guess how little war news there is. There is very little mentioned of the Russian Front these days, so things cannot be going so well. Jock went as a driver to 5th Independent Battery near Southampton. Went out for tea in Corsham.

Monday 22nd May
Roll on leave.

Tuesday 23rd May
Spent the morning practising for my post-war job at Dartmoor by carrying rocks. Kesselring[2] has flung in all his mobile reserves against the Allied advances in Italy. We are now approximately sixty-six miles from Rome. Dortmund and Brunswick were heavily bombed last night. Two thousand planes were out and we lost thirty-five. More travelling restrictions have been brought into force.

Wednesday 24th May
Empire Day. We observed it by having a very peaceful day in barracks. Goodness knows why we have been brought back to Corsham. The Sergeant Major always has to rack his brains to find something for us to do and quite often he fails.

Thursday 25th May
This easy life is making us terribly lazy. One feels put out for the rest of the day if one doesn't get an odd two hours sleep in the afternoon. Roll on the

---

1. The Hitler Line was another name for the Gustav Line.
2. Kesselring was the German general in command of all German forces in Italy.

Second Front. Let's get into France. After all, we joined the Army to fight and this period of inactivity is getting boring.

Friday 26th May
The Allied armies in Italy have linked up with the Anzio beachhead and we are now only twenty-five miles from Rome at the nearest point. Saw the dentist and had one tooth filled: agony to stop the agony. Parliament seems to be occupied with plans for post-war employment for us all.

Saturday 27th May
It's Whit Saturday and a heat wave is beginning. There was quite a crowd at badminton.

Sunday 28th May
Whit Sunday. It's a very hot day. Went for a walk up the North Walk in Corsham.

Monday 29th May
Whit Monday. It's an even hotter day. The papers announce a heat wave in this area. It's 84-degrees in the shade. They're telling us! Allied armies are reported to be sixteen miles from Rome.

Tuesday 30th May
It was a very strenuous day. We have to move from Site 8 to Site 1 tomorrow because a section of Women's Auxiliary Air Force (WAAF) is taking over Site 8. There are literally tons and tons of ammunition to be moved and it seems to be packed in the most awkwardly shaped boxes. We didn't finish until 7.00pm and, by then, our hands were cut and sore. Spent a quiet evening at the YMCA with Bill MacOwen.

Wednesday 31st May
Up at the crack of dawn to move camp. It was one long day of throwing things onto wagons. Goodness knows why the Marines have to transport all this kit about. The new site is very much nearer Hawthorn Cinema and the canteen, but it's a good half an hour's walk to Corsham Badminton Club. I should have been on fire picket, but I managed to sneak off to badminton.

Thursday 1st June
The 5th Army is now only fifteen miles from Rome as shown in the map in *Figure 17*. They are, however, meeting stiff resistance in that area. Nevertheless, I think we shall be in Rome in another fortnight. Russian news is pushed into a corner column now.

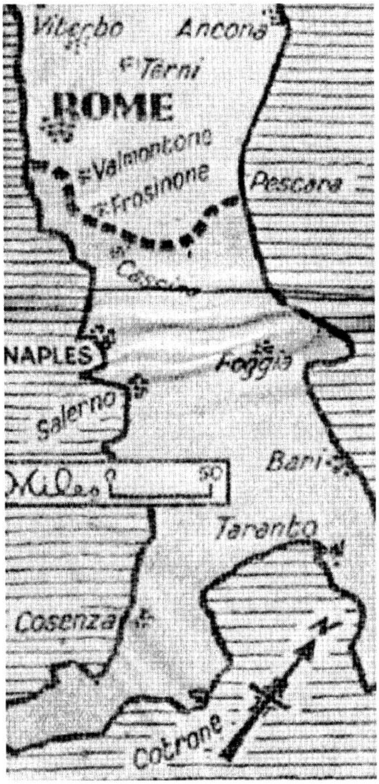

Friday 2nd June
Badmington match: Corsham versus Site 10[1] (away).
Result: Charles and I versus 1st Men's couple LOST 21-15
Charles and I versus 2nd Men's couple WON 21-12
Miss V Crane and I versus 1st Mixed couple LOST 21-15
Excellent supper, provided free, *gratis* and for *nix*.

Saturday 3rd June
Corsham's 'Salute the soldier week' opened, with a ceremonial parade of all the services. ield Marshall Sir Phillip Chetwoode, now Colonel-in-Chief of our Regiment, took the salute.

Figure 17
A map of the southern part of Italy indicating the territory presently under Allied control. (Source not known).

Sunday 4th June
We're only twelve miles away from Rome now. The eyes of the world are focused on Italy. Our armies have pledged safety to the Roman civilians. The fall of Rome is expected hourly. The 'Invasion Coast' in the north of France was again bombed last night. Five thousand tons of bombs have been dropped in the area in thirty-six hours. An ammunition train collided and exploded in a Cambridgeshire market town and five hundred of the two thousand inhabitants are now homeless.

Monday 5th June
We've made it. At 10:24pm, Allied troops have reached the centre of Rome. See *Figure 18*. The newspapers use their largest type since the fall of France.

1. The author was a member of a civilian badminton club and on this occasion they were playing a team from a Forces' camp, Site 10.

BLACKOUT

Daily Herald

No. 8825 • MONDAY, JUNE 5, 1944 ONE PENNY

ks Race Up Highway Six And Storm Way To First Axis Ca

ALLIES IN ROM

ard By Yard Battle

Figure 18

One newspaper's triumphant treatment of the declaration of the fall of Rome to the Allies. (*Daily Herald* June 5th 1944).

Our troops had to fight their way yard by yard through the streets, but most of the German forces had been withdrawn. The civilians welcomed our troops with open arms. The 9.00pm news announces that the 5th Army are now north of Rome, having crossed the Tiber. Actually, the fall of Rome is not as important as may be imagined. The main thing is the destruction of Kesselring's forces. Nevertheless, the fall of Rome will have a great effect on morale. We have had quite a hard day throwing ammunition boxes about.

Chapter 21
The Second Front begins

Tuesday 6th June

It's happened. Great jubilation. The long awaited event has now materialised. Momentous news. Early this morning the Allies invaded France. All England is in a great state of excitement, as, no doubt, are America and Russia as well. Everyone you see in the street is smiling and offers a jovial: 'Good morning'. Yesterday: the fall of Rome; today the invasion. The press has never had such a scoop before. It is as though the fall of Rome took the dust off their large-type in readiness for the news of the invasion. There had been many planes over here during the night and Arthur Glasworthy said that it sounded as though the Second Front had started. I responded: 'For all we know it might have done' and switched on the radio. The first words we heard were: 'This morning, the Allied invasion for the liberation of France began'. We cheered; we jumped for joy. At last it's come.

Over four thousand ships took troops to Normandy on the north coast of France. Strong forces of paratroopers and air-borne troops were dropped round the Seine Estuary, behind enemy lines. The invasion began with a heavy air and naval bombardment of the French coast. General Eisenhower is in supreme command. Bulletins are issued hourly and the whole world listens intently to reports on our progress. It certainly is a great moment. The Prime Ministers and Kings of the occupied countries have broadcast to their countries telling their fellow-countrymen what to do. General de Gaulle[1] advises French patriots to be patient and await the order to strike. The RAF and the Navy are still bombing hell out of German shore batteries. My friends in the Marines and Jock Baillie are over there and, at the very moment I am writing this, they will be pumping shells from their tanks into the German defences. At one time, it was a toss up whether I went with them or not. Oh how I wish I were over there with you Jock. It is terrible to sit here on my bed with all that excitement going on over there. Perhaps we shall soon return to our Regiment and go into France with them. I sincerely hope so as I should not want to come out of the Army without having done anything. This afternoon we had an open-air service for the Marines who are now over there fighting. I offered up a little prayer for Jock. The King's speech at 9.00pm was very brief and said very little, beyond saying that the least we could do was to pray for our soldiers over there and for the liberation of Europe.

---

1. General Charles de Gaulle was the leader of the Free French Government-in-exile.

Wednesday 7th June
Allied troops are now ten miles inland at one point and have almost taken Caen. Landings were made on an eighty-mile front. A strong beachhead has been established and in many places the landing forces have joined-up with the paratroopers that were dropped behind the enemy lines earlier. General Eisenhower reports that everything is going really well and according to plan. There is very heavy fighting in one sector. There is not a single thing in the newspapers except war news and racing. Our forces are still streaming across the channel.

Thursday 8th June
It's the third day of the invasion. Rommel's first big counter-attack in Normandy with massed tanks has been flung back by our troops. General Eisenhower, the Allied Commander-in-Chief, has visited the beachhead. The first contingent of wounded men has already been brought back to England. Paratroopers have been dropped on Cherbourg. It has been officially announced that there are more British troops in France now than there were men in the Royal Navy at the outbreak of the war. Still, that doesn't say much. It seems to me that our greatest advantage is our air superiority. The RAF and USAAF are continually bombing vital transport centres and mercilessly pounding enemy positions and troop concentrations.

Returning from badminton at 11:30pm, we received quite a shock. There stood Bishop and Moss, two of our friends who were supposed to be in France. They had quite a story to tell. Ten miles from the French coast, the barge transporting their tanks developed a bad leak and they were ordered to abandon ship, as it was sinking. They were picked up by a tug just before it went down and being tank-men without any tanks, they were brought back to this country and sent straight here. All their kit went down with the tanks.

Friday 9th June
Enemy resistance is stiffening, but our troops are still advancing as planned. The beachhead is now thirty-five miles wide and ten miles deep. Very heavy tank versus tank battles are taking place three miles south west of Bayeux. German 'Tigers'[1] are involved. The town of Caen was almost destroyed by the big guns of the fleet. General Eisenhower is reported to have said: 'No-one, but a fool, would have attempted to invade in bad weather with a rough sea and that is why I did it'. On the home front, I saw Leary Constantine and C J Barnet[2] in a cricket match at Corsham.

---

1. The German King Tiger Tank was introduced in early 1944. It was the most powerful tank of the Second World War with a powerful 88-mm gun and front armour that was almost impenetrable.
2. Constantine and Barnet were famous cricketers of the day.

Saturday 10th June

The opening of the Second Front has pushed the news of the Italian campaign into the background, and the news that, having taken Rome, we are now over forty miles north of it has not been received with as much enthusiasm as the reports that we have advanced another two miles in France. French patriots are giving increasing aid to our troops. *Figure 19* shows the battle positions in France and Italy on June 9th.

The Beachheads Widen

CLOUD banks resting only about 100ft. above the ground almost completely blacked-out the battle areas in the daylight hours of yesterday.

In contrast with the thousands of sorties flown on previous days, only a few isolated aircraft had been reported operating up to a late hour.

This closing down of the weather meant a big break in the air support plans, but it is not thought that the fighting will be materially affected as a result of it.

Figure 19

Two maps indicating the respective positions of the Allied and German/Italian forces. The Allied forces are occupying the darker shaded areas. (Source not known).

Had the first swim of the season at Bath Swimming Pool. The water was warm from the Roman springs. Saw Betty Hutton in 'The Miracle of Morgan's Creek'. In the cinema, half-pound boxes of strawberries were auctioned in aid of the 'Salute the Soldier' week. Bath's target was nine hundred thousand pounds, but they made over a million.

Sunday 11th June

The 5th Army is now fifty-five miles north of Rome. The German 14th Army has been routed and is in retreat. Germany is now fighting on four fronts: to their east in France, to their South in Italy, to their west in Russia and in the air, where the Allied air forces continually pound battle areas and transport centres. All the beachheads in Normandy have been linked up and the front is now fifty miles wide. Things look good.

Monday 12th June

Tank-carrying gliders have been used successfully for the first time. Many of them landed in France. The tank engine is started up while the glider is still in flight and it runs straight into action, immediately the glider lands. The Russians have launched their new offensive. Heavy tank battles are still in progress between Caen and Bayeux.

We were firing Sten guns and pistols on the range this afternoon when Mr Kilpatrick dashed up to tell us that we have been recalled to the Regiment and we return by train tomorrow. This seems rather ominous. We might be mobilizing for action. None of us want to return as we have had a good time here. I've got to like Corsham and Corsham people very much indeed. I shall miss badminton terribly. Several fellows are courting quite strongly here, especially Tubby Nunns, but they've had it now. Needless to say, we took full advantage of our last night in good old Corsham.

Chapter 22
Rejoining the Regiment

Tuesday 13th June

Churchill has visited the Normandy beachhead and was on HMS Kelvin during an action. MPs are to protest about him doing this sort of thing again. He certainly is a marvel and definitely one of the greatest figures that the war has turned up. The Luftwaffe[1] has made its first appearance in strength over the Allied beachheads.

The usually friendly Corsham Station was not a very pleasing sight when we trundled our kit onto it at 7:15pm. Before we left, a Marines' major made a very complimentary speech and thanked us warmly for the excellent work we had done for them. Jolly sporting of the old boy. The journey from Corsham to Swarland was, as are all Army train journeys, organised chaos. But at least we had a seat all the time and chars and wads at various stations.

Wednesday 14th June

So it's back to the 15th/19th KRH. The card school in our compartment finished at 4.00am. We arrived in camp at 10:30am and breakfast was laid on for us. Our first inquiry was about leave. The answer was simple: we've had it. American troops have captured Montebourg, in their drive towards Cherbourg. This is only the eighth day of the invasion, yet the front is already over fifty miles wide and ten miles deep. Service personnel can now stake their claims to vote by filling in an Armed Forces Declaration Card.

Thursday 15th June

There has been steady progress on all Normandy fronts. Large forces of Lancasters bombed Le Havre, a German E-boat base, and, as a result, no E-boats[2] were seen in the channel today. Hanover had a daylight terror raid. Still agitating for and agitating about leave

Friday 16th June

American troops, on the Cherbourg peninsular, have only seven miles to go in order to cut off the Germans in the northern sector. General de Gaulle received a terrific welcome in Bayeux. For the first time, radio-piloted planes were used over this country. Fire Picket.

---

1. The Luftwaffe was the name by which the German Air-Force was known. However, the literal meaning of the term is the more generic 'air force'.
2. The term E-boat was the name the Allies gave to the German *Schnellboot* (fast craft). It was a small, fast torpedo boat.

Saturday 17th June
The King has visited the Normandy beachhead. As an anti-radio controlled, flying bomb measure, the RAF bombed their taking-off points on the French coast. Local advances have been reported all along the Normandy front. Visited Morpeth with Bill MacOwen and saw the film of Charlotte Bronte's *Jane Eyre*: an excellent film, set on the Yorkshire moors.

Sunday 18th June
American forces have reached the west coast and cut-off the German troops on the Cherbourg peninsular. French forces have landed on Elba and are re-taking the island. The Russians are hammering away at the Mannerheim Line[1] and are meeting fairly stiff Finnish resistance. I feel sorry for the Finns. They are good fighters, but they've chosen the wrong side. A very startling article by Rex North in the *Sunday Pictorial* suggests that, on the whole, the French people do not want to be liberated. He argues that the Germans have treated them fairly decently and have provided good trade for them. It's four years since the Germans took over and in that time the French have got quite used to them and some French women have married German soldiers and, therefore, resent our invasion. Under German occupation things were more or less quiet and life was normal. Now we have come to liberate them, bomb their cities, fight in their streets, commandeer their food and dislocate commerce. Nevertheless, there are still a large number of them who realise that this is the price France will have to pay for her liberation.

Monday 19th June
No startling war news. Guard. Roll on leave.

Tuesday 20th June
Had our first typhus inoculation. It had very little after-effect. All of Elba is now in French hands. The Germans that are trapped on the Cherbourg peninsular are retreating towards Cherbourg and there is only eight miles to go. Today the 8th Army entered Perigia, one hundred and twenty-nine miles north of Rome. And it is only a fortnight since Rome fell. German 'flying bombs' were over the south coast last night and damage and casualties are reported. These pilot-less planes are not radio-controlled as was originally thought, but are operated by an automatic pilot that is set before their take-off. Thus, there is no control over them once they have left the ground. They are jet propelled and have an average speed of three hundred and twenty-five mph.

---

1. The Mannerheim Line was a defensive fortification line on the Karelain Isthmus. It was built by Finland against the Soviet Union. It was named after Field Marshal C.G.E. Mannerheim.

Wednesday 21st June

It has just dawned on me that my next leave, if I manage one, will be my last before I go abroad. Today we signed a paper to say that the Regiment had mobilised and that we realised that if we absent ourselves without leave, we will face court-martial for trying to avoid the draft. My last leave was six months ago, but I suppose I shall only get embarkation leave with the rest of the Regiment. There is a rumour that we are going to relieve part of the 9th Army in Persia or Iraq, but it seems fairly obvious that we are going to France. Our Centaurs are being replaced with Shermans and our lorries are being painted green with the Allied star. I shall have to polish up my French as soon as I can get hold of some French polish. One thing is certain, if I get another leave, I'll take home all my personal belongings – wireless etc. It will be safest to take this diary home too, as it will probably only get destroyed if I take it to France or, wherever we're going, and I cannot send it through the post because it will be destroyed by the censor.

Thursday 22nd June

Squadron Quartermaster fatigues.

Chapter 23
A Secret Weapon

Friday 23rd June

This is the most sudden and secret move that I have ever known this Regiment to make. Coming off fatigues at 7:20pm, I had to pack my kit and put it on the lorry by 7:25pm. I've never bunged stuff into a kitbag so quickly before. That is perhaps with the exception of the time when I had to pack my kit to go on leave. And so we say farewell to Morpeth and Swarland Camp and, in my case, it's not with any regret.

Saturday 24th June

Reveille was at 5.00am. Conveyed to Morpeth Station by RASC lorries at 6:15am. Being a regimental move, we have a special through-train to ourselves. No one yet knows where we are heading and we eagerly follow our route down on the map. Newcastle, Darlington, York, Sheffield, Lincoln, Brandon, Norwich and finally, St Osyth, a tiny village about seven miles from Great Yarmouth on the East Coast. We arrived here at 9.00pm and dinner was served at 11.00pm. We are under canvas in a wood, as usual, miles from anywhere.

Sunday 25th June

In a security lecture this morning, we were told about the type of training we are to do here and the secrecy of it was impressed upon us. We are to be trained to use a weapon never been used before: an amphibious tank, and it is essential that this is kept secret from the enemy. The whole area round the camp and lake is bounded by barbed wire and even civilian mail is censored. Everything possible is done to prevent the enemy knowing anything about this secret weapon. At 2.00pm we went into Great Yarmouth on a passion wagon. It is a fair sized place, much bigger than I expected, and we spent a very enjoyable day there.

Monday 26th June

Cherbourg has finally fallen, after several days hard fighting. Filled in an Army Voting Form. It follows a new Parliamentary Bill that allows members of HM Forces over twenty-one years of age to vote. Swimming in the camp lake this afternoon was very enjoyable. We are settling down to provide our own amusement – swimming, cards, monopoly etc.

Tuesday 27th June

Owing to the possible danger of the amphibious tank sinking, all non-swimmers have to be taught to swim and this afternoon I went as instructor to Yarmouth. Brrrh! It was cold.

Wednesday 28th June

Our intensive secret training began with a 'pep' talk and security lecture by General Hobart. Then, each crew was handed over to an instructor. My crew consists of Corporal Dorricott, the commander, Dave Dewar, the gunner, Pete Ainsworth, driver, and Bud Marshall, the co driver, with myself as wireless operator. These amphibious tanks are weird looking affairs. They look like Heath Robinson contraptions. Nevertheless, it is a very ingenious and simple idea. A waterproof rubber-reinforced canvas screen goes all the way round the tank and is fixed to a thin steel deck on top of the hull. Before entering the water, this canvas screen is raised above the height of the turret by means of several rubber pillars. These are then inflated with air from two cylinders on the front of the tank. It is given strength by the steel struts of the canvas super-structure. The tanks used are Sherman Duplex Drive MKV. When the tank is 'swimming', the water is above the level of the top of the turret. In the water, the tank is driven by twin-propellers that are powered by the tank engine in third gear. A speed of four knots can be obtained.

Thursday 29th June

Tanks that swim and now diving apparatus. At least, this type of training is a change. Today we donned Davies submarine escape equipment and walked around the bottom of a tank, under fourteen feet of water. It is a queer sensation, until one gets used to it. One's mind acts quite logically under that depth of water. Needless to say, this escape apparatus is a safety precaution in the event of the tank sinking. One sits in the tank until it lands on the bottom of the sea, then one calmly lets one's escape apparatus carry one to the top: very sound in theory. Let's hope it works in practice.

Friday 30th June

Lo and behold: she floats. Our tank is seaworthy. We took over thirty two tons of solid steel to the lake edge, inflated the thin canvas screen and, with fingers crossed, took to the water. She chugged around the lake at a steady four knots an hour and scarcely shipped any water. It seems incredible. On landing the canvas screen drops down instantaneously and, hey-presto, there stands a huge Sherman tank. It will certainly shake Jerry when he sees it. So far it has been kept a military secret. I haven't seen a paper or heard the radio since we arrived at this camp, so I can't report on current war news.

Saturday 1st July

Work until 6.00pm, then took a truck into Yarmouth at 7.00pm. Saw the most humorous film this year: Paulette Goddard, Fred MacMurray, Charlie Ruggles and Edward Arnold in 'Standing Room Only'. Vera received a letter from Jack that had been written in September.

Sunday 2nd July
Sailing, sailing, but not home again. Not over the ocean wave either, but just round Tritton Lake. We are becoming more or less able seamen now. Had second typhoid inoculation. Our front in France is quite extensive now. *Figure 20* shows our present position. It is interesting to compare the progress made with the map of their position in France in *Figure 19.*

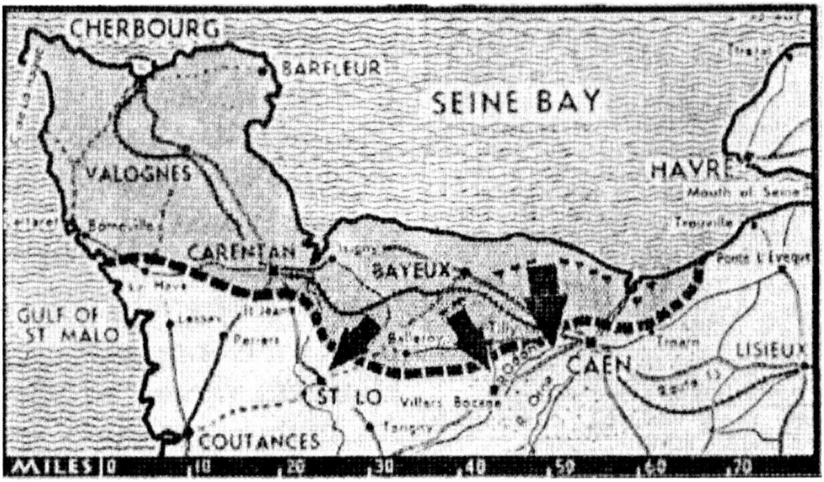

Figure 20
A map indicating the continued progress of the Allied forces in France as shown by the darker shaded area. (Source not known).

Monday 3rd July
Met Sergeant Britnell, a fellow I made friends with at the 53rd Tank Regiment. He is now an instructor on Sherman amphibious tanks. Went through amphibious tanks escape apparatus (ATEA) training**.** For this, we donned the ATEA and sat in a Valentine tank down a fourteen-foot pit. The pit was flooded very quickly and we had to don the breathing apparatus and sit in the tank until the pit was full of water. We then let the oxygen bag carry us to the top. It is a queer sensation watching the water flood the tank and rise above your head. We ought to get danger money for this.

At last I managed to get hold of a newspaper and found out that the Russians are now on the pre-1939 Russian border. *Figure 21* shows the distance that the main Allied armies are from Berlin.

Figure 21
A map showing the distance of the main Allied armies from Berlin. (Source not known).

I lay ten to one that the Russians will be in Berlin before us. However, I don't think that it will be necessary to enter Berlin to win the war. Germany will collapse when we are a few miles inside their borders. Then, of course, there will be Finland, Norway and Japan to deal with. It seems very probable that our training on amphibious tanks is for a second invasion in Holland, Belgium, Norway or Denmark. In Denmark, anti-Nazi riots have broken out and anti-

Nazi demonstrations are being held. I'm on Squadron detail tonight and we are advised to send personal kit home. It looks very much as though we are going to invade without any leave.

Tuesday 4th July

Taking the passion truck to Yarmouth enabled me to see Laird Cregar in 'The Lodger'. It's the best thriller this year so far. Murder films have to be well acted or otherwise there is a tendency to laugh at them. For instance, 'The Bride of Frankenstein' was so fantastic it was funny.

Wednesday 5th July

Training today included driving by periscope. This is used as the tank nears the shore and all the hatches have to be kept closed. There was an M.O. lecture for all operators.

Thursday 6th July

A month today since the invasion started. I wonder how many months it will be before we are in Germany and whether I shall be there.

Friday 7th July

Quite a hot day so we worked stripped to the waist. At the end of it, I was in such a hurry to dive into the lake and cool off that I forgot to remove my wristwatch. It doesn't seem to have shipped much water and goes quite well laid down, but stops if worn.

Saturday 8th July

Up at 2.00am for night manoeuvres in our amphibious tanks on the lake. It was a clear moonlight night and it proved quite enjoyable.

Sunday 9th July

The RAF almost obliterated Caen last night and British and American troops are now fighting on the outskirts. But the greatest news is from the Eastern Front. The Red Army is now several miles inside Lithuania and Poland and is driving on to East Prussia. The 'flying bomb' still occupies a lot of newspaper space. Wait till Jerry hears about our swimming tanks.

Monday 10th July

Our fresh water training is finished and today we made a seventy-odd mile road march to near Clacton-on-Sea. We are billeted in tents about two hundred yards from the sea, in an ex-holiday campsite. The chalets are used as officer quarters, stores, offices etc., and the tanks are parked almost on the beach. We visited Clacton in the evening. It sports six good cinemas, but otherwise seems fairly deserted. Caen was captured by our troops last night. The Russians are now only seventy miles from the East Prussian border, so things are looking up.

Tuesday 11th July

The secrecy of our secret weapon was further impressed on us today although being told this is getting rather tedious. There's still no hope of leave for us.

Wednesday 12th July

Our training began in earnest today with a trip out to sea in our tanks at high tide. We usually train two hours before and two hours after high tide every day, but the Regiment ensures that we have plenty to do at other times with the result that we get about an hour to ourselves before bedtime. The sea was quite calm tonight and our sailing activities were quite enjoyable. No doubt the novelty will wear off.

Thursday 13th July

A force three sea provided quite a bit of excitement today. The waves lashed over the side of our craft, subjecting them to a considerable rocking, but, even then, there was little danger of them capsizing. We had the third and last typhus inoculation.

Friday 14th July

Down to the sea in tanks at 5.00am and 5.00pm. It is getting a matter of routine now. Went to Clacton and saw the film 'Melody Inn'.

Saturday 15th July

Had the full evening off. Played Bill MacOwen at table tennis at the WVS Canteen in St Osyth, a small village two miles from the camp.

Sunday 16th July

It was gloriously hot day so we spent the afternoon and part of the evening swimming in the sea. Being a closed camp one can walk around in the semi-nude.

Monday 17th July

The Red Army is now only fifty miles from the East Prussian border and German officials and civilians are evacuating wherever they can. The capture of Grodno now opens up another road to Warsaw. Laval[1] has given the order to evacuate Paris, and one thousand, three hundred children have already left. Meanwhile, in London, children are being evacuated out of the way of flying bombs. *Figure 22* shows the official picture of the up-dated Cromwell tank.

---

1. Pierre Laval was a French politician who has collaborated with the Germans. He was executed for treason in 1945.

Figure 22

The new version of the Cromwell tank. It was the latest of the British cruiser tanks and they were being employed in Normandy. (Source not known).

Tuesday 18th July

Naval casualties have been so much lower than was anticipated that a considerable number of sailors are now being transferred to the Army. That will shake them. Yesterday, a flying bomb was turned round and sent back over Germany. The sea was too rough for night operations.

Wednesday 19th July

Early this morning several flying bombs passed over the camp. Several people who got up claim to have seen them, but I slept right through. On a night scheme, just before midnight, we observed three doodlebugs[1] flying across the bay in front of us. All one could see was their red tail-glare. A few seconds after their lights flickered out, we heard the dull thud as they exploded somewhere near Brightlingsea.

Thursday 20th July

Had an uneventful day, preparing the tanks for handing over.[2] Spent the night in Clacton.

1. A doodlebug was the name given to a small jet-propelled winged missile that carried a bomb. It was also know as a buzz bomb or flying bomb.
2. Having trained the 15th/19th KRH's on the amphibious tanks, a higher-level decision was made not to assign this weapon to the Regiment. At the time the author and his colleagues were not privy to the reasoning behind this decision. In fact, the following passage in Courage (1949) indicates that even the higher echelons of the Regiment remained in the dark. He wrote: 'About the middle of July it had become clear that, whatever the task for which we have been training, we should no now be required in earnest as a Water Assault Regiment. We never knew what the job was to have been: but the odds were on a diversionary landing in the Pas de Calais or an action as part of Operation Anvil, the landing in the South of France, which started on 15 August' (p 76).

Chapter 24
Back to the day job

Friday 21st July
The Squadron is ordered to move to firing ranges, fourteen miles north east of Ipswich. The water supply comes by lorry from a nearby village. The world was shaken today by the news of an attempt to kill Hitler. The bomb was placed in a brief case on Hitler's desk and, when it went off, a large proportion of his General Staff were seriously injured. Very little news of the affair is being allowed out of Germany, but they are already blaming the Allies for the attack. Simultaneously, with the news of this attempt on Hitler's life, comes the news of a revolt inside Germany, but facts are hard to come by and the German authorities say it was only a minor affair involving a very small group of officers.

Saturday 22nd July
Busy day on the ranges, firing 75-mm armour piercing and HE shells. The tank rumbles up to the firing point and stops. The commander snaps out: 'Action', and the operator yanks the belt through the Browning-30 machine gun and lifts a two and a half foot shell from the rack by his right hand and clamps it into the 75-mm breech. 'Both guns loaded', he yells. 'OK. Driver, advance', the commander says quietly into his microphone. The tank rumbles forward. Suddenly, a target tank starts moving at twenty mph across the range. The commander sees it and raps a terse command into the mike: 'Driver Halt. Gunner traverse right: steady on - 500 moving hornet - Fire'.[1] I'm sitting in the operators seat and see the gunner's knuckles whiten on the trigger. I press myself into the cold unfriendly steel of the turret to get as far away from the 75-mm as possible. I brace myself and tense my ears as the trigger is pressed. There is a terrific roar and it seems as if my eardrums are split. I grope blindly for another shell and ram it into the breech. Once again, there is a terrific roar of flame and the clang and stink of recoil, as the empty case is flung on the floor at my feet. And so it goes on, until firing in that confined space becomes a commonplace event. Now it's quite good fun.

Sunday 23rd July
It's seven months since I went on leave. It's getting cheesing. Dr Ley, the German Labour leader[2], says that the mine used in the attempt on Hitler's life was ordered by the Jews of Moscow and imported from England. As is shown by the map in *Figure 23*, the Russians are fighting in Lublin.

---

1. The figure '500' was a bearing and 'hornet' was code for a moving target.
2. Dr. Robert Ley was chairman of the Nazi Committee for the Protection of German Labour.

Monday 24th July
Dorothy is on holiday at Morecambe, C/O Mrs Jackson, Sunnyside Hotel, Station Road, West Bank near Lancaster. German officers have been ordered to shoot their own men if they 'do not oppose the enemy sufficiently'.

Tuesday July 25th
Visited the dentist at Woodbridge, the nearest town to here. Had three teeth filled and tea in the Methodist canteen. For the size of the town it has a lovely Methodist Church. Woodbridge is the town that has been in the press limelight recently for having patrols of civilians to keep young women off the streets at night to prevent them being picked up by the Yanks. The King is visiting troops in Italy and Churchill is in France.

Figure 23
A map indicating Russian advances on Eastern Front.
(Source not known).

Wednesday 26th July
Spent the day on the ranges acting as operator in the colonel's spectator tank. Luckily, everything went well and he seemed quite pleased. There was a discussion among the troops as to how long it will be before we get out of the Army. The following is a fair estimate agreed by us all: we allow a maximum of six months for the collapse of Germany, four months for the regrouping and reorganising of the armies for the final assault on Japan, six months to finish off the Japanese and one year maximum as an army of occupation, making an aggregate of two years, four months. Thus, I should be out of the Army by the end of November 1946. We shall see how far my estimate is out. That is, if I live to see it.

Thursday 27th July
To say the least, the Russian advances are terrific. They are now one hundred and thirty-five miles from the German frontier and three hundred and seventy-five from Berlin, having advanced two hundred and twenty-five miles in twenty-four days. Our advance in France is much slower, but we have inflicted very heavy casualties on the enemy. Two thousand tons of bombs were dropped on Stuttgart last night.

Friday 28th July
The battle-run with live ammunition today was the nearest thing to real action we have had yet. We remained closed down in our Sherman tanks for six solid hours and fired sixty-five rounds of 75-mm shells and eight boxes of Browning bullets. The turret floor was littered with empty shell cases. At one point we were almost choked by cordite fumes.

The flying bomb still commands much space in the newspapers, but compared to what we are dropping over there, it is a minor danger. Three thousand tons of bombs were dropped over Germany last night. A flying bomb weighs a thousand pounds, so to direct the same weight of explosives at us Jerry would have to send approximately seven thousand flying bombs, which is almost inconceivable.

Saturday 29th July
American forces link up at Coutances. In one re-occupied Normandy village, the Germans poured petrol over two schoolmistresses suspected of harbouring Allied airmen and burnt them to death. God help any Jerrries if I lay my hands on them. Visited Ipswich and saw the film: 'For whom the bell tolls' at the Odeon. It really is a marvellous film with perfect acting by Ingrid Bergman, Gary Cooper and Akim Tamirroff.

Sunday 30th July
Russian troops are now fighting on the outskirts of Warsaw. It will not be long now. It's mostly scandal as usual in *The News of the World.*

Monday 31st July
At long, long last, it has come. After seven long months of waiting, I am allowed to see home again. Yes, seven days of embarkation leave, starting tomorrow evening. We move to a new camp near Bury St Edmunds tomorrow and are allowed to go on leave as soon as we get organised. After careful consideration, I have decided to leave this diary in safe hands at home and to continue in another book for various reasons. This is the last chance I shall have to leave it at home for safekeeping, because this is probably my very last leave before going to France or wherever we are going. I cannot send it through the post because of censorship. If I took it into action with me and anything happened to me, this book would be destroyed and all my good work

wasted. In any case, this diary contains far too much vital information to be taken abroad, hence, my decision to leave this diary at home. If anything does happen to me, at least there'll be some tangible record left.

Led Soldiers
Part II My War

To anyone who reads this book

This is not intended to be a piece of good literature, but merely the jottings of my travels, experiences and thoughts during my service in Europe in the Second World War.

To anyone in England it may seem to be morbid, gruesome, irrelevant, hyper-sentimental or just plain tripe. But there it is. It contains just what came into my mind at the time. One must remember that most of it was written in action and, under mental strain, one writes some queer things. This also accounts for most of the atrocious writing, although the main fault, I believe, is with the writer.

If by any ridiculous chance anything should happen to me, would the finder of this book please send it to:

Miss Dorothy Mewies
10 Milton Street
Skipton
Yorkshire
England

Thanks a lot
D. Mayman
August 1st 1944

The above sounds rather melodramatic now, but there were times when things could have happened to me and I just didn't want my efforts to go to waste. D.M. (This comment was added on April 18th 1945).

Chapter 25
On the move at last

Tuesday August 1st 1944
This second diary should really start on August 1st, where the first one finished, but as I have been on embarkation leave from August 1st to 8th, my diary proper starts on August 9th. To say that I had a marvellous time on leave is inadequate. It was more than that. It was definitely the best leave I have had so far. In spite of having the previous week off, Dorothy managed a full seven days off work again. There were several high spots. We spent a very enjoyable day at Morecambe and had an excellent tea at the Wellington Hotel. Good weather favoured us all the while. We spent another day in Bradford. We had dinner with port wine at a hotel. On the last day, we had a chicken dinner at the Black Horse Hotel in Skipton. Boy! It was good.

Wednesday 9th August
In spite of newspaper tales of huge travelling queues, I had quite a good journey from Skipton to Bury St Edmonds, changing at Leeds and Doncaster. Mother, Dennis and Sylvia saw me off at the station. Return journeys are never very pleasant, and after embarkation leave is no exception. Arriving at the camp at 10.00pm, I had time to get my kit organised before crawling into hairy blankets and laughing myself to sleep.

Thursday 10th August
As a welcome back to army life, we had a very busy day and camped out for the night on the Thetford battle area. We seem to be filling in time waiting for the order to catch the boat.

Friday 11th August
US tanks are reported to be only fifty miles from Paris. Von Kluge's[1] forces are putting up a stiff resistance, but they are being forced to retreat in most sectors. All men between fifteen and sixty-five who are not engaged in absolutely essential war work in Germany have been mobilised for the army. Finished the battle run and returned to camp 9:30pm.

Saturday 12th August
A day always to be remembered and a night that still seems rather like a nightmare. At 5:30pm, as I was preparing for guard, Eric Probin dashed in with the stupendous news that the Regiment is ordered to France immediately and

---

1. Günther von Kluge was Commander-in-Chief of German forces on the Western Front

everyone has been confined to camp. The camp immediately became alive. Jeeps, tanks, half tracks[1], fifteen-cwt trucks, staff cars and 'three tonners' dash hither and thither in a wild orgy of disorder. Everyone seems to have some important job to do as soon as possible. Lorries were sent into Bury St Edmonds to collect all the fellows who had gone there for the evening off. They were rooted out of pubs, cinemas, and canteens and brought back to camp in a bewildered state and a lorry. The air is dense with excitement. We have to be prepared to move any time after 3.00am tomorrow. Spare kit of all descriptions was piled in a heap and set on fire. Blackout regulations were completely ignored in the rush to pack the kit.

Sunday 13th August
The guard turns out to be a farce. At 2.00am I knocked-off in order to pack my kit. At 3.00am we had just got into bed when we were dragged out again to exchange our revolvers for Sten guns and to be briefed. We snatched an hour's sleep between 5.00 and 6.00am. Then we were up again preparing to catch the train to our unknown destination. We actually left Bury St Edmonds in a special troop train at 8:30am. Passing through London, we saw quite a bit of the damage done recently by flying bombs. Families were sitting having dinner in their backyards by the side of their ruined houses, and they cheerfully waved to us as we passed. London certainly gave us a good send off. People all along the line ran to their windows to wave to us. They must have known that we were going to France.

No one knew our destination until we pulled into Fareham station. I never expected to see this place again. The last time I was here was when I was attached to the Marines just before D-Day. This time we went to Transit Camp A6. Within two hours of arriving, we had been issued with Mae Wests,[2] 24-hour pack rations, paper bags to be sick in on board the boat, chocolates and cigarettes and given a hot meal and sleeping accommodation. All our paper money has been changed into francs - two hundred francs to the pound - and we were paid two hundred francs. I now possess eight hundred francs in 100-franc, 50-franc and 5-franc notes and seven shillings and six pence in English silver. Today's paper has startling news from France. General Eisenhower has ordered seventy-two hours of complete secrecy for the great attempt to 'wipe out the Germans in France, once and for all'. A big offensive is about to start, and startling news is expected within the next few days. By that time, I shall be in France. The German 7th Army of three hundred and fifty thousand men faces encirclement by a large pincer movement from Caen and Le Mans. Von Kluge's forces must stand and die or retreat and risk a rout. In Italy we have taken Florence.

---

1. 'Half-tracks' are vehicles with a combination of tracks and wheels.
2. A 'Mae West' is a life-jacket that was named after the famous film star of the period because of her generous figure.

Monday 14th August
Today, we sail for France. I am on board a boat in mid-channel as I write this. It is a glorious, hot day and the sun scorches down on the large convoy under the cover of barrage balloons. Quite a large swell makes writing a little difficult. This morning we were issued with ammunition. I received one hundred and twenty rounds for my Sten gun. Immediately after dinner we were picked up in a RASC wagon and taken to Portsmouth's South Parade Pier. Here we were given a mug full of hot tea and at 4:30pm we boarded boat number UU176. I shall always remember it - 4:30pm August 14th 1944.

Each squadron was allowed one ship and we are packed in the cabins, although it is not too bad on deck. Bully beef and biscuits is our diet at present. I welcome this diversion of going to France. We were all getting cheesed-off with messing around in England. This is a bit more exciting. My address now is pure and simple - British Liberation Army (BLA). I sent a field card home today[1]. I wonder what they will say when they realise I'm in France? Although we boarded at 4:30pm, we did not actually leave harbour until after dark at 11.00pm.

Tuesday 15th August
The sea was exceedingly rough during the night and our landing craft lurched up and down giving one a sinking feeling in the pit of the stomach. More than half the fellows had bad bouts of seasickness and lay around, groaning and belching. I was lucky and didn't feel at all ill, but it was difficult to go to sleep in that confined space with fellows retching all around me. However, I managed it and dreamed about home. Most of us were glad when morning came and we were within sight of the French coast. We alighted on French soil at exactly 11:45am at Aromanches. By the roadside, a sign greeted us: 'Drivers. Remember, this is France. Drive on the Right'. We were marched four miles in the boiling heat in full battle order to Transit Camp No. 60. Gosh! It was hot. After an hour's rest there, we were taken in RASC lorries to an orchard near Bayeux. It was there that I spent my first night in France. It poured down.

Wednesday 16th August
We took over brand new Cromwell tanks and spent the day preparing them for action. These tanks mean life or death to us. They are to be our lifeguard and our home for many months to come. Consequently, we look after them as though they are human beings. Slept under the stars in the orchard again.

1. A field card was a controlled form of communication. It was a postcard that contained a series of boxes that the sender could place a tick in where appropriate. For example, a tick in one box might indicate the sender was in good health.

Thursday 17th August
Today I had my first opportunity to try out the French that I'd learned at school five years ago. Gosh! Did I really leave school that long ago? To my surprise, my inadequate French was understood. We went to the neighbouring village in search of water and had no difficulty in finding it. The people in this district are not at all badly dressed or half starved, as we were led to believe. The countryside here is a little like Norfolk, but perhaps more thickly wooded. Found a German steel helmet in a ditch.

Our Cromwell tanks are now fully prepared for action and loaded with their full complement of ammunition. So at 9.00pm we loaded them on to Canadian tank transporters and set off to find the front line.

Friday 18th August
The Germans are retreating so fast in this sector that we had difficulty finding the front line. We reached the place where the front line was when we set off and were told that it was now ten miles further on. We went there only to find that it had advanced another ten miles. We eventually reached it and took over from the Northamptonshire Yeomanry who had had so many casualties that they are being disbanded. Flers is badly battered by shells and bombs. We passed through it in the early grey light. Outside Bayeux we saw a small cemetery for British soldiers. The Regiment tried to get on to the main Paris road all afternoon, but could not because of an endless stream of traffic carrying supplies to the frontline. We were halted near a wood and, from time to time, peasants ventured out. They had taken refuge there when their homes in Flers had been shelled and they didn't know whether we were Germans or English. They shook hands with each one of us and were genuinely glad to see us. They all had various tales of woe to tell and were convinced that '*Les Boches sont des cochons*'.

Chapter 26
First engagements

Saturday 19th August

Moved at midnight to the battle area. Blackpool illuminations have nothing on the show put up by the Artillery and the RAF. We arrived two and a half miles west of Ecouché at 4.00am and slept until 5:30am with shells whining over our heads. Ecouché was taken by American troops during the morning and, as we passed through, the locals gave us all red wine. We contacted the enemy at 12:30pm. From then until 10.00pm we had several minor skirmishes. This is action for the first time. One's stomach feels empty and full alternately, especially when a shell whistles unpleasantly close. We destroyed seven ammunition lorries and killed several Germans, besides taking many prisoners. Corporal Edwards and Trooper Cornell were killed and seven others were wounded. One fellow is missing. Not a very pleasant first day in action. I wonder whose turn it will be next?

Sunday 20th August

It's been an easy day as reserve squadron to the Regiment. Spent the night just outside Argentan, which the Artillery were shelling with 25-pounders over our heads. Tuned into the 9.00pm news. It is grand to hear the homely chimes of Big Ben, but strange to hear news that we knew several hours before.

Monday 21st August

Received three letters from home. We were the first British troops to enter Argentan from the west, although the Americans had already occupied it from the south. The town is in a rather battered condition after last night's shelling. *En route* to Garcé, we saw three dead Jerries in a machine gun nest in an orchard. They had been dead a few days and had bloated faces and white hair and stank to high heaven. Took part on the attack on Garcé and took several prisoners, including two from an SS Panzer Division.[1]

Tuesday 22nd August

Sent out on a special mission carrying infantry to find an ammunition dump, probably disguised as a hospital. The infantry found the location, but the ammunition had gone. A French peasant gave us a full bottle of *vin rouge* and one of them complemented me on my French. At 7.00pm we heard of a German Panther tank that had been hiding behind enemy lines and was now playing havoc with the transport. A-Squadron was sent back at full speed to deal with it, but when we arrived there, the Americans had taken the job on.

---

1. SS Panzers were an elite (heavy tank) armoured force. They were employed as crack assault units on all the battlefronts.

The Yanks are doing some excellent work over here in France and I admire their fighting spirit. Their casualty list is much bigger than ours. One Yank told me that when they liberated one village, they were given food and while they were having it, one of the villagers sneaked off with one of their guns and returned with three prisoners.

Chapter 27
Catching our breath

Wednesday 23rd August
Forty-eight hours rest behind the lines. We certainly needed it. It's good to have a wash and shave and leisurely cooked meal. A full night's sleep is also greatly appreciated. It gives us time, to write letters. As soon as we arrived in harbour I dashed over to a nearby farm and got milk, butter and eggs. My French was adequate and the farmer's wife told me how the Germans had taken most of their food at the point of a revolver. Consequently, she was more than pleased with the tinned goods we gave her. She invited us into the house and insisted that we had some café crème and calvados. The latter was very strong wine, rather like strong whisky and, although there was very little of it, it almost blew my hat off.

We heard on the 6.00pm news that Paris has fallen. The French Underground and Resistance Movements rose up in arms and re-took the city. Rumania has signed a peace treaty with Russia, Britain and America.

Thursday 24th August
It's our second and last of day of rest. Moved at 5.00pm through L'Aigle and Bourth to the east of Bertieul where we spent the night. When in action it's a matter of sleeping and eating whenever the Boche let you and often we don't get a meal between 6:30am and 9:30pm. We are on guard every fourth night.

Friday 25th August
Moved on towards Vernon and took up a position on a hill covering the northernmost flank. Bought eggs from some French girls.

Saturday 26th August
Went out chasing Jerry, but never saw him. Returned to same harbour as last night. De Gaulle has arrived in Paris. Romania has declared war on Germany. The latter action shows the utter stupidity of war. Immediately it realises that it's fighting on the losing side, Romania has come over to us. The Russians, who have had dear friends killed by the Romanians, now have to recognise them as friends and allies.

Sunday 27th August
No action today. Had a Sunday dinner of stewed steak, diced potatoes and vegetables in mayonnaise, steamed fruit pudding, biscuits, cheese and tea; not bad for the frontline. The nearby villagers turned out in their Sunday clothes to walk round the tanks and greet us this afternoon. Had a bath in a bucket in the middle of the field.

Five Romanian divisions have handed themselves over *en bloc* to the Russians. Bucharest has been liberated. Received a letter from home written last Thursday. Moved at 7.00pm to cross the Seine. In some sectors the Germans are still fighting this side of it, but at Vernon a three mile bridgehead has been established across the river and that is where we're going. The Germans have blown the main bridge across the river, but in twenty-four hours our engineers have spanned it with two Bailey bridges. See *Figure 24* for a map of our proposed route over the Seine at Mantes.

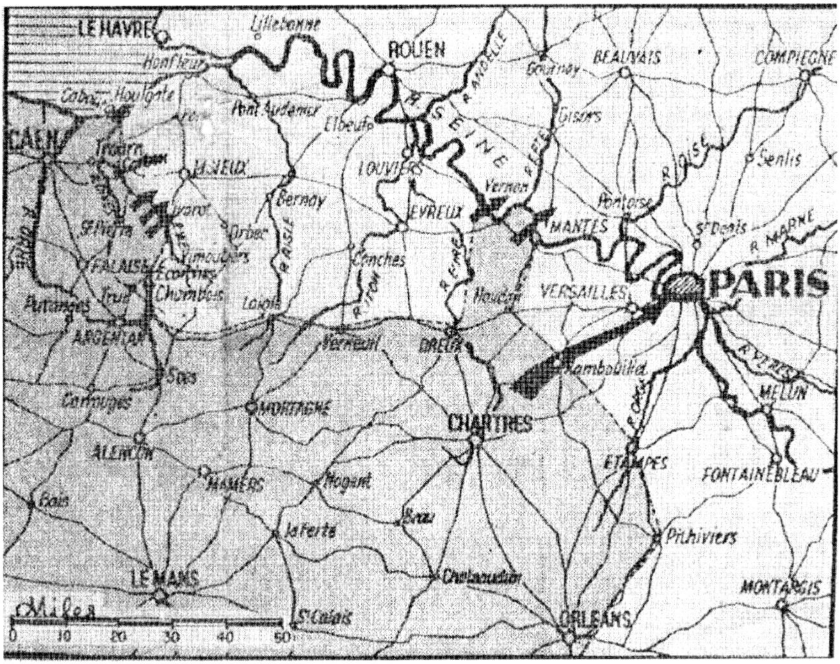

Figure 24

The proposed route by which the author's unit would cross of the River Seine at Mantes (Source not known).

Chapter 28
Crossing the Seine

Sunday 27th August (continued)

We went over in the dark, keeping one hundred and eighty yards between the tanks in order to avoid having too much weight on the bridge at once. We slept the night two hundred yards from the German positions.

Monday 28th August

It was quite a hectic day. Early in the morning we came across a German 37-mm self-propelled gun. A burst of machine gun fire made the gunners dive into their trench and as they did so, Bud Marshall, our hull gunner, splattered one of them through the chest and neck. Our first shell blew the gun clean off the vehicle and our second one set the whole lot on fire. Having thus eliminated the gun, we turned our attention to the gunners crouching in the trench, not more than fifty yards away. We lobbed two HE shells into the trench and splattered it with machine gun fire and left the mess to be cleared up by the infantry. Later on, we came across an apparently innocent cornfield, but there were German infantry in trenches behind each corn stack. We systematically fired at each corn stack and must have killed a few. We then had a good laugh. From behind corn stacks, trees etc., came hordes of Germans stumbling and crawling along, waving supposedly white flags. They were a miserable, sorry sight, yet it was funny to see them crawling along in large numbers surrendering to four tanks. We sprayed BESA machine gun fire over their heads to hurry them up. One fellow, waving a dirty white rag, thought that we hadn't seen him and were firing at him, so he took off his shirt and vest and waved them too. This is the invincible German Army, grovelling in the mud beneath our feet. There then followed an incident that I will never forget. One of our reconnaissance officers came across a group of Germans waving a white flag and, as one of them was wounded, he jumped out to give assistance. As he did so, he was mown down by machine gun fire and died a few hours later. His driver was killed outright. After that, I wanted to mow down every filthy German who waved a white flag, but we could hardly do that. The Regiment took three hundred prisoners during the day for a loss of four men. In one field the Germans had dug deep trenches and put corn stacks on top of them. They were intending lying low until after our tanks had gone, but our infantry came and sorted them out. When they realised that their position was hopeless, they couldn't get rid of their arms quickly enough to surrender. In spite of all this we slept soundly all night. See *Figure 25* for a letter that I had published in my local newspaper, the *Craven Herald*.

A CRAVEN

Cornfield Incident.

An account of a skirmish which took place on the Seine at Vernon is contained in a letter by Trooper D. Mayman, of the Hussars, and formerly of Canal Wharf, Skipton. "The day after we crossed the Seine," he writes, "we came across an apparently innocent field of corn, ready stooked, and as we found out a few minutes later, there were Germans hiding in slit trenches underneath a great many of them. They had not expected our tanks across the river, however, but our Engineers had thrown up a pontoon in record time. So we parked our tank in one corner of the field and fired on them until they were too 'bomb-happy' to fight. Then they came out into the open whining like children—incidentally, many of them weren't much more than 16—a bunch of dejected, ragged wretches." He also relates another incident which happened close by. "One of our reconnaissance officers saw a group of Germans waving a white flag. As one of them was wounded, the officer came out of cover to help him. As he did so he was shot down by machine-gun fire. We are getting 'wise' to them, now though," the writer concludes.

Figure 25

A letter from author to the *Craven Herald* on the 'cornfield incident' (circa late August, early September 1944).

Chapter 29
'Push on, Push On'

Tuesday 29th August
We had a morning's rest after yesterday's fighting. Then we continued the advance and met very little opposition. We took Etrepagny, followed by more cheering, flowers and cider. The people in the liberated villages are deliriously happy to see us. Today, groups of them ran out into the fields without coats or hats to shake hands with us. They were soaked through, yet as happy as children. Of course, they have every reason to be. For them, the war is over. They can rebuild and start their lives afresh. To us, it is just one town nearer Germany.

Wednesday 30th August
'Push on. Push on' is our colonel's favourite phrase at the moment and we do push on at over forty miles today. Our colonel is A.D. Taylor. He uses a shepherd's crook for recognition and is well respected. For photograph of Lieutenant Colonel Taylor see *Figure 26*.

Figure 26
Lieutenant Colonel A. D. Taylor DSO MC (Courage1949: p 72).

Our tank has been misfiring badly and we got the fitters to look at it today. As a result of this, we found ourselves over twenty miles behind the Squadron and had to find our own way up to them. This is a bit tricky using simple French maps, but it was made more exciting by the fact that our advance had been so rapid that small pockets of Germans were left behind to be cleaned up by the infantry and we had to be careful which villages we entered. My French was useful to enquire the way: '*Quel est le nom de cette village?*' and '*Ou est la route a...*' being favourite phrases. We eventually found the Squadron north east of Neufmarche. Our next objective was the fairly large town of Gournay to the northeast of Neufmarche. A-Squadron was sent forward to take it. Ours was the first British troop to enter the town and we went straight down the main road. The Germans had withdrawn a few hours before. We have added it to our list of victories on the tank wall. Flers, Ecouche, Argentan, Garcé, Vernon, Etrepagny, Gournay, and those are only the large towns.

But that is not all. At 9.00pm tonight, we got ready for a big midnight push to Amiens, forty miles away. The ride, in the dark, with pouring rain most of the time, was something of a nightmare. We were dead tired and hungry and only just managed to keep awake. The roads were so jammed with tanks and transport that we could only move slowly and snatched a few minutes sleep every time we halted.[1]

Thursday 31st August

The people of Amiens went to bed last night under German occupation and woke this morning to find that they had been liberated. Rather different from the last war when there was very heavy fighting here for several months. As I write this, Amiens Cathedral is approximately thousand yards to my left. We slept the night, expecting a big German counter-attack from the northeast, but it never came.[2] The map in *Figure 27* shows our advance to Amiens. *Figure 28* provides a newspaper account of our advance and helps to confirm the information contained in footnote 2.

1. While the author uses the term slowly to describe the progress being made, it was in fact much faster than is normally made under conditions of war. They covered some forty miles in twelve hours.
2. Later they were informed that it was British Intelligence that had uncovered a secret German manoeuvre. Since both sides had been fighting at the slow pace of a field at a time, the Germans decided to withdraw a considerable distance on the assumption that the Allies would continue to tackle each short distance as though the Germans were still in occupation. The German's reasoned that the Allied advance was likely to be cautious and this would give them time to dig in for a stronger defence further back. Without Intelligence's anticipation of their plan, this is actually what would have happened. Since the author and his colleagues were not privy to this intelligence information at the time, it was amazing to them that they were ordered to drive at a fast speed down the main road to Amiens.

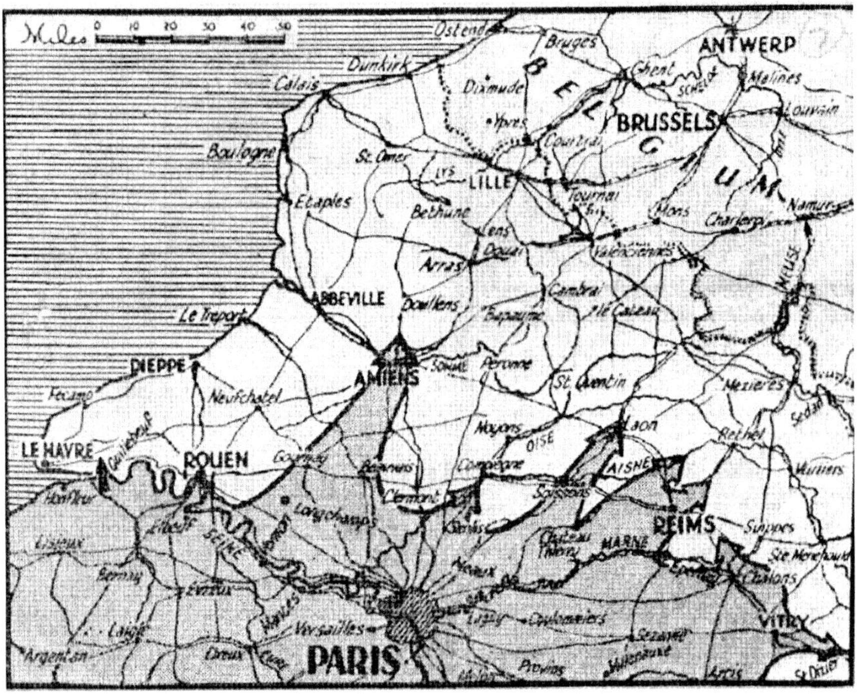

Figure 27

A map showing the Allied forces advance on Amiens (Source not known)

'T WAR' TOC

ipe Out the SS or Our (
Fight Them in 20 Years

BRUSSELS, Thursday.

GENERAL HORROCKS, who commands the British Army Corps which made the spectacular dash from e Seine to Brussels—206 miles in six days against steady pposition—to-day told the story of that historic dash.

But in his tale of victory and success he sounded this ning: "The Germans don't know what troops they ahead of us, but the S.S. are still fighting. Unless we off the S.S. it is sure our children will do it in 20 years' time."

General Horrocks pointed out that the drive to Brussels was not a push round the flanks. All the time defended villages were ahead of us.

Key-point of the advance came when the armoured columns, which had already advanced 25 miles to the Beauvais area, were ordered to push on all night for Amiens.

CLASSIC

SEE MY DIARY AUG. 30TH.

The tanks covered the additional 43 miles during the night and captured the Amiens bridges intact by the first light.

They used the same tactics as in their advances in the desert, and covered the 40 miles in the day leaving their flanks open.

Figure 28

Newspaper account of the advance on Amiens (*Daily Mail*, August 31st 1944).

Chapter 30
Out of Action

Friday 1st September

From Amiens *en route* to Arras, we came across some one hundred and fifty Germans and several guns with ammunition in horse-drawn transport in the village of Gronches-Lucheul. From the high ground to the south of the village, we were able to fire down on them and we wiped out three ammunition wagons and scattered a few infantrymen. The rest retreated into the woods and we were able to report the village clear. As soon as all the Bosch had left the village, the inhabitants ran up to us cheering and shouting. They shook hands with each and every one of us in turn and gave us flowers and fruit. *Vive La France!*

Then came the order to move into harbour. We had not gone more than five hundred yards when the tank engine overheated and caught fire.[1] The Regiment had to go on without us and we were faced with the problem of spending the long cold night alone, less than a mile from the enemy. I went out as translator to liase with the locals and found a farm quite near. The inhabitants were only too glad for us to leave the tank in the farmyard. I asked the farmer's wife if we could sleep in the barn and they insisted that we slept in a little attic in the farmhouse. When we got up there, we found that the good woman had made beds for the five of us – with real clean white sheets and an eiderdown. And this is the battle area. A full nights sleep in a civvy bed was something we had dreamed about for ages. Half an hour ago, we were fighting Jerry – now, we are in a civvy bed, and can stay there, as long we want. The REME tank recovery section is coming to collect our tank, but will not arrive until tomorrow dinnertime at the earliest. And so to bed, subject that is to taking turns keeping guard outside. We had given our map reference to the Squadron Leader, had it confirmed and believed that our tank would soon be recovered. Little did we know, the recovery team had many more tanks to recover before they got round to our one.

Saturday 2nd September

There is nothing to do but wait until REME come, so we did not get up until 9.00am. It had been pouring down all night and we thought of the rest of the Regiment being hauled out of their bivouacs at 5:30am or some other unearthly hour. They probably think that we are out in the wilds suffering countless hardships, yet here we are in comparative luxury. In the middle of the battle area, we are in better billets than we were in England. Apart from the fact that there are still a few Germans hiding in a nearby wood, everything is calm and

1. At first they thought that their tank had been hit and so they all baled out.

peaceful. Nevertheless, we sleep with our revolvers under our pillows. I have a Sten sub-machine gun and a Luger-P38 automatic pistol.[1]

The people at the farm look after us very well and have given us bread, eggs, milk and butter, so we had a collection and gave them two hundred and fifty francs. They have no means of getting any news so I listen in to the BBC and translate it for them. At 7.00pm they had visitors from the village so I got the wireless set out of the tank and tuned it into the French news for them. They were so pleased that they said that they would come again tomorrow night and listen. I don't suppose LAD will have come for us by then anyway.

Sunday 3rd September

This is the fifth anniversary of the declaration of war and the second anniversary of my joining the Army. And thus, we enter our sixth year of war. But it will not go on for long. Germany is collapsing on all fronts. In France their retreat has become a rout and the RAF is taking a heavy toll of their transport. On the Eastern Front the Russians are pushing on through Romania and Bulgaria and the 8th Army is still pushing on in Italy. The Americans have crossed the Mosselle and have taken Metz and Nancy. The Canadians are hammering away at Le Havre and eliminating the Germans who are making a stand at Alville. The British 2nd Army, to which we belong, has crossed the Belgian border and is not far from Brussels. If our tank had not broken down, we would have been with them. Germany is beginning to discover the real meaning of a *blitzkrieg* war. She is having a taste of her own medicine and doesn't like it. If Germany lasts more than three months I shall be surprised. Even if Hitler makes a stand at the Seigfried Line[2], he will not have sufficient men to man it properly. There is still no sign of LAD recovering our tank. Went for a Sunday night stroll to the village of Halloy and the villagers turned out to greet us. My French vocabulary gradually enlarges.

---

1. The author took the Luger from a dead German officer as a souvenir, but later, after consideration, he decided to dispose of it rather than bring it back into England.
2. The original Siegfried Line was a line of defensive forts and tanks built by Germany as a section of the Hindenburg Line in northern France during the First World War. The Germans built a similar defensive line during the 1930s, opposite the French Maginot Line. They call it the Westwall, but the Allies commonly referred to it as the Siegfried Line.

Chapter 31
'The Epic of Violette Brown'

Monday 4th September

Still at the farm and no sign of LAD. Today's entry could well be called 'The Epic of Violette Brown'. This afternoon, Dave Dewar, Bud Marshall and myself walked over the fields to the village of Grouches- Lucheul which we liberated on Friday. There we met a woman called Violette Brown who had lived with her aunt in Norfolk from 1932 to 1939 and who speaks good English. She insisted that we went into the house and shared the meal they were just about to have. Over the meal, I heard the truest story of life under German occupation that I am ever likely to hear. First, let me explain that this woman is 26 years of age and loves England very much. She is an ardent believer in the victory of truth over evil and one of the most sincere people that it has ever been my privilege to meet. Consequently, everything she told us can be taken to be the un-garnished truth and completely unbiased.

She had many stories to tell of the hard life under German occupation. Her father had been taken to Paris to work for the Germans and now that Paris was liberated, they expected him home any day. Her brother was taken to a concentration camp in Germany in 1941 for refusing to work for the Germans, but they had heard from him regularly every three months until recently. They were allowed four ounces of meat per week if the butcher had any in stock and often he didn't. Tinned goods were practically non-existent. There was no coal or coke, except for the Germans, and in winter they had to have wood fires and go to bed early. The price of certain foodstuffs was astronomical – pure coffee was twelve pounds for a kilo (2.2 pounds) and tea was five pounds for the same amount. If anybody refused to work long hours for little money for the Germans they were beaten until they complied.

Her experiences of the British retreat in 1940 were very vivid. On the Doulons Road, she had seen a British Tommy, realising that his situation was hopeless, put up his hands to be taken prisoner. But the Germans tied him down in his seat, poured petrol over him and the lorry and set fire to the lot. She was a Roman Catholic and swore before God that it was true. In the boiling hot summer, the British prisoners who were tired and parched with thirst were marched through the village and the Germans put buckets of water at the side of the road and kicked them over when the prisoners tried to reach them. She gave water to a wounded Tommy and the Germans thrashed her for it. Only nine months ago, five boys, aged nineteen, had found some rifles and decided to start a resistance movement of their own and they wounded one German officer. The Germans caught them and chopped their arms off, before putting them all in a shell hole and shooting them. These and many other stories of Nazi atrocities she told us, but the British are here now and the Germans will never return. I only hope that the British people and Government realise what inhuman fiends we are dealing with and take vengeance accordingly. The next time I see Germans squealing for mercy, I shall shoot first and ask questions afterwards.

Chapter 32
Our sojourn continues

Tuesday 5th September

The British 2nd Army, pushing on from Brussels, has liberated Antwerp. Montreuil, General Haigh's[1] HQ in the last war, has also been taken. Continuing their whirlwind advance, General Dempsey's[2] troops have crossed the Scheldt into Holland. In southern France the Americans have liberated Bourg, thirty-five miles northeast of Lyons. This cuts one of the enemy's main escape routes to the Belfort Gap into Germany. As far as I can gather, our Regiment will now be somewhere near Antwerp, one hundred and fifty miles from here. To catch them up we shall have to go through part of France, right across Belgium and a considerable distance into Holland.

This afternoon the five of us went to the barber in Halloy. *'Le coiffeur'* turned out to be a woman and she was no amateur. It cost us six francs each: approximately six pence. When we returned to the farm we found that three French women were waiting for us to invite us out to tea. We needed no second bidding. These three Frenchwomen of about twenty-six to thirty come from Boulogne, but were evacuated soon after the invasion. As soon as Boulogne is liberated they want to return home and they come here every night to listen to the French news on our tank radio in the hope that Boulogne has been liberated. For tea they gave us toast, cakes and tea with rum instead of milk. It certainly makes a difference. This completes our fourth day on the farm, but still no sign of being recovered. Wrote a letter to Major Pearson, our Squadron leader, telling him that we were still here and that REME had not arrived and we were getting short of rations.[3]

Wednesday 6th September

Last night, Russia declared war on Bulgaria. The Bulgarian Government went into conference overnight and this morning asked for peace terms. Certainly the shortest war on record. It is a pity that all wars cannot be settled by an overnight conference. Russia has also accepted peace terms from the Finns. Yesterday an ultimatum was delivered to the Germans in Le Havre saying that, unless they surrendered, Allied Bomber Command would be sent over. No reply was received and so last night Allied aircraft dropped four thousand tons of bombs on them. Perhaps that will teach them a lesson. German resistance in Holland is becoming a little stiffer.

---

1. Field Marshall Douglas Haigh was Britain's Commander-in-Chief during the Battle of the Somme. He took much criticism for the enormous loss of life suffered by his forces.
2. General Sir Miles Christopher Dempsey was Commander of the British 2nd Army.
3. Such letters were delivered by passing despatch riders.

A section of French Forces of the Interior (FFI) called at the farm today. They were looking for Germans in civilian clothes and also commandeering any kit the Germans had left behind, to help equip their army. They barged into the house as if they had the authority to search it and would have taken anything of military value they thought fit if we had not appeared on the scene. This FFI is a good thing in some ways, but they carry it too far and think that they have authority to do as they please. They don armbands and carry rifles and ride around all day in captured German trucks, which is all very well when Jerry is several miles away.

Thursday 7th September
Je pense que notre regiment a nous oublié. Here we are, still obeying that last order and 'hanging on' until someone recovers the tank. Still, we don't mind too much. For breakfast this morning, we had fried ham, eggs mushroom and onions with new bread, fresh butter and milk. Free French troops have liberated Chalons, seventy-five miles north of Lyons. Canadians are fighting on the outskirts of Boulogne and Calais. Le Havre and Brest were bombed last night. In Italy, the 8th Army has reached Rimini.

Friday 8th September
Today completes our week's stay on the farm, which has been almost like a week's holiday. And as yet, we haven't heard a thing from LAD. Ah well, *c'est la guerre*, I suppose. British tanks have reached the Albert Canal so we suppose that our Regiment will be part of them. German troops are being rushed from Holland to defend the Canal and have blown-up all the bridges. Our troops are meeting stiffer resistance round the channel ports. The British Government must expect the end of the war soon because they have decreed that the blackout will be partially lifted on September 17th and they have put the Home Guard on a voluntary basis once more.[1]

Saturday 9th September
Today is Saturday, but it is like any other day for us, filling in time waiting for LAD. Perhaps the Squadron Leader will send someone back today. But considering they are perhaps somewhere in Belgium, or even Holland, at least two hundred and fifty miles away, perhaps not. No perhaps about it, he hasn't. There are two incidents worthy of note in our day's adventures. The first is that we went out shooting rabbits and couldn't hit a hare at twenty-five yards range with a sub machine gun and the second was almost a catastrophe. Loading his revolver, to go out this evening, Pete Ainsworth accidentally pulled the trigger. The bullet went through Bud Marshall's tunic and grazed Dave Dewar's arm. For a minute, we thought one of them had 'had it'. There is very little war news as General

---

1. The author and his colleagues got most of their information from passing despatch riders who carried British newspapers.

Eisenhower has ordered operational secrecy on the push into Germany through Belgium and Holland.

Sunday 10th September

This morning, Bud Marshall shot a hare and the old lady cooked it for us for tea. I prefer rabbit. In the afternoon, Pete Ainsworth and I went for a walk round Lucheux and Grenches-Luchuel. We met Miss Violette Brown with her English father who had been liberated from Paris. It was a glorious day and we thoroughly enjoyed our walk. At 7.00pm we stopped a despatch rider and asked him to post our mail. When he heard of our stranded luxury, he asked if he could spend the night with us, as he had been travelling all day. We said 'yes' with pleasure, especially as he had Friday's papers with him.

Monday 11th September

In the morning, on hearing of our ration situation, the despatch rider hopped on his bike and went to a Service Corps depot at Mondicourt, three miles from here. He told them that he had been sent by an officer to get rations for eight stranded men. There were in fact only five of us. He returned with a sack full of rations, including real white bread. Once again, our food supplies are replenished. We gave our landlady some white bread and tinned goods and she was more than pleased with them. This morning, by the side of what had been a German officer's truck, that is until the RAF got hold of it, I found a Luftwaffe pay book. See *Figures 29 and 30.*

Figure 29
The pay book of a dead German Luftwaffe officer.

Figure 30

The inside pages of the dead German Luftwaffe officer's pay book.

In the afternoon, Pete Ainsworth and myself hitchhiked into Doulons, the nearest large town to here, six kilometres away. It is one of the most badly bombed towns I have seen so far because the bombing is so concentrated. There is a rail junction there and the RAF have played havoc with it several times, that is even before it was subjected to intense bombing just prior to our troops entering it on September 1st. Near the railway, where houses once stood, are huge bomb craters that could easily hold a horse and cart. The inhabitants are getting their battered homes reorganised and telephone and electricity supply lines are being repaired. Yet in amongst the rubble, clean, well dressed and smartly made-up women parade as thought they were walking down the Champs Elysee. At night, we went to a café in Mondicourt and had six glasses of cognac and calvados each. Although they are as strong as whisky, I didn't feel in the least inebriated.

Tuesday 12th September

The war rushes madly on and we still observe it from the comparative safety of the farmhouse. We are thinking about writing a book and naming it 'The Five Lost Men of the Army' or 'How five men lived for fourteen days on three days rations'. It would make a good newspaper article or BBC news item, beginning something like this: 'somewhere in the heart of France are five men. The last time they were seen was on Friday 1st September in what was then no man's land. It is known that they had, at the most, only three day's rations and they have been missing for twelve days. When last seen, they were wearing dirty khaki and needed a wash or even a bath. Anyone who has seen these unfortunate men, please communicate directly with "The Bureau of Poor Lost Soldiers", otherwise, they will be reported missing, believed killed.'

Wednesday 13th September

Today is the hundredth day after the invasion of France, and American troops are now ten miles inside Germany and the German frontier is threatened in all sectors. Le Havre has capitulated, after five thousand tons of bombs were dropped on it and it yielded eight thousand prisoners. Boulogne, Calais and Dunkirk have been threatened with the same. General Eisenhower has warned German civilians to get out into the country as the Allies advance, as we shall spare no towns or Nazi civilians who linger there. Things look very bad for Germany. Eric Probin becomes a father on December 17th and hopes to be in England by then. At one time, I would have said that he hadn't the faintest chance, but now, I am not so sure. However, it is certain that the end of the war with Germany is very near perhaps only a few weeks away.[1] What a day of celebration that will be. I shall not be in England to enjoy it, but it will be a celebration all the same. No doubt before then I shall be in action again. I shall be very annoyed if I get killed a few weeks or days before the end of the war.

Meanwhile, on the farm everything progresses smoothly and lazily. We give a hand now and again. This morning, four of us walked nine miles to an RASC dump for rations and all they would give us was ten tins of bully beef, sardines, margarine and a pound of jam. We are running short of soap, writing paper, tobacco, ink, razor blades and matches.

Thursday 14th September

The cows still moo, the hens still lay eggs, the turkeys still gobble, the horses still pull the plough, the cocks still crow, the pigs get fatter and we still wait here for LAD and do the same as the pigs. At least this rest gives me chance to catch up with my mail and I wrote to Tommy Holden, Eric Astin and Bobby Horner today. At night, all five of us went to a café in Mondicourt, where the beer is weaker than English cider and only three and half pence per pint. I think it would be impossible to get drunk on it.

---

1. On April 18th 1945 the author made the following note in the margin: 'Oh Yeah. I always said we were too optimistic those days'.

Friday 15th September
Walked over to the RASC depot and indented for seven day's rations. There is still a German loose in the woods behind the farm, but he never bothers us so we leave the FFI to deal with him. The Germans are throwing everything they have got into the battle for Germany and are using old obsolete tanks and guns. Prisoners taken near Aachen include men straight out of hospital with wounds not fully healed, lame, half-blind and deaf and men who have only been in uniform a week or a fortnight. The Hitler Youth Regiments have been brought from Holland and they jump fanatically onto tanks shouting: 'I want to die for Hitler'. And, most of them do. When I get back into the frontline, I shall try my best to grant them their wish.

Saturday 16th September
There's nothing like a nice brisk four and a half-mile walk before breakfast. This morning, Pete Ainsworth and I got up at 6.00am and walked over to the RASC depot.[1] At 8.00am we set off in a three-ton lorry to draw rations from Amiens, accompanied by a captain from the Pioneer Corps, Captain Papers of Manchester, a thoroughly decent fellow and two clerks. I was very much surprised to see that life in the city is almost back to normal again. Trains and buses are running and there are the usual queues. The shops display their various wares, policemen gesticulate wildly, the telephone service functions once more and it is hard to realise that the town was won from the Germans only a fortnight ago. The shortness of the French skirt is quite pleasing to the eye and most French women dress well. As is to be expected, certain commodities over here are cheaper and more plentiful than in England and *vice versa*. I saw large stocks of combs and fountain pens and these are scarce in England. We contacted REME workshops in Amiens and they said they would recover us and take us into their workshops in the next few days, so we shall be back in the frontline in ten days or so. Returning from Amiens, we stopped in Albert and Pete Ainsworth and I had a good look round. At first impression Albert is a very nice little town and I bought a postcard from a local shop. *See Figure 31.*

1. All the time they had been trying to expedite their return to the Regiment.

Figure 31

A postcard of Albert that features the shop with stripe blinds where the author purchased it.

Sunday 17th September

Today the three French women - Marcelle, Antoinette and Huguette - who listen to the news on our radio every night, invited all five of us out to dinner. And boy! What a dinner. There were six courses and the meal lasted for over two hours. This was our menu.

1st course: Soup.
2nd course: Sardines, bread and butter
3rd course: Sliced tomatoes, chopped onions with bread and butter
4th course: Roast rabbit and potatoes
5th course: Thin, underdone steaks
6th course: *Café noir* and cakes

With the meal, we had French beer and wine. At the café afterwards, we had cognac and *vin Mousseux*. It was a very enjoyable day. Clocks put back one hour.

Monday 18th September

Airborne troops landed in Holland near the German border and Allied forces are forty miles from Cologne. Seigfried Line has been crossed in four places. Those were the headlines in the news this morning. Now that the battle of Germany is on, the fighting is fierce because the German forces are more concentrated. But this helps the RAF and the USAAF because they have less to bomb. It must be hell for Jerry at the moment. After reporting our tank to the Amiens workshops we expected to be recovered today, but no one came. I wrote several letters and went to the café in Halloy.

Tuesday 19th September

No one seems to be worrying about our tank or us. We are forgotten men.[1] The lady at the farm seems to be getting a little anxious as to when we are going. I am sure she thinks we are staying here until the war is over. We asked her if she could put us up for one night, but that was over a fortnight ago. However, she still gives us five eggs a day and milk morning and night. We give our mail to despatch riders to post. It is three weeks since I heard from home. I hope everything is all right. Met some of the Dorset Infantry Regiment retiring from the front line to Bayeux. They say that our Regiment will have had a pretty tough time. Perhaps it is fate or, rather predestination, as I do not believe that it was fate that has held us behind the enemy lines like this. Had we been with the Regiment we may have been 'the late Tare-one-Charlie'.[2]

Wednesday 20th September

The British 2nd Army has made a lightning thrust into Holland and has taken Nimegen. But for a burnt-out engine that is where we would have been too.

Thursday 21st September

This morning, Madame Duprés told us that she had heard that Germany had asked Russia for peace so we tuned into the 1.00pm news, but it wasn't true. Calais was subjected to concentrated bombing last night and small pockets of resistance are being mopped up in Boulogne. The Germans are depending mainly on roadblocks for defences in several sectors. In Italy, the Germans are still clinging to their defended positions.

Friday 22nd September

The British Government has issued proposals for demobilization after the war with Germany. As yet they are only proposals and not law. They propose partial demobilization after the war with Germany, mainly on the basis of 'first in first out'. Releases will be awarded on a points scale and one's number of points will be determined by dividing the months of army service by two and adding it to one's age. In a month's time, I shall be twenty-one and will have been in the army for twenty-six months so my points total will be thirty-four. Eric Probin is twenty-six and has been in the Army for fifty-one months so he will have fifty-four points. On this basis, I estimate that I shall be out of the Army in a year to eighteen months, which is a helluva long time.

---

1. At this stage they are very worried about their position. Their last order from their Squadron Leader was: 'we have reported your map reference position to tank recovery. Do not leave your tank.' In spite of this, they had taken secondary action in reporting directly to a newly arrived local tank recovery unit. This is the only way they can get transport to the frontline some hundred miles away.
2. This was the code name of their tank on the day they had broken down.

Our forces are meeting stiffer resistance now that they are in Germany and we expect that when we return to the Regiment, we shall find that quite a few of our friends have been killed. We held a council of war and decided to go to the REME workshops in Amiens tomorrow to ask them to hurry up and repair our tank.

Saturday 23rd September

In accordance with our *council de guerre* of yesterday, we hitchhiked the twenty-nine kilometres (eighteen miles) into Amiens by 1.00pm. We looked round the city until 2.00pm and then saw the REME officer. We had time to see the famous Amiens Cathedral. For postcard picture of the cathedral see *Figure 32*. We also saw the Hotel de Ville, The Prefecture of Police, the Art School and several historical buildings.

Figure 32

A postcard of Amiens Cathedral.

In the REME workshops we saw a Sherman tank that had been hit by an 88-mm shell. Nothing remained of the turret, but a mass of scrap metal. The crew wouldn't have stood a chance. We were told that we would be recovered within forty-eight hours. However, time will tell, as we have heard that story before. After two hours chasing round the town, periodically falling over red tape, we eventually got a chitty signed. It authorised us to draw three days rations. We got back to the farm just before dark.

Sunday 24th September

A beastly day, so we stopped in bed until 10:30am. This life of inactivity is beginning to tell on us a little and we are in need of exercise so we go out for walks. Today, Bud, Dave and I walked to Orville about five kilometres away. We saw an ox that was teamed up with a horse in a plough, but it was the horse that did all the work. My knowledge of farming is not very extensive, but it seems to me that spring is the right and proper time for off-springs, but here the cows have calves, the mares have foals, the ducks have ducklings and the hens have chickens as merrily as though it were May. Most of the French trains are running again, but they are not yet organised from Amiens to Paris. They have three classes - first, second and third - and their first class is about equal to our third class. Most of their third class carriages have bare wooden seats. The Germans have left quite a bit of rolling stock undamaged here, presumably because the lines were cut before they had chance to move it. More civilian vehicles are appearing on the roads, but the civilians tell me that as yet, food is not much easier to get, although the FFI have stopped the notorious 'black market' and prices are not quite so inflated.

Monday 25th September

A REME sergeant arrived and looked over our tank. He is sending a Scamel recovery lorry to take us to the Amiens workshops tomorrow. That means we shall probably be in the frontline again in another week. Ah well, *Sans faire rien comme ci, comme ca.* Finished reading *Mr Priestley's Problem*, an exceedingly humorous book by Anthony Berkely,

Tuesday 26th September

All Frenchmen between the ages of eighteen and forty-seven years of age have to register for national service today. Madame Duprés told me this, as her son, who is twenty-eight, has to register and he is the only one who can work on the farm because her husband was wounded by the RAF and his right arm is temporarily useless. Still, I suppose it is only right that the French help to finish off Germany. We have freed their country for them and they should help us in return. They will no doubt share the army of occupation duties with us too. France is a queer country. The peasants work hard in the fields, while the citizens make merry in the cities. Most French peasants are good, simple folk who have always lived on the land and are content to work from dawn till dusk. Most of their pleasure is in their work. Their life has always been fairly hard and, consequently, under German occupation it was they who suffered the least.

Chapter 33
Amiens and the tank hospital

Wednesday 27th September

Recovered at last. At 10:30am a Scamel lorry arrived to take us to Amiens. We spent an amusing hour manoeuvring the Scamel in order to tow the tank out of the farmyard and, after removing two fences we eventually got it out onto the road and loaded onto the transporter. Brief *adieus* and *bonne chance* to Madame Duprés and we were on our way. I found that it is not exactly warm on the back of a transporter. We arrived in Amiens in time to go to the ENSA Garrison Cinema to see Joel McRea in Buffalo Bill. Just to sit in a cinema is a treat. Our tank is parked on the main boulevard and we are sleeping in the *Ecole Primaire de Filles*, which, to the uninitiated, is - or rather was - a primary school.

Thursday 28th September

The Airborne Division, which landed in Holland, has been forced to retreat, after holding the main bridge at Nimegan. Their losses were exceedingly heavy and only two thousand out of the whole Division of approximately eight thousand came back safely. One thousand two hundred wounded were left behind under the care of members of the RAMC. The authorities say that they did their job satisfactorily and their sacrifice was not in vain. But I smell a slight blunder somewhere.

This afternoon, we looked round Amiens Cathedral, which is supposed to be one of the finest in Europe. The sculptures both inside and out involved excellent craftsmanship. The interior consists of several altars round the main high altar. It is a magnificent setting for the Ascension. In front of this, four priests chant all day long. Their sonorous tones faintly rumbled round the cathedral all the time we were there. On several of the massive, stately pillars are plaques in French and English to the memory of the British, Canadian, New Zealand and American troops who gave their lives in the defence of Amiens in 1918. There is also the flag of the Newfoundland Regiment. The altars are all superbly carved and decorated and everything combines to give a sense of reverence and beauty. In the evening, we saw an ENSA show at the Garrison theatre. The shows change every week. I haven't seen much of frontline ENSA or the Young Men's Christian Association (YMCA).

Friday 29th September

The Luftwaffe has finally plucked up the courage to come up into the skies and fight. They appeared in strength for the first time over the Western Front last night. But that didn't stop the RAF carrying on their concentrated bombing of Germany. Jerry is also bringing new divisions of artillery and self-propelled guns into action. We were paid five hundred francs each today and spent an enjoyable afternoon buying various minor comforts. Quite a number of shops have small cards in the window – 'English spoken here'. Even if it isn't, no one seems to have any difficulty buying anything. Our tank was inspected today, but it cannot go into the workshops yet. *Sans faire rien.*

Saturday 30th September

Russia has now taken the whole of Estonia. It has been decided that Eric, Dave, Bud and myself have to return to the Regiment with only Pete staying with the tank. We are to travel the first stage by train to somewhere in Belgium. I assume that we will get further orders there. We await orders to move and meanwhile, we continue our tour of Amiens.

Sunday 1st October

This morning, a girl of about fourteen appeared at our window and invited two of us out to dinner at her home at 20 Rue de Levassier. Bud Marshall and I went and received an excellent welcome. The family consists of mother, father, daughter, son, aged ten, a cat and a dog. They gave us an excellent dinner – tomatoes, fish, roast beef, onions and gravy, cake and black coffee with rum. The usual red wine and beer was present in large quantities. We did justice to it all. The daughter, Anne- Marie, sang us a French song '*Salut Tommy*' which was written to commemorate our liberation of Amiens on August 30th. Since we were the first British troops to enter the town they insisted that we gave them one of our divisional signs as a souvenir and so I tore the 'bull' off my left shoulder.

In the evening we met a captain from the Fife and Forfar Regiment in our Brigade[1] in a café. He had just come out of hospital. He told us that Mr Bryce, our troop officer, had been killed a fortnight ago. This rather shook us, as we knew him well.[2] We sincerely hope that our friends in his crew are all safe. It is going to shake us when we return to find that several of our friends have been killed. As far as we can gather, the Regiment is having a rough time. We shall know in about a week's time. I hope my mail wasn't on Mr Bryce's tank.

Monday 2nd October

Spent the day under an hour's notice to move, but nothing happened by tea-time, so the five of us went to the ENSA cinema to see 'Broadway Rhythm'. The French civilians are willing to pay fantastic prices for cigarettes and food. I bought fifty cigarettes from the YMCA mobile canteen today. They cost me eighteen francs: I sold them for a hundred. In the same way, one can get twenty francs (two shillings) for a tin of bully beef. Also, if you want to be mean you can get ten francs (one shilling) for a two pence bar of chocolate or a bar of soap.

---

1. A brigade consists of two or more regiments.
2. Mr Bryce was an older officer around 32 years of age, not the normal 22 to 26.

Tuesday 3rd October

Our kit was boarded onto a train at Amiens station by 11.00am this morning[1], but as we had to wait until midnight for an engine, we took full advantage of our last precious hours in civilization. In the evening we went into what appeared to be a normal café by the side of the station, but it turned out to be a café-cum-brothel. These are legal in France. Downstairs is a normal café, but I'll not vouch for what goes on upstairs. We had a cognac and came out quickly. The floor of our cattle truck was not exactly soft, but I slept well all the same.

1. The author and his colleagues were informed that they were to leave their tank in the workshop to be fitted with a new engine and that they were to rejoin their Regiment without it. The author got a letter from a workshop officer to this effect.

Chapter 34
In search of the frontline

Wednesday 4th October
The train of (troop) carriers, some repaired tanks and our two cattle trucks with ten fellows in each, moved off at 2.00am, although I was hardly conscious of the fact. In spite of bad jolting and the cold, I slept until 5.00am and by that time we had passed through Arras and were at Douai, which is very much the worse for aerial bombardment. From there, we crawled along to Lille where we arrived about 2.00pm. French railways seem to be a very slaphappy affair. If the driver feels like something to eat, he just stops the train and sits on the embankment in peace. Once, when we stopped, I asked the driver if we had time to go for a drink and he said that it was quite okay. He held the train up until we came back. At Basieux we had to stop to have all the wagon numbers checked, as it is the last French station before entering Belgium. We stopped again to change engines at Tournay, several miles inside Belgium. As we had half an hour to spare we went into a café, forgetting that we still had French money. However, they accepted it as a favour. Very much to my surprise, I find that nearly all Belgians speak French as well as Flemish. Quite a few of them speak English too. The train pushed on from Tournay and we spent our second night on the train.

Thursday 5th October
We awoke this morning just before the train passed through Brussels. The electric trains and trams are running again. We are well inside Belgium now and some place names begin with 'Z' like Zolder. All notices are written in Flemish and French. For example ' Exit' is written as *Uitgang, Sortie.*
We arrived at our destination Bourgleopold just before dark. It was too late to unload the carriers so we spent our third night in the cattle truck.

Friday 6th October
Under orders from the RTO, we unloaded our carriers from the train. It was decided that we should set off to find our different regiments on the frontline tomorrow, so we went into Bourgleopold to try to change our French money into Belgian, but it couldn't be done. I was surprised to see ice-cream being sold in 'large lumps'. It is a terrible feeling to have plenty of money in your pockets and yet not being able to spend it. At night we went to the cinema and asked if we could get in by paying with French money. They said no, but they would let us in for four cigarettes each. Thus, we saw Stanley Lupino and Sally Gray in 'Cheer up'. It was in English with the Flemish and French translations appearing in print at the bottom of the screen. The two supporting films were in French and Flemish.

Saturday 7th October

We set out in the carriers this morning for Eindhoven, but hadn't gone more than six or seven miles when we stopped for dinner. We stayed there all day and night too. The nineteen of us who were wending our way back to the frontline are now reduced to twelve because the other seven are making their liberty last yet another day. Dinner was cooked by digging a hole in the ground, filling it with sticks, pouring petrol on and igniting them. We opened one tin of each kind of food we had, emptied it all into an old biscuit tin with some onions that we had scrounged and stirred it up into one big stew. It was all right too. As we were sampling this concoction, literally hundreds of heavy bombers passed overhead and we thought that the big push had started. We heard later on the 6.00pm news that three thousand Lancasters and Liberators had attacked numerous targets in Germany. As we have not been able to get any French money changed into Belgian currency, we sold a few of our tinned goods and soap to a 'civvy' and this provided us with the means of spending an enjoyable evening in a café. The barmaid could speak French so I was official translator for the party. We slept the night in a nearby barn.

Sunday 8th October

The straw in the barn was so soft and warm that no one got up until 9.00am. After breakfast and a rough wash and shave, the seven of us from the 11th Armoured Division set off in the two King's Surrey Light Infantry (KSLI) carriers to find our regiments - 'somewhere in the front line'.[1] At 11:20am we crossed the Belgian border into Holland – a red and white striped barrier that is now permanently open - although some Belgian Maquis (the Belgian Resistance Movement) were hanging around. A few hundred yards inside Holland, we saw five burnt-out Sherman tanks. It was not a very pleasant welcome back into action. On either side of the road are groups of British graves with neat white crosses. Some of them have their owner's caps and cap badges on them. There must have been fierce fighting round here.

Already, we have seen many windmills and people wearing the traditional wooden clogs, but as yet, no one with patches on their trousers. In the towns, most of the people wear shoes on Sundays, but on the farms they wear brightly coloured wooden clogs or sabots[2] and have plain ones for weekdays. Invariably, the children wear clogs. In the big towns, however, boots and shoes are the fashion. Passing through Eindhoven, we noticed that the people were quite well and fashionably dressed, but the women were not as attractive as in

1. As the frontline kept moving they found themselves chasing moving targets. All they had to help them find their Regiment were newspaper cuttings of where the frontline was two days earlier. More contemporary guidance came from asking the drivers of passing ambulances and supply vehicles if they knew the location of the 15th/19th KRH.
2. The term 'sabots' is French for wooden shoes.

France. They are heftier and have better natural looks, but they don't seem to bother about them. I haven't seen many of the flaxen haired beauties that are supposed to live in Holland. In a way, Dutch sounds like a kind of pigeon English - drinkwater, warmwater are all the same except that the 'W's are pronounced as 'Vs' and warmwater sounds like 'varrum vater'. The monetary system is different from those of France and Belgium. Both are based on the franc. There are two hundred French francs and one hundred and seventy-two Belgian francs to the pound. A guilder (*een guilden*) is worth about seventeen Belgian francs, which is roughly two shillings.

As the land is very flat, most people own bicycles and there are separate cycle tracks down either side of the road. Most of the roads in the Low Lands are long and straight. We found our new Divisional Head Quarters near Gemert and they gave us the location of our Regiment, but as it was hopeless trying to find them in the dark, we pulled in for the night at a Dutch farmhouse. None of us could speak Dutch, but we made them understand that we wanted somewhere to sleep and the farmer led us to an attic floor covered with straw and this was more than acceptable.

Chapter 35
A sad news day

Monday 9th October

Before we left the farmhouse, the old lady gave us some hot milk. We found our Regiment resting behind the lines not far from Gemert. We said our *au revoirs* to the two KSLI and the Fife and Forfar Regiment chaps who went on to find their regiments, and found our own Squadron Leader, Major Pearson.[1] He was more than pleased to see us and had a tank ready and waiting for us. Then the sad news began to pour in. Many of our friends have been killed: Mr Bryce, Hooky Walker, Arthur Harrat, Pete Clark, Bob Harris, Bill Wayne, Fred Harrison and Pete Ireland. In addition, many others have been wounded by shrapnel: Fred Sheldon, Pete Angel, Bert Peachey, Simmonds, Ashlee, Les Manning, Reg West and Corporal Kingston. This is only in A Squadron. The other squadrons only had five tanks out of eighteen in action. It shook us to hear of all these deaths at once. I have known most of the fellows for eighteen months and, in that time one becomes quite attached to one's fellow troopers.[2]

Someone told us that when Mr Bryce's tank was hit, the shot went right through the rear corner of the tank, blew one side and arm right off Mr Bryce and splattered poor Hooky's head. Ashlee, the gunner, got away with shrapnel in his hand and side and remained conscious all the time. He had to remain with hatches closed down in the confined space of the turret with the two mangled bodies of his friends for three hours before he could get out because of machine gun fire. He and the driver and co-driver managed to get away then, but had to leave the tank in no-man's land. It was four days before anyone could get back to the tank to remove the bodies. They were buried at 11.00pm in the middle of an air raid. When Sergeant Gadd's tank was hit, the shot went right through Ken Harris, the gunner, and hit Pete Clark, the operator. Ken would have been killed instantaneously, but they say that Pete lived for three minutes. Corporal Nicholl's tank was hit and his gunner killed, but he got out of the tank and wandered in a bomb-happy condition down the main road. Regardless of his state of mind, he then had to take over command of the tank containing the mangled remains of Mr Ireland. I bet it took some nerve to do that. Still, this is war I suppose and one must expect such things. It is said that George Horley won the Military Medal.[3] When his tank was hit and Mr McM-Winckley was wounded in the stomach, Horley lifted him out of the

---

1. The author delivered a letter from the Transport Officer listing the reasons for the delay in recovering their tank.
2. The author also heard that on the last day in action before being pulled out for rest, Major Pearson's brother had been killed.
3. The Military Medal is a medal that is awarded to ranks below that of officer.

tank and dragged him one hundred and fifty yards to safety, all the time under machine gun fire. When B Echelon was bombed, 'Blanco' White drove three lorries away from a burning lorry full of exploding ammunition and petrol. Freddie Crump knocked out two Panther tanks in one day.

Chapter 36
Preparing for action

Tuesday 10th October

Spent the day preparing our tank for action. It has been knocked out before, but has now been reinforced by armour plating. The armament as usual is one 75-mm main gun and two Besa machine guns. At the moment our Regiment is resting in a wood four miles east of Gemert. The rest of the Brigade is still in action holding our positions, while all our forces are being consolidated for the Big Push. The German defences are said to constitute one big crust around the Seigfried Line and when that is broken, it is expected that there will be very little resistance inside. General Montgomery hopes to crack this crust before winter sets in. When the Big Push does come, it will be on a scale unprecedented in the annals of history.

Wednesday 11th October

As I haven't received any mail since our tank has been broken down and in workshops, there were forty-two letters waiting for me, and today, I settled down to answer a few of them. It took me three hours to read them all. Amongst them were several newspapers, dated the end of August, saying that the war would be over in five weeks. Some of them even said that it was a matter of days. They are still saying it. However, once the crust of the German defences is broken I don't think it will be very long. The snag is that it is we who have to break the crust and by 'we' I don't mean England, but 'we' personally. Today is the birthday of my mother and Tommy Holden. I wish them both many happy returns.

Thursday 12th October

We are still resting behind the lines. Our new – reconditioned - tank is now almost ready for action. The tank is, but the crew aren't. It is getting too near to the end of the war to be killed in action. Several military strategists think that the Germans will fight on, even if Berlin is taken, but I don't think so. In any case, by that time the Russians will be closing in on the eastern front of Germany. Once Arnhem has fallen there are no more towns to be taken to the northwest and we can cut off the Germans in Rotterdam. The Americans have surrounded Aachen and are approximately twenty-five miles from Cologne. When the push on Cologne begins, the RAF and artillery will bomb and shell the town into an unrecognisable mass if the German troops in it refuse to surrender. The civilians have been warned to clear out into the country. If they stay in the towns, it is literally their own funeral.

Friday 13th October
Thank goodness we are not going into action today – it's Friday 13th. Still, I am not superstitious. We were supposed to go into action this afternoon at 3:30pm, but it has been postponed until tomorrow morning.

Saturday 14th October
Moved off at 3.00pm to the battle area. No sooner had we arrived there than the bolts on the gear selector level sheared off and we had to return to camp to take over another tank. We could only plod along in third gear and it was after dark when we arrived there, so we could not start preparing the new tank. We had a good night's sleep in the barn in spite of the fact that a German fighter plane tried to keep us awake.

Sunday 15th October
We were up at first light this morning and started preparing the other tank for action. We eventually rejoined the squadron at 10:30am and found that they had not moved off into action. It was a case of standing to all day. Just before dark, we moved up to the front and harboured for the night. In the pouring rain and semi-darkness we had to prepare a meal, dig a hole under the tank to sleep in, in case of mortar or shellfire, and fold our blankets into a sort of bed. By the time we had finished everything was soaked including ourselves, but we crept under the tank and lay there until 10.00pm when it was our turn to go on guard.

Monday 16th October
I was on guard last night. Two of us had to stay in the ditch and keep a listening watch, while the other two patrolled the tanks. It was eerie out there in the ditch in the pouring rain, expecting Jerry to pop up any minute. Two hours in a ditch in the pouring rain isn't pleasant at any time, especially when you are soaked to begin with, but that was only a minor problem compared with looking out for Jerries wanting to do or die for Hitler. I don't mind them dying. It's when they try to take me with them that I don't like. I was glad when our spell of guard was finished and I could crawl under the tank again. This morning, somebody accidentally put his foot on the Besa machine gun firing mechanism and seriously wounded Mr Seine of B Squadron. Yesterday he was pinned down by German machine gun fire and managed to escape only to be hit by his own guns the day after.

As I write this entry, a big infantry attack is going in on my right and is being supported by a terrific artillery barrage from the rear. The noise is deafening and one can hear the shells whining overhead. There are rockets, 25-pounders, and all kinds of heavy guns. I am certainly glad that I am at this end of the barrage and not the other. With shelling like this and bombing day and night, it is obvious that Jerry has had it. If only he would realise it and pack in. It will be grand when there is no more danger of being killed or mutilated for life and one doesn't hear continually of friends who have suffered that fate.

Chapter 37
More than a glimpse of hell

Tuesday 17th October

Our immediate objective is to clear a German enclave on our side of the River Maas. For a map of the area and the nature of our task see *Figure 33*.

Figure 33

A map showing the German enclave on western side of the River Maas. It is identified by the author's insertion of a cross (Source not known).

We started on this task in earnest today. We were proceeding slowly down the main road when the enemy started to mortar and shell us. I have never closed those turret hatches so quickly. Several shells landed very close to the tank and we felt it shake. A whistle or a whining crescendo precedes the landing of all the mortar-shells. Therefore, one only has a few seconds warning to dive for cover. We inside the tank were comparatively safe, but the infantry had quite a few casualties and the wounded were taken to the rear on jeeps, one poor fellow was minus a leg. Further along the road, through the periscope, I saw a German mortar shell land right in the middle of a group of German prisoners. Too bad being killed by one's own shells after being taken prisoner. We took quite a few prisoners. Some looked dejected, some worn out, some arrogant, some grinned like Cheshire cats, but all were dirty and unkempt. One group of about thirty men marched in with their officer leading. Contact with the enemy was slight, but grew fiercer towards dusk. It was pouring down again and pitch black when we pulled into harbour and once again, we spent the night between soaked blankets.

Wednesday 18th October

Today, in a German prisoner's kit, we found several items that he had obviously looted from a Dutch farmhouse – spoons, cigars and some women's clothing. A-Squadron was in reserve most of the day. Clegg of B Squadron was killed. Jerry is not a very sociable sort of a guy. This morning we thought we would cook breakfast, but he thought differently and started to send mortar shells all round us. It was a case of eating breakfast in between diving under the tank a dozen times before we managed to finish it. Our nerves are in such a state now that someone has just to whistle softly under his breath and we all dive under the tank. I am becoming a veritable Jesse Owens and can cover the one hundred yards to the hole under the tank at a pace that has never yet been equalled. We ought to be issued with a flying suit and a diving suit, one to wear when flying to the tank and the other to wear when diving under it. Being shelled and mortared is not exactly a pleasant experience, but we have got so used to it that we can detect by the whistle whether or not it is coming our way. Towards dusk we were sent on a potentially dangerous mission around a parallelogram of roads that had not been cleared. Much to our relief, we found no opposition. Two German colonels gave themselves up to 2nd Troop today. It was found that they were Polish and willing to talk and considerable information was obtained from them. We also captured a German staff car, intact, full of maps. For once, it didn't rain at night and we were able to dig our bed-pit in comfort, although we couldn't light fires to cook with because there were enemy planes overhead.

Thursday 19th October

A day I shall never forget. The fact that I am here to write this now seems nothing less than a miracle. Today's happenings still seem an incredible nightmare involving a horrible succession of escapes from death and patching up wounded comrades. I will describe it as best my shattered nerves will allow. A-Squadron stood by until dinnertime and then we were called upon to attack a position north of Venlo. During a bout of heavy mortar fire, an 88-mm anti-tank gun hit Sergeant Jackson's tank and he was killed. This shook us considerably as he was really one of the best, liked by all. A short while after, our Troop officer's tank got stuck in a ditch and Mr Wilson came on to our tank, leaving Eric Probin, our tank commander, to get his tank out of the ditch. No sooner had they done this, then they were hit by an 88mm shell and the tank caught fire instantaneously. Luckily, no one was hurt and they all baled out. Only Keeler, the gunner was burnt, but not too seriously. All five made a dash for safety under mortar fire, but no one was hit.

Meanwhile, we had been ordered to advance on an orchard and clear it of infantry. Sergeant Gibson's tank took up a position not far from a red-roofed farmhouse. He hadn't been there long when an 88-mm shell hit his tank. Marshall, his wireless operator, was badly wounded in the neck and legs. Being an operator myself, this news didn't help to cheer me up, especially as we were not far from him when he was hit. Seeing what happened, John Sutcliffe started to reverse his tank towards the orchard for cover only twenty yards to our right, but he too was hit by the same anti-tank gun and the tank caught fire. They baled out and I could see that several of them were wounded and badly burnt and I realised that our turn would come soon if we didn't get out of it quickly. We reached the shelter of the few trees in the orchard and Corporal Sutcliffe's crew crawled towards us. We stopped our tank and helped them on to its back to take them to safety. John had two very bad wounds on the back of his right leg and his face and hands were badly burnt. Bill Durham's face was so badly burnt that he was almost unrecognisable. He was temporarily blind. We patched them up as best we could and laid them on the back of the tank to take them to the field dressing station. No sooner had we done this than there was a terrific 'whoof' and a blinding flash in the turret. Instantaneously, I realised that we had been hit and baled out of the turret, wondering if I had been wounded. I was very much relieved to see Dave Dewar and Mr Wilson bale out too. Our immediate concern on finding ourselves out of the tank and all right was for the wounded that were on the back of the tank. We got them on to the ground as quickly and as best we could in case the tank caught fire. The engine was still running and we tried to tell Bill Baybutt, our driver, through his visor to switch it off. He was slumped forward and his eyes were closed and, for a moment, I thought he was dead. Mr Wilson ordered me to make a dash to the nearest tank and ask for help. This I did, and found the Squadron Leader, Major Pearson. He pointed out that he could not send another tank to collect the wounded because it would probably be hit too.[1] Then we had to carry the wounded seventy-five yards to the comparative safety of a haystack. On returning to the tank for the second time I was astonished to find that Bill

---

1. Major Pearson asked the author to get back into the tank, look through the hole where the armour piercing shell penetrated and try to get a line on where it may have come from. He did this on the assumption that lightening wouldn't strike twice in the same place. He was able to give the Major a line on a copse not far away.

Baybutt had come round and managed to get his flaps open, and was standing there hoping for help.[1] Dave and I lifted him out and found that his left arm had been badly shattered above the elbow. Dave did an excellent job of first-aid and then he carried Bill to safety. In the meantime Taffy Hughes and I carried Bill Durham away. In spite of the fact that his face was so badly burnt and had no sense of feeling in it, he kept his spirits up wonderfully well and even made one or two attempts at jokes. All we could do for him was put cream on his face before lifting him on to the back of Mr Heathcote's tank. That ride to the field dressing station must have been hell for them. We sat on the back of the tank and comforted them as best we could. On arrival at the dressing station the doctor quickly dealt with them and despatched them in ambulances to base hospitals.

We, the survivors, were sent back to A2 Echelon, issued with survivors kits and told that we would get a week's rest. We certainly need it as we are all pretty badly shaken up. My nerves are not steady even yet. I definitely don't want to go into another tank after that episode. All I can think about is the day's experience and I didn't get any sleep through it. But that is not all. On finding that our tank was still runable, Mr Wilson got another driver and decided to drive it away. He had not gone very far when a second 88-mm shell went straight through the turret and wounded him so badly that he died two hours later. If Dave and I had been in the turret with him, instead of going back with the wounded, we would have had it. Bud Marshall, our co-driver, is the luckiest person on earth. An hour before we were hit, he cut the end off one of his fingers when slamming his door and had to go to the MO. If this hadn't happened, he would be dead now because the first shot went straight through the armour exactly where he would have been sitting.

1. The author didn't know how Baybutt managed to achieve this manoeuvre with only one arm and other injuries: lifting heavy tank flaps would be a challenge even for a very strong person.

Chapter 38
Battle weary

Friday 20th October
I thought I would sleep last night, but the thoughts of the day's experiences made it impossible. We are all very much shaken by the experience and none of us think ourselves capable of going into action in a tank again. In fact, the very thought of it turns my stomach over. This was not made any better when, at 3.00pm, orders came through for five of us to collect another tank from the Forward Delivery Squadron and this, less than twenty-four hours after we were lucky enough to get out of the other tank alive. Still, I suppose we are so short of men that it has to be done. We will be the most cautious crew in the Regiment as we are all still suffering from nerves and all hate the prospect of going back into action. Our crew is now Corporal Probin, commander, Dave Dewar, gunner, Taffy Hughes, co-driver, and Tubby Nunns, driver, with me as wireless operator. We arrived at the Squadron just before dark and bedded down for the night.

Saturday 21st October
Knowing that all our crew had a pretty terrible experience, Major Pearson, the Squadron Leader left us in today, while the rest of the Squadron were in action. The day's rest was very much appreciated.

Sunday 22nd October
This morning, Major Pearson came to see me and shook me by offering to make me up to corporal and become a crew commander. I told him that at the moment, after being blasted out of my tank, my nerves couldn't stand the responsibility of five men. Perhaps I will think differently if the chance of promotion comes again. Eric Probin and Tubby Nunns saw the Squadron Leader this morning and told him that their nerves were so bad that they could not stand going in another tank. Consequently, they were sent back to A2 Echelon for a rest and replaced by our old pal, Boogie Watson as driver, and Tumblety as commander. I now wish that I hadn't refused promotion because I'll have to go in as operator anyway. Several sergeants have reverted back to trooper because they cannot stick crew commanding any longer. The form now is that the Regiment have to hold this sector until November 8th. We are to be relieved for four days by the Fife and Forfar Regiment and we are to rest and make merry in Derne. That kind of warfare is not so bad.

Chapter 39
Holding our position

Monday 23rd October

Today was the first time that I have experienced static warfare or merely holding a position. I must say it is much better than continually pushing on. It is quite funny really. We take the position during the day and the Germans move in at night. They move out before we come up again in the morning. We just park our tank where they can see us. They shell us until we get fed up being shelled and they get fed up of shelling, so we both pack in for the night. We get sniped at when we are trying to make dinner out in the open, but it is all part of the fun of the game.

Tuesday 24th October

I'm pleased with this - another day's rest while B Squadron are up at the front. Saw Bill Kavanagh and had a chat with him. Received a letter from home saying that Ronnie Mayman has got engaged.[1] Things move fast these days. Taffy Hughes, our ex sergeant's mess cook, made us a terrific meal today. Some of the food, we just found. We had potatoes, peas, carrots and fried chicken, covered with thick onion gravy followed by plums cherries and tinned milk. Then, we had tea, of course. Not bad for a tank crew in action.

Wednesday 25th October

Up to the frontline again this morning. We pulled in between two haystacks and camouflaged up. There was the usual shelling and mortaring and we had to dive spasmodically under the tank. That is rather a nuisance when you are halfway through dinner. A sniper took a few shots at us, but apart from that, everything was quiet.[2]

Thursday 26th October

Four days rest behind the fighting line began today. We moved back to the village of Deurne and took up billets in a mill. It is grand to be static for a while; to put ones best suit on and 'civvy' shoes and stroll around the town. Once more we return to a semi-civilised state. At 7.00pm, we went to a cinema show in a civilian cinema run by the Army. The film was 'A Yank at Eton' starring Mickey Rooney and being a non-propaganda film, it took our minds temporarily away from war in all its forms. It is grand to be sleeping in a building and not under a tank.

---

1. Ronnie Mayman was a cousin of the author.
2. They also took some German prisoners.

Friday 27th October
All our hopes for a four days rest were shattered today when we were ordered to move at two hours notice. This meant we could not have our badly needed baths and were not allowed out. Apparently, the enemy have put in a counter-attack in the Venlo area and have advanced four or five miles. Consequently, our rest is cancelled and we have to lend the Yanks a hand to help push Jerry back. Sergeant Gibson is returning to England for a course on the new Comet Tank and leaves this weekend. How we all envy him. Not only will he be out of the fighting for a while, but he'll also get seven days leave after finishing the course. He had quite a lot of kit to take home, so I offered to buy his portable typewriter to save him carrying it. I got it for two pounds. It is quite small and handy to carry on the tank. At last, my friends will be able to read my letters.

Saturday 28th October
Moved into an orchard and stayed there all day as reserve regiment. Chicken for dinner again. The Russians are pushing slowly on in spite of stiff German resistance in East Prussia where the Germans are loosing an average of seventy-five tanks a day. Good show. Our bombers still hammer mercilessly at German industrial towns. On the home front, Eric Wiggan got married at Keighley today. I wish him and his new wife much happiness.

Sunday 29th October
The date sounds familiar. Ah, yes, it's my 21st birthday. I spent the first three hours of it on guard, frozen silly. At the moment, we are being shelled, so it looks like being a jolly birthday. An infantryman has just been hit in the leg by a shell just up the road. Two hundred yards down the road another infantryman has trodden on a mine. There was a hell of a flash and explosion and the wounded are being carried back past us now. In a way it is a marvel how anyone lives in action. We have to contend with shelling, mortaring, machine gun fire, small arms fire, snipers, mines, anti-tank guns, bombing 'Moaning Minnies'[1] and hoards of other fatal weapons. At night, Jerry puts on a firework display especially for my birthday. Jolly sporting of him. Two bombs fell unpleasantly close, but apart from that it was quite a pretty picture. There are flares, star shells, pink and white parachute flares and all kinds of ack-ack tracers, criss-crossing in a variety of original designs: much better than Skipton Gala. Received several birthday cards - presents are waiting until I return home. What a party I will have then.

Monday 30th October
One good thing about all the days being alike is that we don't get that Monday morning feeling. The enemy have advanced two miles in this sector and have retaken the village of Liesel. Refugees are now streaming up the main road.

---

1. 'Moaning Minnies' were the nickname given to screaming shells.

We had quite an easy day as reserve to the Yanks, but we were shelled as usual. No casualties.

Tuesday 31st October

Received a terrific birthday cake from home. The crew and I had a big chunk each for supper. We are at present on flank protection to the infantry attack on Leisel. It is not at all bad. As the weather deteriorates, tank warfare will become more and more static, and therefore, much easier for us, but will slow down the progress of the war. Whilst I am not at all keen to be involved in the fierce fighting, I would like the war to be over pretty soon. It has gone on five years too long already. The newspapers are still very optimistic, but a two or three mile advance makes headlines these days. Mr Churchill said in the House today that the war against Japan is expected to continue for eighteen months after the war with Germany. Good Lord! I hope he's misinformed.

Chapter 40
Killing time and a pig

Wednesday 1st November

Went out fighting as Mr Ridding's wireless operator. The last time I operated for a troop officer, he got killed, but I haven't told him that yet. The infantry put in an attack on Leisel and we gave them covering machine gun fire. They managed to advance much further than had been anticipated and, in fact, it was quite a good day. For a photograph of the tank crew see *Figure 34*.

Figure 34

The tank crew. Top row, left to right: the author, Jack Arkley. Bottom row, left to right: Dave Dewar, Boogie Watson and Mr Ridding (Nov 1st 1944).

Tuesday 2nd November

Having successfully repulsed the German counter-attack at Leisel, we returned to the Venlo sector and spent the day doing odd jobs on the tanks. We were promised a cinema show at night, but it never came off. At about 4:30pm we saw a considerable number of our bombers returning from a daylight raid on Germany. Jerry put up a lot of flak and one of our planes, a Lancaster or a Liberator, I could not quite distinguish which, was hit. We saw it come diving steeply to earth and burst into flames with a terrific roar as it crashed about one thousand yards away, just inside our lines. We saw six parachutes come gracefully down and for a while it was touch and go whether they would land in our lines or in German territory. I believe they all landed in ours. I think a Lancaster or a Liberator has a seven-man crew, so what happened to the seventh man we can only surmise. His end would be instantaneous, if he was in the plane when it crashed. At about 9.00pm, when we were in our blankets under the tank, Jerry started to shell us with 105-mm shells. Some of them fell unpleasantly close and we grovelled closer to Mother Earth as they whined overhead.

Friday 3rd November
We seem to be taking things much easier than before, as we had another day in harbour today. No one really seems to know what is happening. Actually, I am not worried. This position of reserve suits me fine. Received some toffee from Dorothy. My typewriter is going great guns now and facilitates letter writing tremendously. Antwerp has fallen and so has the first lot of snow. The attack on the Philippine Islands is progressing satisfactorily. Guard duty at night was a very tense affair. Dave and I stood out there in the machine-gun pit expecting a mass German infantry attack at any moment. The rustle of grass made by a stray sheep was enough to set our nerves on edge.

Sunday 4th November
It was yet another day taking it easy in harbour. The civilians in the area have been evacuated because there had been too much fifth column work. There have been several pigs wandering around here with no one to feed them, so we were merciful and killed one outright instead of letting it die slowly of hunger. Taffy Hughes once worked in a slaughterhouse, and he made an excellent job of killing the pig and slicing it up. Now we have pork for dinner for several days to come.

Sunday 5th November
It's Guy Fawkes Day. I only hope that Jerry does not put on a firework display. As from today, we only have to cook our own breakfasts. A cold meal is supplied for mid-day and a hot meal is brought up on a Divisional lorry at the end of the day when we have finished fighting. This experiment will be a good idea if the cooks play their part, as it's very awkward for us to cook our own meals in the dark when we come in. We had an excellent fire today of peat. It is very smoky at first, but throws off a good heat afterwards.[1]

---

1. On April 8th 1945 the author added a note in the margin of his diary to the effect that this meal system only worked for six days.

Monday 6th November

Life is still quite easy and, although we were up at the front today, everything was quiet. We did a bit of long-range shelling, but when Jerry started shelling back, we cleared out of it. Once again, I implore any reader to excuse the dirty condition of this book and the atrocious handwriting, but it is almost impossible to keep one's hands clean and, at the moment, it's so cold that writing is a complicated job. This morning, the Squadron scout car hit a mine and the driver was badly wounded, but the officer got off with bruises and shock. Needless to say, the scout car doesn't work any more. Now back to our palace, our haven of refuge - the hole in the ground under the tank.

Tuesday 7th November

C Squadron was shelled this morning and one of their fellows got two shrapnel wounds in the back. It is terribly cold getting up in the morning now. We crawl out of our hole at 6.00am in our underpants and dress in the gale outside. This morning, it was moonlight when we got up and freezing hard. The first diversion is breakfast where we can dash around and fill up the petrol stoves in a frantic effort to get warm. When it grows light, we are allowed to light a fire. Breakfast, like all other meals, is a rather a grubby affair because we haven't got time to wash beforehand. However, Taffy usually makes something very tasty out of our only just ample rations and we all declare it to be the best meal we have ever had. Washing up is always a problem. We usually wipe the plates over with an old rag, on the principle that: 'a bit of clean dirt does nobody any harm'. Washing clothes is also another difficult problem, but recently a mobile laundry that visits the bathhouse at Helmond has solved the problem. There we can get a complete change of clothing. I actually managed to see a cinema show in Deurne tonight. Five men per troop were taken back behind the lines to see the show. The film was 'The Uninvited', starring Ray Milland, Ruth Hussey and Patrick Gale. It was an exceptionally good thriller with excellent acting by all three. It relied mainly on psychological effects rather than horror scenes. One of the most startling coincidences I have ever experienced happened while we were in the cinema. The news film was showing the bombing of Duisberg and a bomb being released from a plane. Simultaneously, a bomb fell outside the cinema and blew all the doors open as well as causing plaster to fall from the ceiling. I couldn't resist turning to Jock Baillie and saying: 'Very realistic film. Isn't it?' On the way back we had to go over a crossroads that is usually shelled by the enemy at that time of night, but we managed it safely and, gratefully, crawled into our blankets under the tank.

Chapter 41
Fighting the rain, the mud and the cold

Wednesday 8th November

We have now two enemies – the cold and the Germans and I hardly know which is the worst, although it is easier to get away from the latter than the former. The newspapers report that Christmas leave will be granted for certain frontline regiments in Holland, unless the 'big offensive' comes off. Leave will be ten days from the time of arriving in England to the time of departure. I'm pessimistic about our prospects for leave. Even so, it is something to look forward to. It is surprising that even the mere possibility, but improbability, of such a thing cheers one up. Walcharen Island, controlling the Scheldt Estuary, is now almost completely in our hands and the port of Antwerp, which we captured almost intact, is working again and will relieve our supply columns immediately.

Thursday 9th November

We moved up this morning into the Vaulen sector and we are to remain here for two days. That is two days too long. We have taken up positions two or three hundred yards from the enemy and are shelled and mortared all day long. Occasionally, a sniper takes a few shots at us and, in retaliation, one of our snipers from the Welsh Guards pots at them through telescopic sights. We picked off one yesterday and one today. Looking at the enemy positions through binoculars from the observation post in the attic of the shelled farmhouse, they look terrifyingly near. We live in a hole dug in the mud under the tank and only move out of it when absolutely necessary. It is extremely awkward cooking under there, but it has to be done. It is too cold to sleep and too cramped to read or write so we just talk.[1] Dave Dewar, our gunner, has been transferred from our crew to 4th Troop, which is being re- formed. A fellow named Jack Arkley has replaced him. Glynn Hughes -Taffy to us - is now gunner and Jack is the co-driver. Boogie Watson still keeps us entertained by his mimicking and blunt wit. At night we moved back three hundred yards into what was originally an orchard, but it is now a sea of mud a foot deep. Two shells fell within fifteen yards of us, but no one was hurt. Once again, we dug a hole under the tank and crawled under the blankets in our muddy clothes. However, at midnight I was hauled out for wireless watch. I am on until 2.00am and it's getting towards that now, for which I am truly thankful.

---

1. One of the reasons the author felt it necessary to venture out from under the tank was to make his diary entries.

Friday 10th November
I shall be exceedingly glad when our stay in this sector is over. Things are much too hot for my liking. This afternoon, I ventured forth from my hole in the ground to collect the mail. On my return journey two shells fell so close that they covered me in mud. I regained the safety of the dugout under the tank, only to find that a moment later, a shell, fell right in front of it and blew the idler rubbers off. There were many shrapnel holes in the bins and mudguard of the tank, but none of us lying underneath it felt the least effect, except perhaps for a slight shaking of our nerves. After that, we kept as close to the good earth as we could. Received my camera from home and letter from Bill Baybutt saying that he is in Swansea Hospital and has his left side and arm in a plaster cast. As I thought, when Dave and I lifted him out of the tank on that fateful day, his left upper arm was broken. The cut on his chin must have been much worse than we thought, as he had not been able to use his jaws to eat for a fortnight. Even then, I wonder if he is luckier than I am. A nice clean 'Blighty' wound[1] seems all there is to live for these days. Corporal Webster got hit by shrapnel today when a shell fell a few yards away from him and a piece of shrapnel went up through his chin, severing his lips and tongue, and then into his nose. It is a rather horrible wound that will probably affect his speech. I only hope that it's not as bad as it looks.

Saturday 11th November
Thank goodness we are out of this sea of mud and shells. We pulled back this morning to Deurne for two days rest. As Deurne is only a small village several of us hitchhiked into Helmond, a medium sized town eleven kilometres away. There, we had tea at our own Divisional Club served by Dutch debutantes who could speak a little English. The meal cost us twenty-five cents, which is approximately six pence. The cinema provided the next two hours entertainment; the film being 'Stage Door Canteen'. The cinema has been commandeered by the Army and is only open to civilians on Sundays. In most continental cinemas, smoking is not allowed because there is no suitable method of ventilation and the smoke spoils the film. Altogether it was a very pleasant day out and a complete change from yesterday.

Sunday 12th November
Baths this morning were very much appreciated. So too was the spare time to write letters. In the afternoon a 'passion truck ' was run to Helmond and once again we visited the Divisional Club, this time having three helpings of food. Electricity in certain sectors of the town had failed, so we had to spend the evening in the Club and wandering around cafés. One café provided

1. A 'Blightly wound' was Army lingo for a wound that was serious enough to ensure hospitalisation in the UK, but not serious enough to inflict a lasting disability.

entertainment in the form of piano and drums. I tipped the drummer ten cigarettes and he let me play for quite a while. We certainly hit the high spots.[1]

Monday 13th November
It's Dorothy's twenty-second birthday. Her surprise present will have to wait until I get back to England, when she will get an engagement ring. But that is between this book and me for the moment.[2] Hitler's new 'secret weapon' - the V2 - is causing quite a sensation in England and commands most of the space in the newspapers. Several of them fell on London a few days ago. They are reputed to travel at three thousand mph and reach a height of seventy miles. Because of their vertical descent, they have not as much blast effect as the V1, but they give no warning noise. We moved back to our position in the Venlo sector this afternoon and for once, got really organised.

Tuesday 14th November
It's been quite an easy day in harbour. Taffy dished up some excellent meals and I managed to write a few essential letters. The 51st Highland Division has put in an attack just south of here and it's going well.

Wednesday 15th November
It's been another easy day out of action. Most of the time seems to be occupied by preparing meals. I never get enough time to write letters.

Thursday 16th November
Guard from 3:30am to 6:30am this morning was a pretty ghastly affair, especially as a white frost formed. We had to walk round all the tanks in ten-minute reliefs, just to keep warm. We were glad when daylight came and we could light a fire and sit on top of it. B Squadron relieved us this morning and we moved back to Deurne. All our crew went to an ENSA show before proceeding to the Squadron jerger. English beer had been saved for the occasion and everyone had a triple rum ration. Entertainment was provided as usual by us. Jock Baillie and I played a boogie-woogie piano piece and an enjoyable evening was had by all.

Friday 17th November
Feeling civilized once more after a bath in Helmond, I mixed with the crowds in search of presents and 'souvenirs of Holland 1944'. Most things are of inferior quality to British goods, though toys are very much cheaper here. Our

---

1. Since the Army gave everybody who was on active service a cigarette ration and the author smokes a pipe, he used his ration as currency with which to buy a range of items.
2. On April 18th 1945 the author added the following entry in the margin: 'She'll get a wedding ring too.'

11th Armoured Divisional Club provided some excellent scoff for tea and a cinema show finished off quite an enjoyable day.

Saturday 18th November
After a morning's maintenance, it was back to Helmond again in search of food and entertainment. We found them at the Divisional Club and Flora Hall respectively. The latter was a 'Stars in Battledress' show featuring Sid Millward and his Band.

Sunday 19th November
It's been a very quiet day writing letters. In the American Presidential Elections Roosevelt has been returned for his fourth term by a large majority. Hitler has not been seen in public or heard on the radio since the attempt on his life a few months ago. Himmler has deputised for him and read out his speeches. The rest is clouded in rumour. Different newspapers have various opinions on what has happened to him. The most popular one seems to be that he has had a throat operation. Let's hope it was unsuccessful.

Monday 20th November
We camouflaged our tank to look like a Christmas tree. Christmas is only five weeks off. Tumblety has bet us ten shillings each that we will be on leave in England before Christmas. I am afraid that he will be out of pocket, but I hope I will be paying him. Started twenty-four hour guard at 12-noon. Roll on 12.00 tomorrow.

Tuesday 21st November
Most of the day was spent recovering after last night's guard. The weather is still terrible. Tomorrow at dawn, we go into action again. We are to go down the main road towards Amerika, a small town held by the Germans. The position is made trebly dangerous by the fact that there is no way of getting off the road or turning round. As things have been static for quite a while, the Germans have laid mines all over the place. Ah well, we'll worry about that tomorrow. In the meanwhile, a precious nights sleep will be appreciated.

Chapter 42
Bogged down and grateful

Wednesday 22nd November

Moving off before dawn and in a gale, we arrived at our assembly point at 7:30am. The REs, who were to have laid the scissor bridge[1] across the dyke for us to advance, had not arrived so the infantry went on without us. After many technical hitches the bridge was eventually laid and we trundled across to the unknown beyond. Usually the rain and mud are our enemies, but today they were our friends. Instead of pushing on into battle, most of our tanks got bogged down and we stayed behind in the mud and safety. It didn't just rain, it poured down. We got soaked from head to foot, water squelching in our boots, shirts and vests damp. What a life! If only my mother could see me now. We slept in our wet clothes and did a couple of hours on guard into the bargain.

Thursday 23rd November

Oh to see a hill. The countryside here is one long, boring roll of flat, bare land, the main product of which is peat. The trees have lost all their leaves now, giving the landscape an even, more desolate appearance. Because of the heavy rains there are bogs and huge pools of water everywhere. It really is impossible country for tanks and I have great hopes that we may be taken out of action soon. We spent all day playing at draughts with the tanks. One tank would get stuck and in the process of pulling it out another one would get stuck. Sometimes we would have three tanks stuck and one out and other times three would be out and one stuck. So the game went on all day, making no progress at all. In fact, it got so bad that when it came dark, we abandoned our tanks and went on the Squadron Leader's tank to Amerika, which by this time had been taken by the infantry. There in the dark we tumbled into houses, which had not been tested for mines or booby traps and laid down exhausted and slept.[2]

Friday 24th November

In daylight this morning, it became obvious that the infantry had rummaged through the houses and, therefore, they were clear of mines. We found ourselves a civvy bed to sleep in then had to walk out to the tanks to try to get them un-bogged once again. Needless to say, it was to no avail. We returned to a double rum ration and it sure was appreciated.

---

1. A scissor bridge was a temporary structure that was capable of being erected quickly. It was so-called because of the way in which it expanded to bridge a river or chasm.
2. At this point the author acquires some German photographs and inserts them in his diary. However, at this distance in time he can't remember how he came by them. See Figures 35, 36, *37, 38 and 39.*

Saturday 25th November

Once again, we spent the whole day trying to recover our tanks, but without success. We floundered around in the mud and the rain and at the end of the day had moved the tanks at least a yard further. The Squadron moved back from Amerika to Zilburg on the railway lines. The roads are so bad that the railway lines have been filled in. It is rather bumpy in a lorry and a tricky business driving between the lines. On the side of the railway were two dead Germans whom we had seen three days ago. They stunk to high heaven, but someone had turned them over and looted them. One of them was badly mangled too. We arrived in Zilburg just before dark and managed to get the same billets as we had last time.

Sunday 26th November

After a day in the mud, with the aid of two Sherman Armed Recovery Vehicles (ARV) and a Scamel, we managed to un-bog our tanks and returned at dusk up the railway line to our billets. It was a glorious night and I really appreciated the beauty of it - the soft wanness of the moon and the falling mist combined to make the most beautiful picture I have seen so far in Holland. It's strange that in the ugliness of war, one should notice these things.

Figure 35

A souvenir of the war; a photograph of Hitler saluting his troops.

Figure 36
A souvenir of the war; a photograph of a Nazi rally.

Figure 37
A souvenir of the war; a photograph Hitler surveying his troops from a balcony.

Figure 38
A souvenir of the war; a photograph of Hitler presiding over a march past.

Figure 39
A souvenir of the war; a photograph of a column of German troops.

Chapter 43
Static warfare

Monday 27th November

We are still static and so we have more opportunity to write letters, but nothing interesting to record.

Tuesday 28th November

Baths in Helmond provided the day's highlight. They were followed by tea in the Divisional Club and a visit to the News Theatre. Compared with the number of British troops in Helmond, the British entertainment there is insufficient. All one seems to do is queue. Still, one can spend quite an enjoyable evening there.

Wednesday 29th November

Moved from Zilburg to Horst, only a mile or so from the River Maas and the remaining German pockets. The form at present seems to be five-weeks of static warfare, with us probably returning to the same billets every night. We are billeted in a farm a few kilometres to the east of Horst. We park our tank in the farmyard.

Dutch farms are very different from English ones. Most of the bourgeoisie or peasant farmers are fairly poor and invariably wear cheap wooden clogs. Their clothes are usually simple, well worn and smell of the good earth. By nature they are slow and inquisitive and seem amused because we wash so often, although they never look very dirty themselves. They are not as excitable as the French and have less spirit and *joie de vivre.* As in the rest of the continent, the children start smoking at the age of ten. An average number for a family is eight.[1]

Some families keep their farmhouses scrupulously clean and the others simply stink. The one we are in at present is a cross between the two. Their barns are all part of the farm house and it is not uncommon to find a pigsty next to the living room. Water is supplied by pump or well and bucket and very few farms have electric light. Bicycles are an essential part of the homestead and are kept in the front room.

Sanitation is generally bad. The WC's are often open ones and no one seems to mind if the rest of the family look on. I have yet to see a coal fire in Holland. Peat is plentiful and they burn it in stoves and it throws out a fairly decent heat. Angora rabbits, with their queer pink eyes, are an integral part of their

1. The author doesn't remember how he acquired this information.

livestock. Entertainment beyond family life seems non-existent and the standard of living is very much lower than on English farms. For a photograph of the crew in a light-hearted mood in the Dutch farm see *Figure 40.*

Figure 40

The tank crew on alternative transport. Standing, from the left to right: Steve Booth, the author and Ted Hipkiss. Seated in the cart, from left to right: Boogie Watson and Taffy Hughes. On the horse's back: Jack Arkley.

Thursday 30th November

We thought that things would be quiet here, but today's activities were far from it. The worst incident of the day was when my friend, Dave Dewar, who has been in the same crew as me since we left England, was hit by shrapnel and had a piece taken out of his lip and nose. It bled considerably, but it is not as serious as it could have been. I sincerely hope that it doesn't disfigure him, as he is a very good-looking fellow. Still, plastic surgery does marvels these days.

Today, B and C Squadrons put in an attack with the Monmouthshire Infantry Regiment on a castle in order to clear all the Germans from this side of the Maas. Opposition must have been stronger than expected as our Squadron was called in to give assistance in the afternoon. Enemy shelling was considerable and Sergeant Major Lara was wounded. Taffy Hughes and I were standing on top of the turret when there was the terrible whiz of a sniper's bullet. Taffy and I were in the turret much faster than the proverbial greased lightening. We took quite a few prisoners, which we handed on to the Infantry to march back to base. The Monmouth's lost a considerable number of men and the medical orderlies were working all night. I don't mind seeing dead Jerries, but a dead

Tommy is always a distressing sight. At 4.00pm we shed a track, after firing smoke across the river, and after several unsuccessful attempts to replace it, we thought we would have to spend the night out there in no-man's land with Jerry patrols prowling about. But on the Squadron Leader's orders, we abandoned the tank and rode back on the back of his tank with five prisoners.

Friday 1st December
We went out to recover our tank with a B squadron recovery vehicle. It was slow work as we were under shellfire most of the time, but we eventually managed it and got a half-tracked ambulance out too. Nearly all our MO's vehicles were busy collecting our dead. War is a horrible thing when you see it like that. On October 19th Sergeant Jackson was killed, the same day that our tank was hit, and today was the first day that we could get to his tank. A party went out to bury him and they found that he was unrecognisable with no eyes and very little flesh left on his face. Yet the Jerries had lifted him out of the tank and taken everything out of his pockets, leaving him to rot in the mud. Two C squadron fellows were buried too and they were in a pretty bad state, one mass of putridity after six weeks in the open. I certainly didn't envy the gravediggers' their job.

Saturday 2nd December
A considerable part of the countryside here is under water and only the main arterial roads can take heavy traffic. The secondary roads, which are nothing but mere tracks in most cases, are one mass of mud. The main roads in Holland are exceptionally good, usually long and straight but they are very scarce. Today, I found myself on road-making fatigues, which meant collecting a load of bricks from the remains of bombed houses in Horst and dumping them on the muddy track. It was a slow and tedious process. The form now is that we sit here in case of a German counter-attack across the Maas, which is quite a good job, unless the counter-attack comes off.

Sunday 3rd December
Late reveille at 7:30am was appreciated. So was having the afternoon off. The people at the farm where we are billeted gave us a cup of hot milk each this morning. At nights we monopolise their table and paraffin lamp, while the family sits round the room just watching us. They laughed when we laughed and showed considerable interest in my typewriter.

Monday 4th December
Guard last night was not exactly exciting, but it is not so bad when you know that the enemy is five miles away as opposed to only five hundred yards, as it often is. In the afternoon four men per troop went to the cinema in Horst to see 'Four Jills in a Jeep'. By luck of the cards, I was one of the four. Wrote to Tommy Holden.

Tuesday 5th December

It was another uneventful day. Finished reading *Ragged Banners* by Ethel Mannin, a very intellectual book about the futility of thought and the absolute in poetry: an extremely good book.

Wednesday 6th December

Usual maintenance. It is officially announced that leave for the forces on the Western Front starts on January 1st and must be finished by April. It is at least something to look forward to, although I don't suppose we shall get it for two or three months yet. A newspaper account of these arrangements is presented in *Figure 41*.

LEAVE FOR OUR
Out-of-the-hat ballots by Montgomery's wish

WEEK AT HOME: FIRST COME NEXT MONTH

21st ARMY GROUP H.Q., Monday.

THOUSANDS of British soldiers who have fought and slogged all the way from the Normandy beaches to Holland are to go home on leave next month. The scheme starts on January 1.

Special steps are being taken to see that they are given all comfort and facilities to and from their homes. Trains will be waiting at stations, tickets and vouchers will be issued before they embark, and the period of leave will be determined from the time they set foot in England.

On an average a man will be away nine days. He will not be home for that period. If he arrives in the United Kingdom on D-Day he reports back to the port on D plus 8.

The soldier who lives in the Midlands—and that is a representative distance—will have seven nights at home. The man who lives in Southern England will have eight nights, and a man who lives in the North of Scotland slightly less.

Extra for distance

The leave of those who have to travel to Ireland or the Orkneys and Shetlands will be calculated from the time the soldier arrives on the island. If he arrived on D-Day he starts back on D plus 7.

Two factors may cause delay or upset the time-table—weather and operational needs.

Here are the points of the scheme:

Figure 41

A newspaper account of how leave is to be arranged (*News Chronicle*, December 5th 1944).

Thursday 7th December

It has now been announced that we shall be in these billets for another six weeks, unless the Germans counter-attack. This is the first time we have had static billets since leaving England. Consequently, preparations are going ahead for a good time on Sahagun Day. Last year we had turkey and chicken. This year I suppose we will have looted pigs and chickens. This period of inactivity gives me very little to report, but it is better that way.

Friday 8th December

Our principal job at the moment is road-making which sometimes provides an opportunity for finding collectable things among the rubble. So far, nothing has materialised.

Saturday 9th December

This morning my tank was hit by an 88-mm German tank gun, we ran over mines, were under heavy shellfire and took 35 prisoners – all in theory on a sand table. It is much easier than in actual action. Pity our politicians cannot fight all wars out on sand tables. It would save a deuce of a lot of misery and unhappiness. This afternoon I took part in a practice game of rugger and, in spite of the fact that I hadn't played for ages I still thoroughly enjoyed it. There was some controversy about whether we played Rugby League or Union. It ended with the Unionists winning.

Chapter 44
Forty-eight hours leave in Brussels

Sunday 10th December
Cheers! We are going to Brussels for 48-hours leave on Tuesday. Preparations are in full swing. Played cards and won three guilders.

Monday 11th December
Tomorrow we visit Brussels. That is the only important thing about today. See *Figure 42* for the Brussels Leave document which included the advice on 'Do's and Don'ts' shown in *Figure 43*.

ISSUE No. 5 SCHEME B

BRUSSELS LEAVE
BILLETS

NAME L/Cpl [illegible]

Your Meeting Point is marked with a Cross below

	Address	Map Ref.	Your Meeting Point
1	67, Ave Jupiter - - -	A 15	
2	192, Ave Moliere - -	E 16	
3	36, Ave Albert Elizabeth -	Off Map at M 8	
4	I, Square Francois Riga -	Off Map at M I	
5	172, Rue Marie Christine -	Off Map at F I	
6	Cinquantenaire - - -	M 8	

YOUR FEEDING CENTRE IS SHOWN ON YOUR MEAL TICKET

TRAM SERVICES connecting your Billet Area with your Feeding Centre are also shown on your Meal Ticket

FIRST AID BOXES are held at each meeting point

Billets are reserved exclusively for personnel of the Special 21 Army Group Brussels Leave Scheme

UNITED SERVICES WELFARE CENTRE, BRUSSELS GARRISON, is at 45 Boulevard Bischoffheim (corner of Rue Royale). Map Ref. G.4

NOTES

Do not talk about where your unit is or what it is. Do not discuss equipment, losses or battle experiences. The people of Brussels are very hospitable and will do all they can to make your leave enjoyable. Enjoy yourselves with them but do not tell them anything.

You are warned of the high prices of casual refreshments. Ask the price before you order. Your accommodation and meals are free, but purchases in all canteens must be paid for in cash. You must not buy food in civilian restaurants. Haversack Rations will be supplied for return journey to unit.

ISSUED BY ARMY WELFARE SERVICES AND EDUCATION BRANCH HQ BRUSSELS GARRISON

Figure 42
The author' Brussels leave pass.

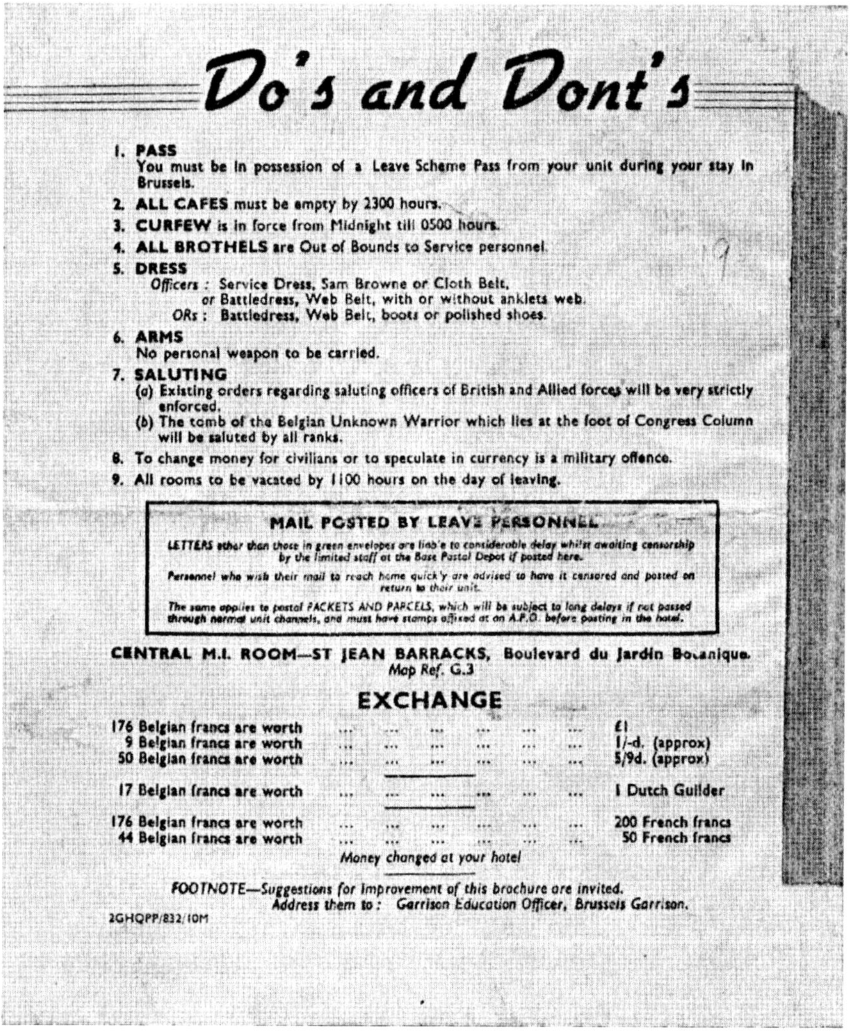

Do's and Dont's

1. **PASS**
You must be in possession of a Leave Scheme Pass from your unit during your stay in Brussels.
2. **ALL CAFES** must be empty by 2300 hours.
3. **CURFEW** is in force from Midnight till 0500 hours.
4. **ALL BROTHELS** are Out of Bounds to Service personnel.
5. **DRESS**
Officers : Service Dress, Sam Browne or Cloth Belt,
or Battledress, Web Belt, with or without anklets web.
ORs : Battledress, Web Belt, boots or polished shoes.
6. **ARMS**
No personal weapon to be carried.
7. **SALUTING**
(*a*) Existing orders regarding saluting officers of British and Allied forces will be very strictly enforced.
(*b*) The tomb of the Belgian Unknown Warrior which lies at the foot of Congress Column will be saluted by all ranks.
8. To change money for civilians or to speculate in currency is a military offence.
9. All rooms to be vacated by 1100 hours on the day of leaving.

MAIL POSTED BY LEAVE PERSONNEL

LETTERS other than those in green envelopes are liable to considerable delay whilst awaiting censorship by the limited staff at the Base Postal Depot if posted here.

Personnel who wish their mail to reach home quickly are advised to have it censored and posted on return to their unit.

The same applies to postal PACKETS AND PARCELS, which will be subject to long delays if not passed through normal unit channels, and must have stamps affixed at an A.P.O. before posting in the hotel.

CENTRAL M.I. ROOM—ST JEAN BARRACKS, Boulevard du Jardin Botanique.
Map Ref. G.3

EXCHANGE

176 Belgian francs are worth	... ...	£1
9 Belgian francs are worth	... ...	1/-d. (approx)
50 Belgian francs are worth	... ...	5/9d. (approx)
17 Belgian francs are worth	... ...	1 Dutch Guilder
176 Belgian francs are worth	... ...	200 French francs
44 Belgian francs are worth	... ...	50 French francs

Money changed at your hotel

FOOTNOTE—Suggestions for improvement of this brochure are invited.
Address them to : Garrison Education Officer, Brussels Garrison.

2GHQPP/832/10M

Figure 43

A list of 'do's and don'ts' when on leave included in the Brussels leave pass.

Tuesday 12th December

It was a crisp, clear sunny morning when we set out in the back of a three-ton lorry on the one hundred and fifty mile journey to Brussels. By we, I mean five men from each of four squadrons. Our own particular party consisted of Jack Arkley, Taffy Hughes, Boogie Watson and myself, with Sergeant George Buxton of Bradford in charge. The journey down was uneventful. We passed through Deurne, Helmond, Eindhoven, Burg Leopold and Louvain, watching the road signs and advertisements change from Dutch into French. A few miles inside the Belgian border we actually saw a hill, which is a very rare occurrence in this part of the world. The number of kilometres to Brussels - or Brussel or Bruxelles - on the signposts gradually dwindled and at 4.00pm we found ourselves in the centre of the city. With each of the four parties being billeted at different places, it was almost 6.00pm by the time we found our place.

We were billeted in what had been an institute for the deaf and dumb. It was a truly magnificent place, consisting of tiled, well windowed, modern buildings facing on to a tiled courtyard. There is no official blackout in Brussels and the light streaming through the thin silk curtains of the large windows onto the courtyard presented a glorious spectacle. It was a truly impressive building. In spite of the fact that it was pitch dark and with us not knowing the layout of the city, we jumped on a tram and found the high spots. In the Trocadero (club-cum-café) we had an egg-flip each, and in various other cafés we sampled various kinds of wines. I have not yet visited Paris, but it cannot be any worse than Brussels for immorality. We had quite a lively evening and returned to our billets by 11:30pm. A good supper was waiting for us and we did full justice to it. For a photograph of me outside our accommodation in Brussels see *Figure 44.*

Figure 44
The author on leave in Brussels.

Wednesday 13th December
Up early this morning, we clung onto tram-27 and found ourselves in the shopping centre - veritably, a woman's paradise - rows and rows of well laid out shops displaying their wares invitingly. Watches of good Swiss makes are in abundance at reasonable prices - fifteen jewel Pontiac watches could be bought for one thousand, six hundred francs - approximately nine pounds. Unfortunately, I hadn't enough Belgian currency. There were plenty of good makes of English pens, which seemed strange because they are so scarce in England. I bought Dorothy a gold crucifix, a few toys for Dennis and Sylvia and several odds and ends as souvenirs.

Another thing unobtainable in England, but plentiful in Brussels, is ice cream. We had it in large quantities - vanilla, raspberry, chocolate with peaches and pears, apples and cherries - lots of them. There were cakes too - cream puffs, meringues, éclairs and all kinds of fluffy delicacies. We made short work of them all. Brussels is a gay city. Everyone is well dressed and gads around on trams in a carefree way. Nearly all women have fur coats and fully-fashioned silk stockings and know how to use their make up to the best effect. They are invariably good looking too. In spite of the fact that nearly all cafes have an 'upstairs' business, one would not call Brussels an immoral city. The people are just broadminded in a happy sort of way. For them life seems to be a carefree, happy go-lucky thing and they make the most of it.

Thursday 14th December

Spent the morning sampling more ice cream and visiting historic places. We climbed the two hundred steps of the Congress Column and had an excellent view of the city; that is after we had recovered from the dizziness of a spiral ascent that seemed interminable. We saluted the Tomb of the Unknown Warrior and noticed that civilians raised their hats as they passed. The Botanical Gardens - *Les Jardins Botanique* - provided some amusing settings for snaps. We returned to our billets for dinner and were ready for the return journey when, more by design than accident, I suspect, the fan belt of the lorry broke and could not be repaired until tomorrow morning, much to our joy. This gave us the opportunity to see a Harry James film at the ENSA Cinema.

Friday 15th December

The fan belt on the lorry having been replaced, we bade our farewells to the gay city at 11.00am and set off on our return journey. Reaching Burgleopold without incident, we dined in the NAAFI there and were on our way again. On arrival back at the Regiment, I found to my astonishment that I had been a Lance Corporal for two days. The main advantage is that I get an extra one shilling and three pence a day. This puts me on six shillings a day, forty-two shillings a week with no income tax.

Chapter 45
Holding on

Saturday 16th December

It was a day to settle down, after Brussels, otherwise, free of incident. The situation in Greece is very sticky at the moment. British tanks and paratroops have attacked the EAM[1] headquarters in Athens. The rebels hold nearly all the heights in Athens and the RAF have been strafing concentrations of them on the outskirts. The Fascist-minded civilians make this their way of objecting to our occupation and the new Government. It is estimated that there are fifteen thousand rebels inside the city and ten thousand outside. Field Marshall Alexander has been brought in to take command of the situation.

Sunday 17th December

We moved from the Horst sector to the Roermond sector, but we're still only holding the front and not pushing on. Our billets are very much better and the people much more sociable. As orderly corporal today, I had to find RHQ in the dark with a message for the adjutant. By the time I had finished detailing guard, transport etc., it was bedtime.

Monday 18th December

There is quite a lot of enemy air activity over this sector. This morning, several ME-109s[2] flew over here quite low. A fairly good ack-ack barrage was put up, but with no result. Jerry is using quite a few jet-propelled planes in this sector as well. It was great to see our fighters patrolling the sky. Apart from air activity and shelling, we are not likely to see any action for a while yet.

Tuesday 19th December

Today came the disconcerting news that the Germans have advanced thirty miles into Belgium and that the Americans have had to give way, but the Yanks are now holding them. The strategic importance of this new German thrust cannot be seen yet, and news of it is being kept back. The Germans are giving us no trouble in our sector and we had a route march for exercise this afternoon. What a war!

---

1. The EAM was the largest and most militant Greek resistance movement. The initials stood for National Liberation Front.
2. ME-109s were Messerschmitts; German fighter planes.

Wednesday 20th December
The situation in Greece gets no better. No one seems to know exactly who-is-fighting-who and our soldiers are having a rough time. In Italy the fighting is exceedingly slow, but with progress on our side all the time. On the Russian front there is also steady progress, the main drive being around Bucharest. Our activities, as reserve regiment, are confined to tank and physical maintenance.

Thursday 21st December
It's Sahagun Day. It's held in honour of the Battle of Sahagun, won by the Regiment in Spain in eighteen hundred and something. In England the anniversary is usually an occasion for great rejoicing and celebrating and it was still celebrated on the frontline this year. Regimental sports were held and we spent quite an enjoyable morning watching them. The officers' tug of war was especially interesting. Sahagun Dinner was of quite good quality and quantity. Moreover, the officers and sergeants served the dinner, as custom would have it. We had pork chops *a l'Argentan*, braised steak *a l'Amiens*, creamed potatoes *a l'Antwerp* and pudding *a l'Amerika* with rum sauce a the 'good old Angleterre': Quite a good stuff (good meal). The afternoon was utilised to sleep the dinner off. The dinner was followed by a jerger, but we didn't go because we didn't want to leave the warmth of the farmhouse front room.

Friday 22nd December
The position of the German break-through is a bit clearer now. They have made an advance of forty miles to Leige in Belgium, apparently with Brussels as their objective. The main German Army has been used and it rather looks as though it is a last determined attempt. Several Panzer and SS Divisions have been used. The Americans appear to have got over their initial confusion and are now holding most sectors. This is one of the occasions when time is going to be a deciding factor and, with careful strategy, this attack can be turned against the Germans. On the one hand, if the attack cannot be repulsed it will mean serious consequences for us. But if we can stem it and cut it off, it will be a great advantage for us because, for once, the German Army has come out into the open where we can get at it. We await further news with interest. In the meantime, we have been warned to keep a sharp look out for enemy paratroops. Many of them have been reported to be wearing American uniforms. Also we are at an hour's notice to move into action if needed.

Saturday 23rd December
I received nine letters and I sent Dorothy her present from Brussels by registered letter. New auxiliary motor fitted in the tank.

Sunday 24th December

It's Christmas Eve -1944. What a contrast from last year when I was home on leave. This year, I am spending it in the front room of a Dutch farmhouse. The family gave us an excellent Christmas Eve supper of custard and fruit pie with delicious drinking chocolate. They make us really at home and there is no awkwardness about the situation. It is surprising how easily the language difficulties are overcome. I would not mind visiting these people again after the war. Our two troop sergeants turned up in rather a happy state at about 9.00pm with a bottle of brandy. We joined the rest of the fellows in the other billet, so the brandy did not go far, but we had quite an enjoyable singsong.

Chapter 46
Peace and good will?

Monday 25th December
Christmas Day. Last year on this day, I wrote up this diary in the comfort of home, wondering where I would be this Christmas. Unfortunately, now I know. Even on this day of peace on earth and goodwill to all men, shells are whining across the skies on their errands of destruction. And, not very far from here, two large armies of men are trying desperately to kill each other. I thank God sincerely that on his day I am not in action. The Hermans family were at Kirk this morning by 8.00am. I attended a church service at RHQ at the less strenuous hour of 11.00am. We sang carols lustily and it was an excellent service.

Christmas dinner was quite an elaborate affair, dished up by the corporals. We had pork chops, tinned turkey, roast spuds, mashed spuds and peas, followed by plum pudding with rum sauce and mince pies and cheese. Quite well cooked too, for a change. I wonder what they are having for dinner at home? No doubt Dennis and Sylvia will be dashing around the house wildly excited about what Father Christmas has brought them. If only I could see them. I hope that all at home are having a good Christmas. Considering that I am on active service, I am having an excellent one. At Christmas one automatically looks forward and back. Last Christmas I believe I said in this diary that the war should just about be over by this Christmas. Since then, I have seen quite a bit of action and know more about the various elements controlling the progress of the war. Now I give the war with Germany until the end of August. Thus, next Christmas should definitely see the end of the war, but I do not expect to be demobilized by then. Christmas comes but once a year - pity it doesn't come more often.

Tuesday 26th December
Boxing Day. It's a normal working day for us, although we are not doing much at the moment. In the evening I was one of five fellows in the Squadron privileged to go to the Phillips Concert Hall in Eindhoven and hear the Halle Orchestra. It was a marvellous performance and I sat enthralled throughout. The orchestra of seventy players was led by Lawrence Turner and conducted by John Barbirolli with Mr Arthur Grumiaux as violin soloist. He gave a marvellous performance in the E minor concerto. The full programme was as follows:

Overture Leonora No. 3	Beethoven
Violin Concerto in E Minor	Mendelssohn
Interval	
Unfinished Symphony	Schubert
Valse Triste	Sibelius

Cappriccio Espagnol	Rimsky Korsakov
Encores	
Londonderry Air	
Radetzky March	Johann Strauss
Overture Die Fleidermaus	" "
Tales from the Vienna Woods	" "

After the advertised programme, the audience clapped the conductor back for three bows and an encore. After the first encore, they simply would not let him leave and the applause was so terrific after each piece that he played four encores. It really was appreciated and I more than appreciated and enjoyed it. For once I felt myself lifted by the sheer beauty of the music and I left greatly exhilarated.

Wednesday 27th December

Today, Boogie Watson and I took a truck to the park for derelict tanks near Eindhoven. All the canals and, indeed, almost everything is frozen solid and we saw many couples on their way to the skating areas. They dress up for the occasion and all carry their skates slung round their necks, fastened together by a piece of string. Most of them are good skaters. The winters here seem much more severe than in England. When I get up in the morning, my towel and toothbrush are usually frozen and we go to breakfast over fields covered in frost as thick as snow. When I came to fill my pen, I almost broke the nib - the ink was frozen solid. Half a mug of the cold tea left by my bed one night came out in one piece the next morning.

Thursday 28th December

I commanded the tank to the ranges near Lommel in Belgium, about sixty miles away. It was terribly misty and one could hardly see the tank in front. To make matters more complicated the road was covered with ice and the tanks slithered all over the place. Once they started slipping, they were uncontrollable and it was surprising that we didn't pulp any lorries. We went *via* the main roads so map reading was quite easy. A twenty-minute halt in Bree provided an opportunity for dinner. We reached our destination near Lommel at 4:30pm, filled up with petrol - a mere sixty gallons, cooked ourselves a meal and found ourselves billets. Luckily, I knew the Dutch phrase for: 'Can we sleep in your barn please?' In the event, we found ourselves sleeping in the house. For a photograph of the tank crew see *Figure 45*.

Figure 45

The tank crew. From left to right: Boogie Watson, Jack Arkley, the author and Dave Dewar (December 28th 1944).

Friday 29th December

Because the Bailey bridge over the Escaut Canal was insecure, we had to go by a circuitous route for thirty miles to get to the ranges, only five miles away. It seems rather ridiculous pulling us out of the frontline to go practice on a range sixty miles away when we could advance a few miles and lob shells into German occupied territory. However, we fired our shells and the results were quite good. At 6.00pm we set off back to Leverooi on a Squadron lorry. We slid most of the way, but arrived safely.

Saturday 30th December

There's a photograph of Germany's new Tiger Tank in today's *Daily Express*. See *Figure 46*.

Figure 46
A photograph of Germany's new Tiger tank (*Daily Express* circa late December 1944).

I sincerely hope that we don't meet many of these chappies when we go into action again. The Belgians in the re-occupied territory are having a rough time of it. The Germans are shooting civilians and all that sort of thing. The advance has been pushed back twelve miles, the Americans are hammering at the flanks and our air forces are giving German communications a terrific pounding. Pushing back this counter-attack will definitely lower German morale as the German soldiers were told that they would soon be having leave in Brussels again. Such an advance would probably be the beginning of driving the Allies completely out of Europe.

Sunday 31st December
Churchill assures us of full and final victory in 1945. Hitler says victory for Germany in six months. They ought to get together and thrash it out. It is reported that Major Glenn Miller and his whole band are missing after the sudden German push into Belgium. *Figure 47* is a newspaper story reporting on one of the many Nazi atrocities.

AN American soldier looks down on the body of a boy aged about six. More bodies are in the background.

According to the caption with the picture, which reached London from the Western Front last night, the boy and other Belgian civilians were shot by the Germans in Stavelot.

Below, John Wilhelm, Reuter's special correspondent with the United States First Army, gives his version of the same or a similar incident which he places near Stavelot.

Figure 47

A newspaper account of one example of Nazi atrocities (Source not known).

God! When we go into action again, I will not be taking any prisoners. They all ought to be exterminated. That is a rather extreme statement for a Sunday, but it is in the cause of Christianity.

It's New Year's Eve. The people here, being devout Catholics, stayed up until midnight and chanted in the New Year. We felt ourselves in the way, so we retired at 10:30pm.

Monday 1st January 1945

New Years Day: the beginning of yet another year of war. At least this year should definitely see the end of it. We said that last New Year's Day, but we hadn't invaded the Continent then. I wonder just what this year will bring? A New Year means very little really. True, it can be a fresh starting point; for turning one's back on the old and facing the future with a clean sheet, but one is irrevocably linked to the past and the old things must go on. A job left unfinished yesterday in 1944, still has to be finished in 1945. In reality, one cannot shut ones mind on the old year and start refreshed on the new. Life this year still has the same problems that afflicted the last one and what has been done in the past cannot be undone. I suppose one must have year-ends to wind up accounts and banks to pay interest etc., but they seem have little social importance beyond that, unless it is as an excuse for merry-making. As an old-Dutch custom, Mrs Hermans dished us up oatcakes today. Apparently they have them on New Year's Day in the same way that we have pancakes on Pancake Tuesday.

Tuesday 2nd January

Spent an uninteresting day on the Besa range. Saw an excellent 'Stars in Battledress' show in the town of Weert.

Wednesday 3rd January

As Sergeant Nicholls is away at the moment, I have taken over command of the Challenger tank. This means very little at present because we are static, but it does mean more responsibility if I have to command it in action. We spent the morning on the Sten gun range and the afternoon playing basketball.

Thursday 4th January

A sergeant from Bovington, the capital of 'Tankland', gave us an excellent lecture on tank recognition this morning. The details about the King Tiger are even more formidable than its picture. The Germans are always far ahead of us in tank design and production. We only beat them by sheer numbers. Germany brings out a new gun, so we decide to bring out something to equal it. As soon as the gun is produced, Germany brings out an even better gun and so we go on.

Today was a glorious day; one of those days that really makes you feel alive. It began with a clear, dry frost and when we trooped across the fields for breakfast, the sky was a clear deep blue with the moon still held there, as if reluctant to leave the sky's refreshing beauty. The frost turned into myriads of multi-coloured lights as the new morning sun brought them to life. At noon, the sun was really warm, exceptionally so for December. Yet we turn this beautiful and peaceful world into a horrible inferno of war. Oh that man would see his folly.

Friday 5th January

Today we heard surprising and sad news about Paddy Slattery, one of our fitters. Apparently, he and Jerry Selby set out to test a three-ton lorry and ended up taking a Dutch civilian to his home, near the frontline at Venlo. The civvy and Jerry Selby went upstairs to collect some clothing, leaving Paddy downstairs. When they came downstairs, Paddy wasn't there, and, they presumed he had gone for a stroll somewhere outside. The civvy wanted something from the cellar and as he opened the door, he heard 'hands up' in German. He promptly slammed the door and beat it, followed by Jerry Selby, who had not bothered to take his personal arms. He hung around outside for a while shouting for Paddy. Getting no response, he got the aid of a platoon of our infantry who were some distance away. When they arrived they searched the house thoroughly, but found no trace of the German or Paddy. Therefore, it can only be presumed, that the German killed Paddy or knocked him unconscious or took him prisoner while the other two were upstairs and then, made good his escape, while they were fetching the infantry. Thus, Paddy is reported missing for the moment, but he could either dead or a prisoner-of-war.[1] We must now be on the lookout for German spies wearing our uniforms, speaking excellent English and knowing quite a bit of regimental history. One was captured in our Regimental clothing not long ago at a café near the ranges and if they have got Paddy, they have another uniform to masquerade in.

1. Paddy Slattery is listed as having been a prisoner of war in Courage (1949, p 258).

Chapter 47
Time for contemplation

Saturday 6th January
It was a very quiet day that culminated in a game of chess with Tony Booth.

Sunday 7th January
Attended church service at RHQ. The padre was rather a flop and would have done much better talking to little children than to frontline fighting men. The church proper will have to buck its ideas up if it is to play a vital part in world reconstruction. They talk about the Lord making the rich poor and the poor rich in a world where it's anything but that. Such flowery language as: 'The Lord make his countenance to shine upon you' is hopelessly out of date. More practical language should be used. The world of business must be met on its own terms and the basis of religion explained in simple terminology so that it can be better understood. Less sentiment and more logic should be introduced. Religion is not a thing to be solemn and sad about, as is the popular opinion today, but something to rejoice about and that side of it should be stressed more. I could go on and on, but it is a minor form of hypocrisy. Anyone can suggest improvements when it means no inconvenience to them.

Monday 8th January
Today's mail brought news that Mrs Davies passed away last Tuesday evening. Understandably, Vera is very upset.[1] Time will be a great healer. During the night several inches of snow fell and a miniature blizzard raged all day. It's quite impossible weather for tanks. However, if it freezes I shouldn't be surprised if we see action again in a few weeks time. The first leave party goes on February 15th. Roll on England.

Tuesday 9th January
Activity here is very much curtailed by the heavy fall of snow. We seem to spend most of the time in our billets, which is quite a good thing. This afternoon, however, our troop officer took us on a compass march.

Wednesday 10th January
Being orderly corporal today meant the usual dashing around detailing fellows on an ad-lib basis. Still, it is very much easier than doing guard duty. Troopers do guard and full corporals and sergeants guard commanders, but lance corporals, just do orderly corporal duty. This only applies when we are not in action. In action everyone does guard.

---

1. Vera was the wife of Dorothy's brother, Jack, and Mrs Davies was her mother.

Thursday 11th January
Last night was the coldest of the war - 16 degrees of frost. I had to thaw my toothbrush and shaving brush out before I could use them. The rest of the fellows are sleeping in the barn on top of a huge stack of straw. But as there was no room for me up there, I was sleeping on the floor until today. The 'old lady' has presented me with a room of my own, complete with 'civvy bed'. Whether it was because she thought it was too cold for me in the barn, because she has 'taken a fancy to me' or because I am the Non-Commissioned Officer (N.C.O) I do not know. Training films at Weert made a fairly pleasant morning. A quiz programme occupied the afternoon.

Friday 12th January
Re- visited Helmond; this time to see the film 'Cover Girl', and an enjoyable day was had by all.

Saturday 13th January
Today's paper gives the good news of a new Russian offensive towards Silesia. The attack is going well and Stalin declares that this will be the final campaign of the war. He intends to go right through to Germany. If he manages to capture the industrial district of upper Silesia, it will be a great strain on Germany's war effort and the end of the war will be in sight. I should think the Russians will get a lot of support from the workers in the industrial areas as they are mainly Poles and Russians, imported as prisoners and doing forced labour for the Germans. I hope that they take retaliation for such atrocities as Lublen in Poland where the Nazis murdered two hundred civilians, including women and children, just before they evacuated the town. Incidentally a new Polish Government has been set up there.

The German advance into Belgium has been pushed back considerably now. Compare the present position with the one on December 30th. German losses are estimated at forty thousand prisoners and fifty thousand dead against the American losses of forty thousand and these are nearly all prisoners. In Athens hostilities will cease at one minute past midnight on Monday morning. Discussions between the Greek Government and the EAM-ELAS will then take place.[1]

Sunday 14th January
Went to church at RHQ. We now have a new padre - an MA I believe. He talks good sense, not religious sentiment. He has thought about religion seriously. We could do with more fellows like him.

1. ELAS was the army of EAM. It meant Liberating Greek People's Army.

Monday 15th January

The REME captain peered down our big gun and just managed to see the other end. Verdict: it has to be de-coppered. The gauge would not even go in the barrel because the copper was so thick. Still, it is only to be expected, as it is one of the original tanks that we got in France.

Tuesday 16th January

The Intelligence Officer's lecture put us in the picture about the war situation. It is certainly much brighter than a fortnight ago when we were being pushed back in Belgium. The British 2nd Army has put in an attack on Roermond near here, but the eyes of the world are upon Russia. The more tanks Joe knocks out, the less there are for us. Good old Joe.[1]

Wednesday 17th January

As a sequel to the series of First Aid lectures we have had, this morning, in lieu of an examination, we had an inter-troop competition. We tied with FHQ for the prize of six hundred cigarettes. I've learnt more about First Aid in this series of informal lectures by an RAMC corporal than from all the MO's lectures. I now consider myself fairly competent.

Thursday 18th January

The majority of the infantry regiments in our Division have been so badly under strength and have been re-enforced by young soldiers that they are now doing extensive and intensive training. As part of this training, we went on an infantry-tank co-operation scheme today. Perfect co-ordination between the infantry and tanks would save many lives, but it tends to be neglected, mainly by the infantry. Infantry without tanks often means heavy casualties when a couple of tanks could easily silence the machine gun nests with HE's and BESA fire. On the other hand, tanks without infantry support often means loss of tanks and the lives of the tank crews because they are unable to sort out enemy bazooka men in deep slit trenches. Bazookas are much more deadly than 75-mm or 88-mm because the second explosion takes place inside the tank. An 88-mm is a solid shot and rips the tank open, but there is more chance of surviving than with a bazooka.

Friday 19th January

An exercise for A Squadron was supposed to start at 8.00am, so we got up an hour earlier than usual and trooped down to the cook house for an early breakfast only to find that the scheme had been cancelled last night and no-one had told us. Boy, did we curse. Since it was snowing heavily, all we could do was have map reading exercises in the billet.

---

1. 'Joe' was the affectionate name by which the British public referred to Joseph Stalin. The USSR was an ally in the war and little was known in the West about his internal policies.

Saturday 20th January

Our second infantry co-operation scheme proved much more exciting than the first. We went into attack through a smoke screen at full speed, thus livening things up a bit. Beyond that and receiving a letter from Dorothy, the day was uninteresting.

Chapter 48
A gunnery course

Sunday 21st January
We left Leverii at 9.00am for the Regimental Gunnery School at Lommel in Belgium. I am here to do a week's crew commander gunnery course. To my surprise, I found that I was billeted where I stayed the night when we came down to the ranges. The occupants of the house, where four of us are billeted, are an old lady and her two daughters. A curious thing about the people here is that they have nothing to do and get up at 6:30am to start doing it. Nevertheless, they are very good to us.

Monday 22nd January
Our course started in earnest this morning with an elaborate drill parade. Gunnery is an extensive subject and there is plenty to learn. In an all too short seven days, the course covers 75-mm, 95-mm, 17-pounders, Besa, Browning, testing and adjusting of sights, range finding, sight instruments, ammunition, indirect firing, observation post work and extensive mine instruction. The time between 1:15pm and 1:20pm is all our own.

Tuesday 23rd January
Made my first intimate association with the Bar and Stroud Range Finder. It is an ingenious device that gives you two convergent images that allow you to judge your distance from the target.

Wednesday 24th January
There is certainly plenty to learn here. We dash around from one lecture room to another, stripping guns, delving into the intricacies of ballistics, finer adjustments on sighting instruments and involved theories on testing and adjusting of gun sights.

Thursday 25th January
Today came the exhilarating news that in approximately a week's time, the Regiment is moving back to somewhere on the Belgian-French border for training and re- fitting with the new Comet tanks. These are the very latest British tanks and they are fitted with the new secret 77-mm gun. It incorporates all the best designs and gadgets of British tanks and the 77-mm gun is supposed to be as good as the 17-pounder, with high penetration power. It is about time we got a decent tank. We are always well behind the Germans in tank production, although our engines are by far the best. The Russians have the new Victor Tank, which is the equal of the dreaded German Tiger. For a photograph of this tank see *Figure 48*.

Figure 48
A photograph of the USSR's Victor Tank (Source not known).

However, we are now one up on the Germans in terms of anti-tank ammunition. The principle of our Sabot ammunition is a small exceedingly hard steel projectile with three sabots fitted around it to fit the size of the bore. When fired, the sabots fly off by centrifugal force and, therefore, the small projectile has the same power behind it as a shell twice its size and weight.[1]

Friday 26th January

The news from the Eastern Front is really terrific. The Russians are now only one hundred and forty miles from Berlin. East Prussia is entirely cut-off and Konignsberg is expected to fall soon. Breslau and Poznam are menaced and they are as important to Germany as Sheffield and Coventry are to England. There is a direct menace to Berlin and each news bulletin brings details of further Russian advances. It seems as though the German's last defence-line will be the River Oder, and that runs only twenty miles from Berlin. German morale must be fairly low now, with the Russians only one hundred and forty miles away and our air forces giving them a terrific pounding. There is no saying what next week's news will bring. The end of the war is now definitely within sight. It seems quite probable that instead of waiting for a spring

1. In this context the term sabot doesn't refer to a wooden shoe as earlier. It was a device that ensured the correct positioning of a bullet or shell in the barrel of a gun. It was attached either to the projectile or insider the barrel and fell away as it left the muzzle.

offensive, we shall now push in everything we've got in an attempt to finish the war quickly. The British 2nd Army's offensive in Roermand, which is only a few miles from here, is going well. The British 2nd Army usually includes us, but they're doing without us on this stint. We aren't cribbing (complaining).

Saturday 27th January

Our gunnery course finished today with a fairly stiff test. Pens and brains squeaked simultaneously. I managed 70%, which is average. On the whole the course was very interesting and I have enjoyed my week here. A visit to the town of Mol this afternoon provided a welcome diversion. An excellent jive band plays in the NAAFI there. Jack Arkley and I had five francs worth of civvy cinema. The films shown by most cinemas over here are in English or American. The sound tracks are in English with translations in French or Flemish printed at the bottom of the film. The film in this case was 'The Heart of the North' and we enjoyed it very much.

Chapter 49
Bogged down again

Sunday 28th January
Farewell to Belgium - for a while at least. Our course finished, we arrived back with the Squadron in Holland in time for dinner. The little Belgian currency we had left we saved for our second visit to Brussels, which we hope will come soon. My watch is *caput*, so I hope to buy a new one there. A trip to Brussels is rather a drain on finance and several people are refusing to go the second time because they want to save all their cash for their leave in England.

Monday 29th January
It's Auntie Jessie's birthday. I wish you all the best, Aunt. The Russians are still advancing and are now only one hundred miles from Berlin and forty-five miles from Stettin. Poznan has been encircled in this drive. The Volkssturm,[1] with only fourteen days training, are being used by the Germans to try to stem this Russian avalanche. South of Poznan, the Russians have a bridgehead across the River Oder and are pouring troops across it. And on the Western Front we are taking it easy. Unfortunately, our time will come later, although it would be grand to have the war finished without having to go into action again. Our troops are now doing extremely well in Burma and I am hoping that BLA means the British Liberation Army and not 'Burma looms ahead'.

Tuesday 30th January
I'm orderly corporal again. A regimental advance party has gone into Belgium, so we must be moving back soon.

Wednesday 31st January
I am commanding a tank on the Squadron Infantry co-operation scheme this afternoon. I tried to take it through a frozen stream, which only seemed to be shallow water. A wave of fifteen feet and pieces of ice, a foot thick, flew into the air as we plunged in up to the mudguards. Poor old Ginger Morrison, the driver got soaked. To an outsider, it may have looked funny, but to us it wasn't. At the same time, we could see the humorous side of it. There we remained, nicely bogged down, until the recovery vehicle came to our rescue.

1. The *Volksstrum* consisted of all able-bodied men and some women between the ages of sixteen and sixty who were not already employed in defence of the Fatherland. In practice, it was an *ad hoc* and ill-equipped national militia.

Thursday 1st February
I start this month by wondering what the end of it will bring. The Russians are still advancing on Berlin and the situation at the end of this month should be very interesting. Unless the Russians are held up at the Oder, this month could possibly see the fall of Berlin. It is, of course, a debatable point whether Germany will collapse after the fall of Berlin. Hitler says that if Berlin falls he will take his armies into the Bavarian mountains and the Black Forest and hold out there indefinitely. This may be wishful thinking, although it's obvious that a country is not beaten just because its capital falls; its army also has to be defeated.

Friday 2nd February
During the night we had our first thaw for two months and it was grand to see the countryside green again and feel the warm air as we went to breakfast. Instead of biting cold wind, the air was comparatively warm and still and we felt the thrill of life in nature once more. A breath of spring - how I long for summer in England. We're back to Belgium, but only for two days this time. Left Leveroii at 2.00pm and arrived Hommel at 3:30pm. We passed a terrific convoy *en route*. There must be a push somewhere. Slept the night on the floor of someone's front room.

Saturday 3rd February
The Russians are now only forty-five to fifty miles from Berlin. Their terrific progress is shown in the map in *Figure 49*.

Figure 49

A map demonstrating the USSR's military progress.

We wait tentatively for each new bulletin. The Germans seem to have changed their propaganda. In France, they reported that we were at a certain place when we were in fact miles past it. In contrast, on the Eastern Front, they reported that the Russians had reached a town before they had. The only plausible reason for this seems to be that they can then say that they have retaken a town. Either that or the speed of the Russian advances is confusing their communiqués. In practice for our next push, we fired 75-mm and 17-pounders today. The shooting was fairly good with most of the targets being knocked down. We are back in Holland by 6.00pm.

Sunday 4th February
A torrent of rain today turned all the tracks into three inches of mud. We wade through it to meals and stand in it while we consume them. When it is raining, we endure the stench of the pigsty. We bring spare bread back to the house and toast it. The farmhouse is quite snug and with sixteen people in the front room every night it gets quite warm. When the 'civvies' dash out for the evening meal we dash to the fire and toast our supper. We can always tell when they are finishing by the long monotonous chant they have for grace and by the time they re-enter the front room from the kitchen, we have monopolized the table for reading and writing.

Monday 5th February
The confusion of the communiqués from the Russian front is obvious by the fact that today's *Daily Herald* says that the Russians have reached the line of the River Oder, but have not crossed it, while the *Daily Mirror* states in block letters: MANY GAPS IN ODER LINE. However, one thing is confirmed by all this coverage, namely, that the Russians are now only thirty-six miles from the outskirts of Berlin. On the Western Front, Boogie Watson and I changed the tank idler in the pouring rain.

Tuesday 6th February
The Army Welfare Centre has presented the Squadron with a radio. As each troop is in different billets, it goes round in turn and it is now our privileged possession for three days. Needless to say, it is on all day. At last we are up-to-date with our news. Churchill, Roosevelt and Stalin are in conference near the Black Sea. This seems to signify that we will be pushing on soon, since every time the 'Big Three' meet, there is a big push shortly afterwards.

Wednesday 7th February
I acted as troop corporal commander on a troop scheme this afternoon. Holland! Gosh! What a country. One cannot dig down more than two feet without finding water and it is almost impossible country for tanks. So much so that the troop schemes today turned out to be de-bogging schemes. Several tanks of the troops that started before us were bogged, but we managed to finish the scheme with only one tank out of the four bogged. We were pleased with this and I was ready to take my crew and tank home, when we were called on to tow out one of the bogged tanks. That did it. First the Squadron Leader's tank got bogged and then ours suffered the same fate. We got ourselves un-bogged and used the tank to anchor a second tank, which had appeared on the scene, while we gave a hand with the proceedings. There were six tanks all bogged in one little valley and small wonder. If one stood still for a couple of minutes, one got stuck in the mud. One fellow got so badly stuck in his gumboots that the only way he could get out was to step out of his gumboots and pull them out quickly before he sunk

in again. But the situation soon lost its humorous touch, when we were wallowing around in the mud after dark in the pouring rain. It is not very funny when you are soaked to the skin and the mud and water squelches over your boots. We managed to un-bog three of the tanks and then the situation became so hopeless that the Squadron Leader put a guard on the tanks and we returned to our billets and a very welcome rum ration.

Thursday 8th February

We were wallowing in the mud again at 9.00am this morning. But this time it wasn't raining and dark, so it produced results. All the tanks were un-bogged by 1.00pm. We were the first away and managed to get over all the difficult country only to get bogged twenty yards from the tank park. That was soon remedied, however. The news from the Eastern Front is good as usual. On Tuesday and Wednesday the Russians knocked out one hundred and forty-nine German tanks and took eighteen thousand prisoners. They are now only thirty-three miles from the suburbs of Berlin and have a strong bridgehead over the Oder near Breslau. Last night, seven hundred Mosquitos[1] bombed German positions not very far from here.

1. Mosquitos were RAF planes constructed of heat-formed plywood over a wooden frame, with sections glued and screwed for extra strength. They were built of Ecuadorian balsawood sandwiched between Canadian birch, a particularly strong and lightweight grade of plywood.

Chapter 50
Self-inflicted wounds

Friday 9th February

A very unfortunate accident occurred on the ranges at Lommel today. The full details are not yet known, but this is what I gather happened. Armour piercing shells are usually solid steel with a tracer[1], but a few experimental ones were made with high frequency (H.F) charges inside. However, these are now obsolete and are supposed to have been returned. Regardless of the fact that there might still have been one of these left, to prove that a trace in a solid shot wouldn't go off without being fired, one stupid fellow threw it into the fire. Nothing happened for half an hour and the fellows who knew about it went away to fire the guns. Meanwhile, the party that had finished firing came and sat round the fire of old ammunition boxes, planks etc., to get warm. Seeing the round in the fire, Sergeant Angel tried to get it out with his stick and the thing went off, hurling nails and shrapnel all over the place. Strangely enough, Sergeant Angel wasn't hurt at all. Carrington of our troop was hit in the wrist and leg by shrapnel, but not at all seriously, and Curley Rae was hit by a couple of nails and had his hand and face slightly burnt. The worst injured was Lewis of 2nd Troop. He had half of his foot blown off and was hit in the leg by so many nails and shrapnel that his leg had to be taken off below the knee joint. It is bad enough for that to happen in action, but when it is entirely due to someone's utter stupidity one could remain bitter for the rest of one life. Taffy Lewis had got through five months action without a scratch, only to lose his leg through someone else's stupidity. Still, these things happen and at least he is safe back in England, which is more than I can say.

Saturday 10th February

An attack has been launched from Nijmegen, pushing eastwards, and an advance of ten miles has been made. South of here, the Americans have taken Schmitt and are trying to capture two important dams near there. The Russians are now menacing Frankfurt on the River Oder. A message to all troops from the Commander-in-Chief, 21stArmy Group, wishes us all the best in our last round to knock out Germany, so it looks as though we will be in again soon.

Sunday 11th February

A glorious lazy day spent just writing and writing and writing. Being some sort of Dutch celebration today, the landlady provided us with an excellent supper of oatcakes, biscuits and coffee.

---

1. A tracer was a flare marking the trajectory of the shell's flight.

Monday 12th February

I had a routine day as orderly corporal. There is nothing of interest to report, which is perhaps just as well.

Tuesday 13th February

Pancake Tuesday doesn't means much to us stuck here. I sincerely wish that I could write as yesterday - nothing to report. Unfortunately, there is something to report. We were working on the tank this afternoon and 4th Troop were being instructed on PIAT anti-tank gun nearby.[1] There was a blinding flash and men scattered in all directions. We realised that an accident had occurred and I grabbed the first-aid box from the tank. The PIAT shell had exploded in the gun barrel, making a horrible mess of the gun and the three fellows standing by it. Mr Cruickshank, who fired the gun, was laid on his back with blood oozing from his shoulder and the back of his head. His left arm was lying by his side with a huge piece ripped out of it just above the wrist. Tommy Sutton, from Leeds, had a nasty stomach wound. It was pretty painful. The instructor from the Monmouthshire Regiment was in a bad way too. His legs were peppered with shrapnel and he had nasty wounds in the stomach and face. There was plenty of assistance and we soon had them all bandaged up. By the time we had finished dressing Mr Cruickshank's arms, we had to change the dressing on his head because it was saturated with blood. All three men had to be given morphine and a tourniquet had to be applied to Mr Cruickshank's arm. All three are seriously injured and it seems a shame that it happened on training. This time it was a pure accident. The shell exploded prematurely and it is just dammed bad luck that it should have done such damage.

1. PIAT stood for 'Projector, Infantry, Anti-Tank'.

Chapter 51
Push on Joe

Friday 14th February

We had an enjoyable morning popping off bottles on the rifle range. The weather has improved greatly recently. Today has been almost like summer and the ground dries up quickly. In the British and Canadian push from Nijmegen, Cleve and Gennep have been captured. Resistance appears to have been fairly stiff, although Germans have been giving themselves up in large numbers. Russia continues to make progress. General Konev[1] is now only forty miles from Dresden and Marshall Zhukov[2] eighteen miles from Stettin. Push on Joe.

Thursday 15th February

The decisions of the ' Big Three' in the Crimea Pact have been announced. See *Figure 50* for a photograph of the Allied war leaders and *Figure 51* for an account of their meeting.

The Daily Sketch

NEWS AND PICTURES

TUESDAY, FEBRUARY 13, 1945

ONE PENNY

ALLIES TO DIVIDE GERMANY INTO FOUR CONTROL ZONES

Figure 50

A photograph of Roosevelt, Churchill and Stalin at their meeting in Yalta (Source not known).

1. General Konev was the Commander of the 1st Ukrainian Forces and later of the 2nd Ukrainian Forces. He played a particularly prominent part in the Soviet offensive of 1943-1944.
2. Marshall Zhukov played a central part in the defence of Leningrad and Stalingrad. He commanded the Russian Army in the offensive against German forces and accepted the Nazi surrender in Berlin on May 8, 1945.

Crimea Pact By 'Big 3' | **France To Be Invited** | **Full Meetin On April 2**

DEFEATED Germany is to be divided into Allied zones of occupation, her General Staff broken up, military equipment removed or destroyed, and her war-potential industries eliminated.

These are among the measures decided on at the Crimean Conference of Marshal Stalin, Mr. Churchill and President Roosevelt to ensure that Germany will never be able to plunge the world into war again.

The conference was held at Yalta, a health resort near the south coast of the Crimea. Its decisions were announced in a nine-point communiqué last night. These were:

1 DEFEAT OF GERMANY: We have considered and determined military plans for the final defeat of the common enemy. Our combined plans will be made known only as they are executed.

Meetings of the three staffs will be continued in future whenever the need arises.

Surrender Terms After Defeat

2 OCCUPATION AND CONTROL: Common policies and plans have been agreed for enforcing the unconditional surrender terms which will be imposed on Nazi Germany. The terms will not be made known till Germany is defeated.

Forces of the Three Powers will each occupy a separate z of Germany, with a central control commission consisting of supreme commander of the three Powers in Berlin.

France will be invited to take a zone of occupation participate as a fourth member of the control commission shc she so desire.

Swift Justice For War Guilty

We are determined to disarm and disband all Gern armed forces, break up for all time the German Gene Staff, remove or destroy all German military equipme eliminate or control all German industry that could used for military production, bring all war criminals justice and swift punishment, and exact reparation kind.

It is not our purpose to destroy people of Germany

3 REPARATIONS: Germany to be obliged to m compensation for the damage in kind to the great extent possible.

Peace Charter Conference

4 ALLIED CONFERENCE: A United Nations conf ence will be called at San Francisco in April, 1 to prepare a charter of peace and a security organisat on the lines of the Dumbarton Oaks talks.

China and France will be consulted and invited join in the invitations to the conference.

5 LIBERATED EUROPE: Declaration providing concerning the Three Powers' policies and for jc action on political and economic problems has b drawn up.

Rebuilding of economic life must be achieved . . . the principle of the Atlantic Charter—the right of peoples to choose the form of Government they w

Turn to Back Page

Figure 51

A newspaper account of the Yalta meeting of the 'Big Three' (Source not known).

Friday 16th February

Rumour hath it that we may be going into action in a few days. Flap on. Queer feeling in stomach again. Hope rumour hath it wrong. In a war area anything can happen. I am sorry to be leaving Leverii and the Herman family as we have spent a very comfortable seven weeks here. For a photograph of the Herman family and the crew taken outside the family's front door see *Figure 52*.

Figure 52
The Hermans family with the tank crew. The crew standing left to right:
Ted Hipkiss, the author, Tony Booth, Steve Hamilton and Boogie Watson.
The family seated: 'Pa' Hermans, Wilhelmina, Mathieu, Margaret and Harry.
The remaining members of the family were either too cold or too shy to appear.

Saturday 17th February

Moved off at 7:15am in the grey morning mist under wireless silence. The Regiment must have stretched for at least a couple of miles. We covered the sixty-odd miles north westwards to Hertogenbosch in record time and arrived at our concentration point four kilometres from Hertogenbosch just before 12.00-noon. The first thing that struck us about the place was that flying bombs were passing dangerously low overhead at regular intervals. They must be launched from German occupied Holland and are only just gaining height as they pass over here. I hope that none of them have faulty mechanisms. The rumour of action seems untrue for a while at least. The whole Regiment is billeted in a monastery or school of some sort, which has been a German barracks. There are drawings of Jerries in action on the walls and numerous swastikas and slogans like: 'The Führer's will is our command' all over the place. The artist knew his job too. It was strange to be in barrack rooms again. The order of the day is spit and polish. Are we getting ready for a change in status to an army of occupation?

Sunday 18th February

The barracks have been left in a terrible state by the Canadians who were here before us and we spent today cleaning it up.

Monday 19th February

I have received no mail for six days. Wake your ideas up Army Post Office. Saw Bill Kavanagh. He is number sixty-six on the HQ Squadron Leave Roll. A-Squadron has not drawn up its leave roll yet. Hope we can manage to go together. June seems most likely.

Tuesday 20th February

The buzz bombs[1] still rattle the windows as they pass over and one or two have dropped fairly near here. When it's clear, as it is today, one can see them tearing across the sky on their terrible mission. By their direction, I should say that they were heading for Antwerp. The Nilmegen push, Konev's push towards Dresden and the Cleft Chin murder case[2] occupy equal portions of the newspaper space.

Wednesday 21st February

I set out in the evening for Hertogenbosch with Tony Booth and Tumble Tumblety. A fairly large proportion of the town is damaged, presumably mainly by bombing. We had heard rumours that Germans shelled the town at night, but we didn't take much notice. That was until a shell landed close by and proved the rumour to be correct. Civvies dashed for shelter, but very little happened. Nightlife is very quiet with a curfew at 8.00pm.

Thursday 22nd February

At last, we have some definite news about leave. Out of one hundred and twenty-three eligible for leave I came out a number thirty-five on the Squadron ballot at 4.00pm tonight. The Squadron allocation for March is fifteen and so numbers one to fifteen will go. The allocation for April is bound to be at least thirty, so I should be on leave about April 22nd, I hope. That good news was followed by bad. We go into action again in a few days time.

---

1. As mentioned in a previous footnote 'buzz bombs' was a popular name given to V1s. They were also called doodlebugs.
2. The cleft chin murder occurred in 1944. It was so-called because the victim, a taxi driver, had a cleft chin. Elizabeth Jones and Gustav Hulten, a GI, were tried for the murder at the Old Bailey in January 1945 and found guilty. Hulten was hanged in March 1945, but two days before she was due to be executed, Jones received a reprieve.

Chapter 52
Into Germany

Friday 23rd February
We move up to the battle area at midnight tonight. The newspapers aren't at all encouraging. They tell of stiff fighting against Panzer divisions in the area where we are going. So this is goodbye to Holland. I shall be inside Germany itself soon. At one time that would have been quite a thrill, but going into action again isn't at all pleasant. We shall have to watch the German civilians too.

Saturday 24th February
From here on, my diary becomes rather dirty and brief as we are in action again. We undertake a long tedious route march through the night to two-thirds of the way to our destination. By route march I obviously mean in the tanks. The gunner and co-driver slept on the back. As soon as it came light, we harboured in a wood and after camouflaging up, got under way cooking breakfast of bacon and eggs, which we had scrounged. The afternoon was fairly warm and we made up for our loss of sleep by going to sleep in the open. As soon as darkness descended, or ascended as pilots would have it, we moved off again. At 8:45pm I entered Germany. If a year ago anyone had told me that I would be in Germany today, I would not have believed him, but here I am. Small world isn't it? At midnight we passed through Cleve, which was won from the Germans less than a week ago.

Sunday 25th February
We arrived at our destination at 1.00am and took up temporary positions in a small orchard near a couple of houses. Dave and I are on guard. In France, Belgium and Holland I had sympathy for the refugees and their war-shattered houses, but here, I just don't give a damn. The Germans started this war and if it hadn't been for them, I would be in a comfortable condition, so they can jolly well pay for it. If I want a fire, I shall not think twice about using German furniture. When a Canadian tank was knocked out near here, the civvies dashed out with sticks and started beating the dazed crew as they baled out, so they deserve everything that's coming to them. Received a letter from Dorothy saying that she will marry me next leave, which makes me very happy. Details too intimate to record here.

Monday 26th February
We are under an hour's notice to move into action. Had a look at the knocked out German tank near here. The tank had brewed up[1] and the crew of five had all been killed. There were three graves nearby and two charred bodies inside

1. The term 'brewed up' was Army lingo for 'hit and on fire'.

the turret. One was almost unrecognisable as a human body - just a black mess with a few charred bones. The shape of the other body was recognisable, charred black with the knee bone protruding. All it needed was a notice: 'This might happen to you - Take Care'.

Tuesday 27th February

Up at 4.00am under notice to move into action, which did not come until 4.00pm. With some men from the Monmouthshire Regiment - an infantry regiment - on the back of our tank, we pushed on through the village of Udem, which the Canadians had taken just a few hours before, and Germans were still hanging around in cellars and attics. It was a horrible sensation going through the town, expecting a Jerry to lob a grenade from a window or blast you into eternity with a bazooka. I became all clammy with sweat, but worse was to follow.

Wednesday 28th February

Last night still seems one horrible nightmare. At 8.00pm, we were ordered to push on in the moonlight, straight down the main road through the enemy's lines and A Squadron was to be the leading Squadron with first Troop the leading troop. This made Sergeant Gibson leading tank and mine second. The infantry were to support us and *vice versa.* Tanks are almost useless in the dark. You cannot hear a blasted thing because of the engine and you cannot see anything until you are twenty yards from it, so it is a matter of who gets the first shot in. You seem to be fighting an invisible enemy, an unknown horror bent upon your destruction, and you have a sickly feeling in your stomach because you know that, at any moment, you may be lying on the floor of the tank with a gaping hole in your guts or, if you're lucky, just with a limb hanging off. The first casualties were Jack Danby and Bob Banfield who were both killed by a shell that landed on top of their turret. It's a hell of a pity as they were both good blokes. By this time the roof of my mouth was like a block of salt and my hands warm and moist. Round a corner, by a group of farmhouses, we ran into a group of Jerries in slit trenches. One of them fired a bazooka at us. For the uninitiated, a bazooka is a horrible anti-tank weapon, which pierces the armour and explodes inside the tank making a mess of everything including the crew. If that bazooka had hit us, I should not be here to write this. Luckily it hit the ground just in front of us and we sprayed the slit trenches with machine gun fire as we reversed out of a horrible predicament. Out of range of the bazookas, we came under heavy shellfire and many of the infantry who were with us were hit. Sergeant Gibson advanced a little further and found that there was an anti-tank obstacle and mines across the road, so it was decided to send an infantry attack to the right flank. The infantry were so shaken up by the shelling and spandaus[1] that

1. Spandaus were German quick firing machine guns.

they took a lot of organising, but they eventually set off and we supported them with our big guns and machine guns. They must have had heavy casualties in the wood. It seemed like mass suicide to me, but perhaps they caught some of the Jerries sleeping. Even then, I was not in a happy state, peering into the darkness expecting a Jerry to creep up on us with a bazooka. By this time it was 4:30am and it would soon be light. We had to get out of the valley before dawn or risk being picked off by the German anti-tank gun, which we knew was on the opposite ridge. We just sneaked out as it was coming light. This sounds like one of those war tales that one reads about in fiction: a group of tanks creeping several miles behind the enemy's lines in the moonlight and have to get out again before dawn. Yet here I am writing it and still alive to tell the tale. Yes, truth is often stranger than fiction. It was a horrible experience and I would not like to have to go through it again.

Chapter 53
Another sleepless night

Thursday 1st March

Whilst holding the high ground, which was our objective, a C Squadron, Challenger tank was hit by a shell from a Panther tank and blew up immediately. One fellow was rather badly hurt, but the other four were lucky. We pulled back to replenish our ammunition and petrol and were shelled while doing so. Two jeeps and an ammunition lorry were hit and ammunition was flying all over the place. At 6.00pm we picked up the Herefords[1] and, as soon as it was dark, we moved into action with them, this time with C Squadron leading. Good Lord! More night fighting and as yet no signs of getting any sleep. It's one hell of a life isn't it? Still, I suppose it is helping the war effort.

Soon we encountered the enemy. We experienced heavy mortar fire and the infantry sustained a good few casualties. However, we pushed on with the few infantry that we had left and a terrible anticipation of the deadly bazooka[2] awaited us. None came. But as we neared the village, which was our objective, armour piercing (AP) tracing shots started whistling across our front. There were several horrible seconds of suspense as I saw one coming straight towards the tank. I didn't know whether to bale out or stay put. I was sure our end had come. However, it passed several yards to our left and we reversed out of the arc of fire. With Dave Dewar suffering from battle weariness, Taffy Hughes took his place. We were then sent to chase an SP gun[3] and, in doing so, the tank shed a track and got bogged. Mr Ridding took charge of another tank and left us to wait for assistance when it came light. Incidentally, the SP we were supposed to go after was found by a B Squadron tank that fired an HE at it by mistake. The HE didn't even scratch the heavy armour of the SP but the crew of the SP must have thought that the shot had penetrated and they bailed out, leaving the tank intact.

Friday 2nd March

Dawn brought a clear morning and lots of AP fire. Boogie Watson, Dave Dewar, Taffy Hughes and I made a lightening move and took cover in a nearby wood with the infantry. Much to our surprise, we found that the Squadron was harboured there too. We did without breakfast, because our rations were on the tank and it was under sniper fire. And after all this, came yet another nasty

1. The Herefords were an infantry regiment.
2. The bazooka was one of the first anti-tank weapons. It was nicknamed a 'bazooka' because of its vague resemblance to the musical instrument.
3. SPs were self-propelled guns. In effect they were mobile gun platforms that were used for defending transport columns against air attack.

experience. At about 3.00pm, the wood was heavily shelled and mortared. It seems as though Jerry had concentrated all his artillery on that one small wood. Boogie, Taffy and myself were lying, shivering in a slit-trench, thinking that it is only needs one to land in the trench and we've all had it. Sure enough, one landed right by its edge and Taffy yelled out: 'my leg. I'm bleeding horribly. Stop it or I'll bleed to death'. By now the bottom of the trench covered with blood. Luckily, Sergeant Gibson and Lance Corporal Tumblety realised that something was wrong and they came over to give assistance. It was a horrible job getting Taffy out of the trench, as both his legs were shattered and he was in very great pain. However, we gave him chloroform and got him out of the trench as best we could. As we carried him over to the Squadron Leader's tank, more shellfire came down and we had to drop him and dive for cover. After a second dose of chloroform, we eventually got him on the back of the tank and he was taken straight back to a field hospital. The tot of whisky that Sergeant Gibson offered me immediately afterwards was very welcome indeed. We laagered[1] for the night well clear of the wood, but I didn't sleep much.

Saturday 3rd March

The rest of the Squadron went into action again today, so since I had no tank, I took shelter in a B Squadron tank. Sergeant Gibson saw a farmhouse door open and two jars of fruit standing on the table inside. When he went in to get them, he noticed that two German civvies were sitting in the corner. He remarked: 'Good morning. Heil Churchill. I've come for the fruit'. He gathered it up off the table and went out. A and B Squadron recovery vehicles were un-bogging tanks, when several shells landed right in amongst them. Corporal Howard received a nasty cut on the head and Chatfield was slightly injured. Mr Eyles caught shrapnel in both legs and had to be carried away. Apart from that, it was an uneventful day.

1. The term laager means camp. Laagered is a synonym for harboured.

Chapter 54
Well, somebody had to stay with the tank

Sunday 4th March
At last: a day of rest. We took full advantage of it to have a much needed wash and shave, turning from something resembling dirty gorillas into more or less recognisable human shapes. A good scoff (meal) did not go amiss too.

Monday 5th March
The Regiment moved off today, leaving me in charge of the damaged tank, which is now minus a track and has a terrific water leak. I have plenty of rations, tobacco, writing paper and books, so am not worried how long it is before REME recover me. I remember once before in France… A tank can be made quite comfortable really. I am thoroughly settled down here. With my bed in the driver's compartment, I can eat, sleep, read and write at will. By this time the Germans are three miles away, so I needn't worry about them, but if some low-down German civvy comes snooping around the tank, I have my Sten gun ready to put a stop to his inquisitiveness.

This operation seems to be going quite well, in fact, much better than expected. We have linked up with the Yanks and a fair portion of the German Army is likely to be trapped. The Americans are already in Cologne and the pocket of Germans this side of the Rhine is dwindling. Whether the Americans will carry on and cross the Rhine remains to be seen. If the Americans are not up to strength and, therefore, not prepared to cross the Rhine, I think that we shall do the same as we did on the River Maas, namely, take-up our positions, re-group and re-fit.

Tuesday 6th March
My isolation on the tank did not prove to be too long because, at 2.00pm today, a Sherman recovery vehicle towed it away, to one hundred and fifty-nine Brigade Workshop in Udem. The workshops are actually in what appears to have been a bomb factory and I am billeted in what remains of a fine German house. Huge family albums indicate that it was the home of a well-known German family. The silverware and ornaments, still in the cupboards, go to show that it was a fairly rich family. Well, they've had it now. Udem itself is in a terrible state. I didn't see one house untouched by the bombing and shelling. Three civvies were still living in a very badly battered house, which they had patched up with tarpaulins etc. They didn't seem too happy about it either.

Wednesday 7th March
It's quite a novel experience being in workshops with a tank. The REMEs start work at 8.00am and finish at 5.00pm, but where they work, I really don't know. One can never find them when one wants one. I had a look at the tanks in the tank 'graveyard' this morning. They present a gruesome sight and tell an even more gruesome tale. By the position of the holes in the turret, one can almost tell how many people were killed or injured in it. Those 88-mm shells seem to be able to tear through almost any thickness of solid tempered steel.

Thursday 8th March
Boogie Watson arrived at the workshop with a 4th Troop tank. Captain Bentley told him to take the ruddy thing back, but Ernie Main took it instead. Heard the glorious news that the Regiment is pulling back to Louvain in Belgium for three weeks rest. Not wishing to be left behind, we fixed the track in our tank and I acted as commander, while Boogie drove it at breakneck speed back to the Squadron. It involved a good bit of map reading on my part too, if I may say so. We arrived back at the Squadron in time to cook tea just before dark. For want of a better place, we slept in the tank.

Chapter 55
At rest

Friday 9th March
After a breakfast of bacon and beans, bread and marmalade, we set off in a regimental column for Nijmegen where we are to await transporters to take us to near Louvain in Belgium for our rest. As we halted in Nijmegen before dark, we were able to procure civvy billets for ourselves.

Saturday 10th March
Transporters are not arriving until tomorrow, so we took advantage of it to take a look at Nijmegen. Not a very exciting place, although Nijmegen Bridge is rather an impressive sight.

Sunday 11th March
We loaded the tanks onto the transporters at 1.00pm and arrived Hertogenbosch at 6.00pm. Our original intention was to stay here for the night, but owing to the danger of shelling, it was decided that we should push right on through the night to our destination, four miles from Louvain. We tried to sleep under the canvas of the transporter, but we were cramped and our mouths were filled with dust and our stomachs with diesel oil fumes, so we just lay there in a dazed state. At 1:30am we arrived at our destination and with our eyes bunged-up with sleep and dust, we tumbled out and unloaded the tank. We left the tanks by the side of the road outside the billet for the night and had a welcome cup of char from the cookhouse, before crawling into our blankets and sleeping until 8.00am.

Monday 12th March
The pocket of German troops at Wesel has now been eliminated and the Rhine is cleared from north of Nijmegan to Coblenz. The American bridgeheads over the Rhine have linked up and trapped twenty thousand Germans. Essen has been shelled and bombed so much that it is said to be absolutely flat. This rest is just what we needed and is appreciated very much, but I am dreading the time when we have to go into action again. I want to go on leave and I hope that it will be in about five weeks time with me in one piece. I don't fancy life without a limb. Poor old Taffy lost his leg. Dave Dewar is off tanks because he's battle weary. So, out of the original crew that I came over to France with, I am the only one left on the fighting echelon. God knows how those fellows, who have been in the fighting since the beginning of the war, go on. I have had my fair share of it now. I should go home in five weeks' time and for two weeks of that time we should be on rest. It's what can happen in those other three weeks that worries me.

Tuesday 13th March

Len Stone and myself, together with two drivers, went to Louvain at 7:30am this morning to collect two new Comet tanks. As the train bringing them from Ypres did not arrive until 12.00-noon, we had a good look round the town. It is a fair sized place and quite pretty in parts. Trams run from there to Brussels. It makes me long for leave to see all the cinemas and other luxuries of civilisation. Trains are running again from here and it is the main departure point for leave in this area. In Lubbeek, eight kilometres from Louvain, where we are billeted, nearly everyone speaks Flemish, but in Louvain French is the most spoken language.

Wednesday 14th March

Had the long awaited bath this morning. It feels grand to have a change of clothing too. In the afternoon, a Belgian ENSA show proved to be very good entertainment.

Thursday 15th March

Started a two-day Comet course under Sergeant Nicholls. Otherwise, things are very quiet. We took some trucks to Louvain. It is good to be out on rest, but it makes my diary rather uninteresting. However, I prefer it that way.

Friday 16th March

I had quite a busy day on both the Comet course and as orderly Corporal. Discovered that George Bell has lost my typewriter, which is very annoying. I could have sold it for 100 guilders. Still, such are the hazards of war. Easy come. Easy go, I suppose.

Saturday 17th March

Visited Louvain and saw the film: 'After the Thin Man'. 'Tiny' Finlinson and I were on guard at 7.00pm and had to get back for then. We hopped on one of the rickety trains that often run alongside the roads on the continent. They are very crude and primitive affairs, but serve the purpose of delivering milk etc., to the various villages. They also act as a tram service for the villagers to and from town. Well, to return, we hopped on board this train affair at 5:15pm, giving us an hour and three quarters to do the six-mile journey back to Lubbeek. At 5:45pm we were two miles out of Louvain. At 6:15pm we were just half way and the train had stopped at the bottom of a gradient to get up steam and wait for another engine to help it up the ascent. If we had waited for the train, the guard would have mounted minus one man and one commander, so we abandoned the train and hitchhiked back, arriving just in time to dash on guard.

Sunday 18th March

The Gough case, involving Dennis O' Neill, an evacuee, aged thirteen, being beaten to death by Reginald Gough, a Shropshire farm labourer, is still in session and occupies considerable space in all the newspapers. That and the

Cleft Chin murder case have caused quite a distraction from war news. The Russians have taken Stettin and the American bridgehead over the Rhine is now five miles deep and fifteen miles wide. The British and Canadian bridgehead further north is steadily expanding.

Monday 19th March

Yesterday, Berlin was subjected to the heaviest day's assault of the war when two thousand seven hundred tons of bombs were dropped in one raid. It is estimated that a ton of bombs every second hit rail and industrial targets in and around Berlin. One thousand three hundred U.S heavy bombers were used. A minor crisis is being caused in England by the meat shortage. Most of Britain's meat is being sent to feed the occupied countries. America is rather short as well and, consequently, is cutting down on her shipments of Lend-Lease meat. John Llewellin, Minister of Food, and Mr Oliver Lyttleon, Minister of Production may go to Washington to discuss the situation.

Tuesday 20th March

The famous Remagen Bridge over which many of our troops crossed the Rhine has collapsed. The eastern upstream support had been cut in several places by enemy shells and this was being repaired when the bridge collapsed. Because of these repairs, the bridge was closed to traffic. The only casualties were the engineers who were working on the bridge. The Allied air forces are doing great work in cutting enemy supply lines.

Wednesday 21st March

The first day of spring and it is true to type. It is a truly glorious day and the trees are bursting into bud and all that sort of thing. Oh to spend spring in England.

Tuesday 22nd March

Ah Brussels! Another three days leave in that glorious city. Arrived at 10:30am with Dave Dewar and went to the 'Blue Pool', a Canadian club, where we had a leisurely shower, followed by my first swim of the year. It was a gloriously hot day and it was grand to relax in the clear blue water. We emerged two new men, and did full justice to the excellent meal. We were supposed to sleep at the Hotel De Sermonde, but it turned out to be a dirty, drab brothel. However, in the afternoon we visited the people whom Dave was billeted with the last time he was here and they insisted that we stayed with them and we gladly accepted. They are exceedingly nice people and could not do enough for us. We found ourselves in a civvy bed with real white sheets and an eiderdown and after seeing the film: 'Up in Arms' at the U.S. Army Theatre, and a supper provided by the family, we made good use of it.

Friday 23rd March
It is really glorious weather and really too hot at times. It is surprising how the weather affects one's spirits. The weather today gives one a sense of exhilaration, appreciation of the sweetness of life and desire to live. So much so that action seems so remote and one longs for a continuation of this glorious life. Were it not for the fact that we have been in action on days like this, it would be hard to realize that men are being mutilated and are dying on the battlefield not so far away. It seems too glorious for that. However, here we are in Brussels and we really do appreciate it. Bette Davies and Miriam Hopkins in the film 'Old Acquaintances' occupied the afternoon. Brussels seems to be even gayer than ever in the bright sunlight. As a women's fashion centre, I should say it almost equals Paris. The women are certainly well dressed and made up and most of them are very attractive too. I should think that a woman who isn't well dressed in Brussels would not stand a chance of getting on. Food is still rather scarce, but if one is willing to pay for it, one can get cream cakes galore. Even before the war, one could not get such stuff in milk bars in England.

Saturday 24th March
It is another glorious day. Saw Pygmalion for the first time. Never knew what Pygmalion stood for. Apparently he was a fifteenth century sculptor who created a woman so beautiful that he willed her to life. In the evening, we saw a film: *Le Couple Invisible*. On the streets, we were caught for a twenty-franc donation to some religious organisation. And, thus, our second glorious visit to that gay wide-awake city - the capital of Belgium - comes to an end. We have had a marvellous time and leaving here is like returning from leave at home.

Sunday 25th March
Returned to the Regiment and the good news that my leave has been put forward to Wednesday April 18th - just three weeks on Wednesday. Roll on that date. Spent all day getting two brand new Comet tanks out of grease. I wonder what the rush is? The attack to the east of the Rhine is going extremely well and I should not be surprised if we go back to Germany.

Monday 26th March
There are now eight bridgeheads over the Rhine and Allied forces are already thirty miles east of it. German opposition seems to be weakening. A thousand bomber raids are still going on every night and Germany must be feeling it. There are signs that this will be the final campaign of the war. Certainly everyone is optimistic about it. It looks as though we are going to be in at the kill too, as we are working all hours to get these tanks ready.

Tuesday 27th March

The news is even better. Things seem to be happening rather quickly. All the British bridgeheads have linked up and resistance is reported to be weakening. I am glad to hear this news because that's where we're going and it's too near leave and the end of the war to be wounded or killed. Took over Comet No. 347 and worked till dark to get it ready for action. The crew is now - Tiny Finlinson, commander, with me as wireless operator, Ken Kirkley as gunner, Boogie Watson as driver and Ken Slack as co-driver.

Chapter 56
Back into Germany

Wednesday 28th March

Germany here we come. We were loaded onto transporters at 3.00pm and moved off at 5:30pm. The news is very encouraging. Main headlines are: 'The Allied Armies push into Germany against rapidly disintegrating resistance'. Four major generals and one hundred members of the German general staff have given themselves up. Prisoners are rolling in. They now realise that it is too near the end of the war to throw away their lives needlessly. It certainly looks as though the end of the war is very near. Frank Gillard of the BBC gives it three weeks. I hope he is right. With the comfort of this news, I had a pleasant sleep, in spite of the jolting of the tank as we travelled on through the darkness into Belgium and Holland and then into Germany.

Thursday 29th March

We unloaded the tanks near Issum in Germany and were cooking breakfast by the side of the road when Field Marshall Sir Bernard Montgomery pulled up in his jeep. He wished us good hunting and dished out the daily newspapers. *The Daily Mail* states in bold headlines: 'This is the collapse!' The world is agog with excitement. The end of the war is at last within sight. There is a security blackout on our movement in the north, but we are at least fifty miles over the Rhine and, in the south, the Americans are eighty-five miles east of it. Another month should see it over. It may even be finished by the time I go on leave. I hope so, but I don't think so. At 11:30am we crossed the Rhine. It is a very wide river with a moderately fast current. We crossed it on a single-track pontoon bridge, keeping ninety feet apart, so that the rubber pontoon boats supporting the bridge would not sink too far. As we crossed it - listening, incidentally, to the BBC - I thought: 'So this is the Rhine; the river that all the fuss has been about. I never thought that I would be crossing it. Neither did the Germans I should think. Hope the bridge doesn't collapse. Wonder if it's deep? This is quite an historic moment. Note the time and date: 11:30am March 29th 1945. The next time I cross it will be to go on leave on April 18th, I hope'. Such were the thoughts of a tank Lance-Corporal on crossing the Rhine. Might be of interest to the *Daily Mail* under the heading: 'What I felt like when crossing the Rhine, by one who was there'.

On the east bank of the Rhine, we passed through Wesel, or the remains of it. I didn't see many corpses, so most of the civvies must have cleared out. We slept the night by the side of the tank, not far from there. A very good sleep I had too.

Friday 30th March
It's Good Friday, but as a day of celebration it means nothing to us, as we are well inside Germany. We set out this morning to take a certain place only to find that units ahead of us had taken it already and pushed on another fifteen miles. On the way there we passed quite a few dead Jerries: the only good ones. One or two were rather mangled, but no one has time to bury them. Prisoners keep coming down the road in large groups, happy to be out of it by the looks of it. They know that the war will be over soon and they want to make sure that they live through it. The only way of making sure of that is by becoming a prisoner. It is rather annoying. At least they are safe until the end of the war, which is more than we can say.

Saturday 31st March
Gosh! What a way to spend Easter. We set off after breakfast to take the village Wettringen. We didn't know what enemy resistance we would encounter, but we soon found out. I suppose it wasn't very heavy really, but they certainly gave us a hectic time. The worst thing is the suspense. One's stomach feels empty, yet one doesn't feel like anything to eat. If you let your imagination run riot you would soon become a nervous wreck. I have to keep a firm hold on myself. Going down a road with open spaces and woods on either side, one is faced with the dilemma of either keeping one's head out of the turret looking for enemy tanks, mines, guns or bazooka-men and risking the snipers, shells and machine gun fire or keeping well down in the turret out of the way and risk not seeing the bazooka-men. Personally, I go into action with my head out. I like to see what is happening and look out for these horrible chaps with bazookas. One continuously hears of tanks who have been knocked out and fellows who have been wounded and it doesn't cheer one up at all. My only consolations are that the war is definitively nearing its end and I go on leave on April 18th. After several skirmishes with infantry, we entered the village of Wettringen. We were the first British troops to enter the village and we had to fight our way in. After we had cleared it, we sat on the outskirts, looking out to the east by the side of a church. When the civvies realized that the shooting was all over, they came timidly out of their cellars waving white flags. We were the first English they had seen and they peered at us as though we were curiosities, no doubt wondering what was going to happen to them. They seem quite willing to fraternize and gave us beef sandwiches and cheese. We were even offered German sausage. They all say that the war will be over in eight days and gesticulate wildly trying to show the horrible things they are going to do to Hitler. No doubt yesterday, they were going to do the same to us. Most of them do seem to be glad that it's all over, though some of them wave and cheer almost as though it were an occupied country we had liberated. One old German, however, spat contemptuously on the ground as we passed. We could have shot him I suppose, but we are far too lenient. The Volksstrum

(German Home Guard) is quite a problem. They wear all kinds of uniform and one cannot tell whether they are neutral or civvies or as hostile as the Army. As they are not in the army proper, they cannot be taken prisoner and, therefore, have to be disarmed and sent back home. There are plenty of these Volksstrum in German uniform wandering up and down the roads and it seems strange to just ignore them. I suppose several of members of the regular German Army get back home that way.

Most of the German civvies were scared stiff that there would be more bombing and shelling and Tiny, who speaks fluent German, told them that they could definitely stop worrying because there wouldn't be any more, unless the German soldiers came back during the night. In which case the village would be blown to bits. I don't know whether any did come back, but if they did, they would be pleaded with by the civvies to go away and save them from being shelled again. There certainly weren't any there when we came back early next morning.

Chapter 57
Leave confirmed, survival problematic

Sunday 1st April

It's April at last and I now have the satisfaction of knowing that I go on leave this month, another eighteen days to be precise. There is so much to arrange, yet these blasted Jerries don't give me any opportunity. It is a full-time job keeping myself alive. We returned to Wettringen about 7:30am and pushed on past there. We were the leading troop and didn't know what lay ahead of us, so it was a big strain on our nerves. We were under orders to clear the enemy from a crossroads, but when we arrived the enemy had already retreated. The strain of battle is not so much in the battle itself, but in the expectation of it. Our nerves were put on additional edge when there was a terrific explosion under Jock Baillie's tank. We wondered how many had been hurt and whose turn it would be next. I alternately scanned the countryside with my binoculars for anti-tank guns and the woods nearby for lurking bazooka-men. There was a horrible silence when we tried to get Jock's tank on the air. We thought that the commander and operator must have had it and wondered if the same anti-tank gun or bazooka-man would get us next. After an agonising five minutes of receiving no reply, Sergeant Jack Burton, who is acting as Troop leader in the absence of an officer, went on foot to find out what had happened. We were very much relieved to hear him report over the air that it wasn't an anti tank gun or bazooka at all, but the tank had run over a mine and sustained damage to the track and road wheels. The crew were a little shaken up, but otherwise unhurt. Having thus discovered what we wanted to know, namely, that the road was clear of enemy, but had a few mines, we pulled back a little way and cooked breakfast, or rather dinner and breakfast combined. On the way back, a scout car ran over one of the mines. The front wheel was thrown into the air in little pieces and the driver and commander were thrown right out of the vehicle, but were unhurt. As the rest of the Division were a good distance away, we thought that the day's excitement was over, but we thought wrongly. The 23rd Hussars were having a sticky time in a gorge over the Dortmund-Ems Canal and we had to do a road march and take up their positions for the night. We crossed the canal in the pitch-black darkness. The Bailey bridge had only been built just over twenty-four hours ago. That fellow Bailey can claim a good share of the credit in helping to win the war. They certainly are marvellous bridges and can be erected in a few hours. We harboured and filled up with petrol in the dark, then crept into our blankets and slept like logs. Physical exhaustion overcomes mental exhaustion.

Monday 2nd April

It's Easter Monday and Grandma's birthday. For me it was a fairly hard day in action, at least it was a nerve-racking one. We awoke to find ourselves at the neck of a long valley, no doubt picturesque in peacetime, but a grim military objective now. Our line of advance lay down the centre of the valley and on our left was a high range of hills, overlooking all the way we had to go. It was thickly wooded with hundreds of perfect hiding places for anti-tank guns. It was our Squadron's turn to lead too. I went down that road, literally expecting that the next time I woke up, I would be playing drums in a harp band in the heavens. Or perhaps I would just have an arm or a leg off. Much to my surprise, all went well until we came to a village - in the excitement, I've forgotten its name. There, we were held up by bazookas and small arms fire coming from houses in the village. The bazookas were a deadly nuisance, but the infantry in the village were dealt with easily. Whenever we saw anything move, we just blasted a hole in the house with our big guns or splattered the whole area with machine gun fire. It is much easier in Germany because one doesn't have to worry about civilians. After a pretty good plastering, quite a few Jerries came out and gave themselves up. The odd bazooka-men still lurked about though and we had several anxious moments before they all came out. Unfortunately, not many were killed. Most of them were taken prisoner and seemed glad to be out of it. They were mainly lads of seventeen or so from a Luftwaffe Training Regiment. In the afternoon, C Squadron came through us and probed the gorge. At the top they ran into a heap of trouble, mainly from bazooka-men. They had the choice of staying on the edge of the gorge for the night, with enemy infantry crawling all over the place, or fighting their way back down again by a different route. They chose the latter and were extremely lucky to get away with only one casualty. Meanwhile, we had cleared the village and harboured for the night, just northeast of it.

Tuesday 3rd April

I saw the Squadron Leader and pleaded 'battle exhaustion', so I was sent back to the A1 Echelon[1] and my place in the tank was taken by Charlie Hills who has just returned from leave. Life is very much safer in the non-combatant echelon. The only worry is from the air.

Wednesday 4th April

Arrived back at A2 Echelon with Glasspool and Chatfield who are going on leave. Boogie Watson and Dave Dewar, both former members of my crew, are already back here with battle exhaustion. Life is quite pleasant away from the fighting. Moving further into Germany behind the tanks, enemy planes made us dive for the ditch once or twice, but we were not actually attacked. Slept on the technical stores wagon.[2]

1. The term echelon was the name given to the follow-up support for the tanks.
2. While the author didn't record it at the time, these planes were so low and he was so annoyed that they were attacking a defenceless column that he stood on the cab of a lorry and fired his Sten gun at them 'ineffectively'.

Thursday 5th April

We seem to be pushing on again now. The war cannot last very long at this rate. The Yanks are only seventy-five miles from the Czech border and, in one place, they are only one hundred and forty miles from Berlin. The Russians have almost encircled Vienna and British troops have taken Munster and Osnabruck, so there isn't a lot of Germany left. He cannot have much war material left to leave places like the gorge we were in undefended. Capitulation is expected to come from a group of high-ranking army officials who will have to be recognised as the official government. Our Division has pushed on into the Hanover sector and we followed up behind them until midnight, then we pulled in for the night by the side of a railway station. The place was littered with Nazi flags. Good job we never got to the stage of having passports to travel in England; fancy applying for a permit to travel from Skipton to Leeds.

Friday 6th April

We are now only a few miles west of the River Weser and our tanks are actually up to it. There is an infantry bridgehead over the river and our tanks are to go over at 7.00am tomorrow. Thank God, for the fact that this once, I am not with them. The war in general seems to be going very well and most people say that it will all be over in a fortnight. Allied forces are now twenty miles from Hanover and ten from Berlin. He obviously cannot last long at this rate. Jerry planes do occasionally engage in a bit of strafing, causing us to dive for the ditch, but apart from that, everything is quiet back here.

Saturday 7th April

Roll on a fortnight today. Rollo Riley came back to the echelon today with the distressing news that Sergeant Fred Crump's tank has been 'bazookad' and all three in the turret have been killed - Fred Crump, Powell and Beard. Fred Crump had just returned from leave and the other two were new fellows who had not been over here long. It certainly is time that this war was finished and this needless waste of good lives ceases. Rollo Riley got out from the tank to collect some prisoners and was marching them back, when one of them picked up a rifle and shot him through the thigh. He saw the Jerry who did it and splattered him with his Sten gun. Luckily, Rollo only received a minor wound, two clean holes where the bullet had gone in and out.

Sunday 8th April

It's a glorious day; one that makes me long all the more for England and leave. Germany is quite a beautiful country. It's is a pity that this beauty is marred by its barbaric inhabitants. Yet there are pretty German girls, well dressed too. We were fools to believe all the dope that was pumped into us about the poor standard of living of the Germans. For the past few years, they have been living off the fat of the land, not their own, but that of the occupied countries. Certainly none of the civilians here looked ill-fed or badly clothed. The old farmer, at the farm where we are sleeping the night, had the cheek to ask me for cigarettes. They have been told that we would raze their farms to the ground, shoot all their little children and rape their daughters and when they find out that we are amicable, docile harmless sort of people, they try to take advantage of it. They profess to be violently anti-Nazi and then you find pictures that strongly suggest otherwise. For example, I came across a photograph of Hitler in a deserted bomb-damaged house. See *Figure 53.* What can one do with a race like that? I have a good suggestion, but it is not fit to print here.

Figure 53

A souvenir of the war; a photograph of Hitler found in bomb-damaged and deserted German house.

Monday 9th April
Crossed the River Weser at 10.00am. It is a fairly wide river. Germans have been attempting to bomb our bridge, but so far without success. A few fighters could play havoc with our columns, but we usually only see the odd one or two. If we see more than three planes together, it can generally be guaranteed that they are ours. A burial party was sent to bury Fred Crump's crew today. The bazooka had landed on top of the turret at the gunner's side and blew half the gunner's head off before entering the commander's stomach. The blast had also taken the top of the operator's head off. Such is war.

Tuesday 10th April
It's still marvellous weather. Moved up into an area southwest of the River Liner. SS men[1] are reported to be hiding in the woods nearby. One of our search parties found two German ack-ack soldiers in a nearby house. Hope that there isn't any SS prowling around tonight because I'm guard commander.

Wednesday 11th April
Quiet night last night, although the SS raided the next village. Hanover has now fallen to the Yanks and we have established a bridgehead over the Aller; two major events. In Vienna the Russians have captured three railway stations and the arsenal. However, the British 2ndArmy was encountering stiffening German resistance.

Thursday 12th April
Armoured units of the American Army are reported to be on the Elbe, only seventy miles from Berlin, and one hundred miles from the Russians. Groups of SS are being left behind and, occasionally, they do a bit of sniping and nuisance raiding, but they're not a major danger.

Friday 13th April
The death of President Roosevelt was announced today and the world mourns. I suppose that Dewey will take over now. It seems a pity that this should happen when Anglo-American relations were so secure with the Churchill-Roosevelt friendship. However, there is no reason why they should not continue in this way. Leave is drawing near now and I am getting listless and impatient waiting for it. After eight months away from home, who wouldn't feel this way?

Saturday 14th April
Taffy Thomas arrived back at the echelon today with battle exhaustion and the sad news that five of my friends have been killed. A sniper killed Corporal Len Stone, but the rest of his crew are all right. Sergeant Sam Dibble's tank

1. SS stood for the Schutzstaffel. It meant 'protective squadron' and it was a large security and paramilitary organization of the National Socialist German Workers Party

was 'bazooka'd' and burst into flames and killing him. The other four members of the crew managed to get out, but as they did so, snipers picked off three of them - Eric Hayhoe, Ted Martin and Tropper (Garnet) Hide. The co-driver was the only one in the crew who wasn't killed and he had a nasty gash in his thigh and had to lie under the tank for over an hour before anyone could get to him. Eric Hayhoe has only been back off leave four days, Ted Martin was a pal of mine from Leeds and Tropper Hide should have gone on leave with me next Wednesday. Two more days and he would have been out of the fighting. Why should all this have to happen? It is all very well for people in England to talk about the war being over. Maybe it is for them, but over here, it is still a horrible reality. Besides the above, Sergeant Jack Burton was hit in the face by a sniper's bullet, but, as far as I can gather, it's not too serious. Jack Boag was hit in the foot by a sniper's bullet, but he'll be all right in time I imagine. The tank that I was in, up to a few days ago, was hit twice, but all the crew got out okay. As I go on leave on Wednesday, the fellows advise me to dig a hole and bury myself until then. Not a bad idea either.

Sunday 15th April

My idea of yesterday would certainly be a good one, especially after last night's episode. Bud Concannon and I were sleeping in the wagon when we were awakened by the deathly whine of a shell coming in our direction. I thought: 'There goes this wagon and my leave with it', but it landed nine yards in front of us and although a few bits of shrapnel flew around, we were perfectly okay. By the time we had found our socks, pants and boots the shelling had stopped, but after that we slept in the front room of a nearby house, just in case.

Chapter 58
Still in Germany

Sunday April 15th (continued)

At 6:50pm we crossed the River Aller, at a place called Essel, due north of Hanover and not very far from Hamburg. Each time we move makes it further for me to go on leave and I already have about eight hundred miles to travel. The country we are in at present has not been fully cleared. Our armour has only gone up the main roads and, for all we know, there may still be large pockets of enemy infantry hiding in the woods to disrupt our communication and supply links. Also, now that we are well inside Germany, a few German planes are appearing and strafing the convoys. Consequently, it was with misgivings that we harboured for the night in a clearing between two large woods. For a while, there was indecision as to where was the best place to sleep. Some preferred slit trenches away from the lorries and possible shelling and bombing and others preferred slit trenches near the lorries and away from possible patrols. In the end, Bud Concannon and I got so cheesed off that we slept in the lorry. As I went to sleep, I comforted myself with the thought that next week at this time, I wouldn't be sleeping in a dirty old lorry, wondering if I'll still be in this world when I wake up in the morning. What a contrast the luxuries of home will be.

Monday 16th April

'%*&&^%£! and *%^$!' My leave has been put back one day owing to bad sailing weather. This means that I shall have to get married on the Monday instead of the Saturday. It will mean a lot of chasing around for Dorothy to get everything altered in time, but there is nothing I can do about it and, as it is a wartime wedding, we must expect this sort of thing. I don't grumble too much because I know that it is only by the grace of God that I am alive to go on leave at all. All the same, it is very annoying for those at home.

Tuesday 17th April

We are now at a place called Hermansburg, due north of Hanover and are moving further into Germany. The Yanks are now only thirty-eight miles from Berlin and are attacking Nuremberg and Leipzig, two important centres of Nazism. Things are certainly moving rapidly. A prisoner-of-war camp near here has been liberated and British and American soldiers stream down the roads, waving and cheering. The worst resistance that is met comes from groups of SS fanatics. I imagine that they will keep fighting for ages yet, even when the main body of the Army surrenders. Leave is very near now and it gives me the greatest of pleasure to get my kit packed. It will be grand to see home again, dirty old familiar Skipton station, scene of glorious re-unions and not so glorious partings, Dewhirsts Mill, with her aloof yet warm greeting, familiar streets and places and the smiles of people I know saying: 'Hello, you here again'. When do you go back?' I wonder how much Dennis and Sylvia have grown up and whether or not they will still know me? I long for Sunday when I shall once again be home and with all those dear to me.

Moving further into Germany, we passed a Russian prisoner-of-war camp, which had just been liberated. They were dressed in all kinds of patched up clothing and cheered us wildly. One could see the gratitude and joy written on their faces. They waved at every single lorry and tank that passed and when we threw them cigarettes, they dived after them as though they were diamonds. Many of them had started the long trek back to Venlo and from there they would to be taken back to Russia. But first they have a two hundred mile walk in front of them. Some have bicycles, some farm tractors, but most of them have to walk. It is a hot dusty road and all that most of them have is a blanket and a water bottle. When we gave them biscuits and our cookhouse dished them up soup, the way they gobbled it down showed that they hadn't had a good meal for days, perhaps weeks. It was a glorious sight to see and yet, in some ways, a piteous one. We passed old fellows in rags who could hardly stumble along, yet they were doggedly dragging themselves along in the desperate effort to get to the repatriation point and back to Russia. I have never seen such expressions of joy as there were on some of their faces. I know absolutely no Russian, but one fellow made me understand that he came from Moscow and that their German guards used to smoke cigarettes to half length then throw them on the ground where all the prisoners could see them and crush them with their heels, so that they couldn't pick them up. Consequently, he was overjoyed with the packet of twenty cigarettes, which we gave him. We also passed a lorry load of liberated British prisoners-of-war. They were all looking well and very pleased with life. It's still marvellous weather here. Hope it's like this on Monday.

Chapter 59
Home James

Wednesday 18th April

Have re-read this diary up to here and added a few comments in the margin. I find several of my entries rather ridiculous now. This is the last day we shall be with the Regiment before going on leave as we depart at 6:30am tomorrow morning. I am packed-up ready and can go at a moments notice. We shall leave in a spick and span condition, but by the time we arrive home, we shall be anything but that, as we have a two hundred mile journey in the back of a lorry before we even board the train to take us to Calais.

Thursday 19th April

Leave started today with a twelve-hour journey over hot, dusty roads with no food and only one stop of ten minutes. Good roads in Germany are a myth; most of them are nothing more than glorified cart tracks. The few good ones there are pitted with bomb and shell craters. It is just like riding in an ox-cart with square wheels.

Corporal McConnell, Vick Guest, Jack Brownlee and myself constituted the Regiment's leave party and we were up at 5:30am, although I concede it was no effort as excitement made it difficult to sleep. We left the Regiment at 6:30am in a B Squadron lorry and did the thirty miles to the Divisional UK 'Leave Embussing Point' by 7:45am. At 8.00am, we boarded Service Corps lorries and set off on a two hundred mile journey through Germany to Gennup Transit Camp in Holland. We crossed the Aller, the Seine, the Dortmund-Ems Canal, the Weser and the Rhine in that order. We noticed that most of the villages, just inside the border, were completely in ruins, but well inside Germany there is only occasional village, which had been flattened. It makes things much easier for us when the village is taken without firing a shot, but the Germans get off too lightly. We arrived at Gennup at 8:30pm absolutely covered with dust, but a wash and shave and mug of tea soon remedied our travel worn condition. That is two hundred miles done and only another seven hundred to go.

Friday 20th April

This morning, we were sorted out into zones and now await the loudspeakers in the camp to announce which train we catch for Calais. There are no trains until after dinner, so we have no alternative but to lie here in the sun until the time of the train for our particular zone is announced. It is a glorious day again and I hope that it keeps like this for Monday. This camp deals with quite a large number of leave personnel. The queue for breakfast was four hundred yards long and four deep. We joined it at 7:30am and were served at 8:30am. I hope that no one says to me: 'Did you have a good journey?' Still, no one cares how long it is because we are going on leave and every mile is a mile further from the frontline, and a mile nearer home. I wonder what Dorothy will say when we first meet? Certainly not: 'What, You here again?'

Saturday 21st April
It's 6.00am. We left Gennup Transit Camp at 4.00pm yesterday and travelled by 3rd class train to Calais where we arrived at 4:30am, some one and a half hours ago. The twelve-hour journey wasn't as bad this time, even though there were hard, wooden seats, which we counteracted by sitting on our blankets. At least the train hadn't got square wheels and there was no dust. We spent the twelve hours reading and dozing alternately. At Tilburg Station, a crowd of civvies gave us terrific welcome. It was almost like being in England. The people of Brussels turned out to wave to the 'leave train'. A halt of twenty minutes at Lille at midnight provided a very welcome break for chars and wads, which were ready waiting for us on the station. It felt grand to be on a train again, rattling towards home. On arriving in Calais, we were paid out in English money and changed our foreign currency. Let's see, how does this British monetary system work? Twenty shillings to the pound I believe. It's much easier to work things out in francs where everything goes up in tens and hundred. Nevertheless, the feel of an English pound note is good. So was the chance to have a wash and shave before breakfast at 5:15am. We now sit in Nissen huts; awaiting the loudspeakers to announce which boats we have to catch.

Everyone is allocated a coloured ticket according to his home district. The North and East Ridings of Yorkshire come under a different zone from the West Riding. This arrangement is to my advantage because I'm allowed to go through London and will be able to catch a London- Leeds express. It is now 6:30am. The first boat doesn't leave until 9:30am and, depending on what boat I can catch, I should stand a fair chance of being home before midnight. Home tonight. I can hardly express my thoughts on the subject. 3:45pm. England. England. At last! We left Calais at 9:30am and the white cliffs of Dover hove into sight about 11.00am. There was indeed cheering, but I didn't see any bluebirds. So this is really England. As one of the Canadians said: 'It sure looks swell.' One's feelings on the joy of being home again simply cannot be conveyed. When we disembarked instead of the cheering, which I expected, there was an unbelievable silence as each of us was left to his own thoughts. One fellow, every so often, is subjected to a customs search and I kept my fingers crossed for my binoculars and other things, which are classed as loot. I need have had no fear, however, since the customs official didn't even glance at me. An express with a NAAFI canteen on board took us non-stop to Victoria

Station where special buses were waiting to take us to Kings Cross and St Pancreas. I am now writing this last entry on the train in Kings Cross Station. In a few minutes, it will be pulling out and I shall be on the next to the last stage of my journey home.

So ends my diary.

Postscript

It is now 62 years since my diaries were concluded, and it may be of interest to some readers to know what happened to me over the intervening period. I was lucky to survive the war intact and I have already paid tribute to my less fortunate colleagues in my *Dedication,* but let me reiterate my respect for those whose lives were taken away so prematurely and to those who suffered long term disability. I am aware that the opportunity to go on to have a family life and career after the war was due to the monumental slices of luck I enjoyed during my service.

As already recorded, I arrived home on leave from the Western Front late on Saturday 21st April 1945, the day I was originally due to marry. However, because of my return being postponed by a day, the wedding had to be rearranged for the following Monday. For a photograph of us on our wedding day see *Figure 54.*

Figure 54

The author and his bride, Dorothy, on their wedding day (23rd April 1945).

When I reported back to my Regiment on the frontline, I vividly remember approaching a tank and hearing from a pair of headphones that were hanging on the outside: 'Don't shoot, unless you are shot at. We think it is all over'. That was on 4th May 1945 and the official Victory in Europe Day was declared on 8th May. The media gave this blanket coverage, a flavour of which may be gleaned from the example of a newspaper's presentation of these events in *Figure 55.*

Daily Mirror

MAY 8

Tuesday, May 8, 1945
No. 12,911 ONE PENNY
Registered at G.P.O. as a Newspaper.

VE-DAY!

IT'S OVER IN THE WEST

TODAY is VE-Day — the day for which the British people have fought and endured five years, eight months and four days of war.

Figure 55

An example of the press's treatment of the Victory in Europe Day celebrations *Daily Mirror*, May 8th 1945).

Soon after VE Day the Regiment was moved to Kappeln in northern Germany as part of the Army of Occupation. The British Army set up an army education scheme to assist the rehabilitation of soldiers after six years of war. Major Dawes was appointed Regimental Education Officer and I became his Education Corporal. Mind you it wasn't all work. I had some good times there with my Skiptonian friend Sergeant Major Bill Kavanagh. The photograph of the two of us in *Figure56* shows us in a more relaxed mode.

Figure 56
The author relaxing with his friend Sergeant Major Bill Kavanagh in Kappeln Bay.

In the autumn of 1945 the decision was taken to move the Regiment to the Egyptian-Palestinian border in order to help to keep the peace. As part of the Advance Party I was flown to Cairo in the empty bomb rack of a Lancaster bomber, hoping that the pilot wouldn't press the bomb release button by mistake. It was in Egypt that I was promoted to Sergeant and took over the running of the Regimental office as Orderly Room Sergeant. The photograph in *Figure57* shows me engaged in one of my duties.

Figure 57
The author manning the radio in Egypt

After some twelve months in the Middle East I had a pleasant surprise. Stanley Mason, my old boss at the Ordnance Factory, informed me that he could secure an early Class B Release from the Army for me to play a part in the rejuvenation of the British textile industry. I grabbed the opportunity with both hands and was demobbed on September 8th 1946. I also became the recipient of a grey demob suit with a white chalk stripe. I joined Stanley at Hindley Brothers Limited, Nelson in Lancashire where he was Finance Director. I passed my accountancy finals in January 1948 and later became Company Secretary. Our first daughter, Merron, was born in the same month in which I passed my final exams and our second daughter, Joy, was born in July 1950.

Hindley Brothers went through a series of mergers/takeovers and eventually became Carrington Viyella. At this point, I left to join Thomas Marshall plc as Finance Director, under the leadership of Donald Parr. This company was then taken-over by William Baird, where I continued to enjoy working for Donald. In this capacity I was chairman of a number of subsidiary companies. By then I was a Fellow of the Chartered Institute of Management Accountants and I served as a Council member for several years. I also became a Fellow of the Association of Chartered Certified Accountants and published several papers on financial control. Looking back, I appreciate how fortunate I was to work with Stanley and Donald who were good men and good leaders.

I retired in 1987 at the age of 64 and changed my formal business card to that shown in *Figure 58*.

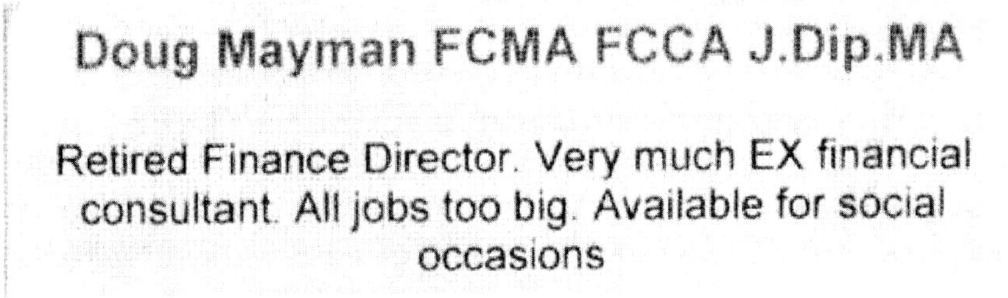
Doug Mayman FCMA FCCA J.Dip.MA

Retired Finance Director. Very much EX financial consultant. All jobs too big. Available for social occasions

Figure 58
The author's retirement version of his business card

Dorothy and I have now been married for sixty-two years. We have four grandchildren, four great grandchildren and another due in 2008. Dorothy is not in the best of health now, but with the help of our daughters and all our good friends, Juliet, Doreen, Jean and others, we have a reasonable quality of life.

After reading through the diaries after some sixty years, I have been surprised at many things, but I must limit myself to two central ones and two lesser ones. The lesser ones relate to my frequent cinema attendance and to the ethos of smoking that prevailed at the time. Both of these might puzzle the younger reader. In those days the range of entertainment was very limited and cinema going was a central element in most people's leisure time. Even so, the frequency with which I attended the cinema was not typical of servicemen. Larger numbers found the pubs or service clubs more to their taste, and on occasions, I joined them. But, for me, my love of films and music, were more useful diversions from the horrors of war. The second issue I want to touch upon is smoking and how widespread the habit was in those days. The practice was for everyone in the frontline to be issued with a cigarette ration. Those who didn't smoke, or like me at the time smoked a pipe, used them as *bono-fide* currency. All this of course is a far cry from the Government imposed smoking bans of today. Yes – "smoking kills", but then so too does war.

The central issues, as is so often the case, relate to politics and religion.

So what of politics? I find it astonishing that at the age of nineteen I was thrust into a situation where I was required to kill and risk being killed in the name of freedom and democracy, yet I wasn't deemed to be responsible enough to vote. In my late teens and early twenties my political views seem to have been quite fluid and I concede to being surprised by reading of my support for the Common Wealth Party. I have been a free enterprise man for so long that I have come to believe that I have always been of that persuasion. However, it should be said that such views were consistent with the prevailing political climate of the time.

And what of religion? What surprised me most of all is that I make no explicit mention in the diaries of a major event, namely, that it was during this period that I lost my religious faith. I suppose this oversight was because it happened gradually, not in a blinding flash. As my editor makes clear in the *Foreword,* I didn't come from a really religious family, but my parents still thought it appropriate that I should attend a Methodist church.

I suppose that prior to my military service some doubts had begun to creep in, perhaps in relation to my reflections on why God should have seen fit to deprive me of my mother when she was twenty-five and I was only three. It goes without saying that my life would have been so much richer had God spared her. Then during military service, my faith was further undermined by a number of anomalies I witnessed, for example, our padre blessing us and our tanks before we went into action and praying for our victory, while his German equivalent no doubt performed an identical rite. To whose prayers did God give most weight? It troubled me that while we were blasting ourselves to pieces, the padres retreated to their respective officers' messes and prepared themselves to administer to the dying. If our cause was worth fighting for, why did they not see fit to join us or were their lives more highly valued than ours? Again, in discussions with my religious colleagues, they often expressed the view that one's time only came when it was God's will. He decided when a bullet or a piece of shrapnel would have one's name on it. I thought what a curious God. How did he select who was to be a victim? What were his criteria for deciding who would live and die? Did he only punish the wrongdoers and spare the righteous? Not in my judgement. None of these arguments should be interpreted as in any way detracting from the lasting admiration I have for my wartime colleagues, many of whom, perhaps because of their faith, did brave things regardless of the danger to their lives. Nor do I think any the less of those with deeply held religious convictions. To coin a phrase: 'May your god go with you'.

The Second World War ended some sixty-two years ago and since then not a single day has passed without a war raging in some part of the world. The lives wasted, the resources consumed and the damage done to the environment are so monumental as to defy estimation. Yet politicians and generals continue to justify war as a legitimate aspect of policy, and in doing so, continue to place multitudes of civilians and led soldiers in harms way.

Doug Mayman.
December 2007

Appendix A
List of abbreviations

ABCA: Army Bureau of Current Affairs
AEC: Army Education Corps
AFV: Armour Fighting Vehicle
AP: Armour piercing
ARV: Armoured Recovery Vehicle
ATEA: Amphibious Tank Escape Apparatus
BLA: British Liberation Army
ENSA: Entertainments National Service Association
FFI: French Forces of the Interior
FHQ: Forward Headquarters
HE: High Explosive
HF: High frequency
KRH: The King's Royal Hussars
KRR: King's Royal Rifles
KSLI: King's Surrey Light Infantry
LAD: Light Aid Detachment
MI: Medical Inspection Room
MO: Medical officer
MP: Military policeman
NAAFI: National Army Air Force Institute
NFS: National Fire Service
NCO: Non-commissioned officer
OCTU: Officer Command Training Unit
RAC: Royal Armoured Corps
RAMC: Royal Army Medical Corps
RASC: Royal Army Service Corps
RE: Royal Engineers
REME: Royal Electrical and Mechanical Engineers
RHQ: Regimental Headquarters
ROF: Royal Ordnance Factory
RSM: Regimental Sergeant Major
RTO: Rail Transport Officer
R/T: Radio Telephone
SQMS: Squadron Quartermaster Sergeant
USAAF: United States Army Air Force
WAAF: Women's Auxiliary Air Force
WVS: Women's Voluntary Services
YMCA: Young Men's Christian Association

Appendix B[1]

Roll of Honour $15^{th}/19^{th}$ The King's Royal Hussars 1944-45

Killed in Action

Name	Date	Place
Cpl F. Edwards	19 Aug 44	Moulins-sur-Orne, France.
Tpr B. Cornwall	19 Aug 44	Moulins-sur-Orne, France.
Sgt R. Bray	21 Aug 44	Gacé, France.
Tpr T. Dakin	28 Aug 44	La Chappelle St. Ouen, France.
Tpr H. Drake	28 Aug 44	La Chappelle St. Ouen, France.
Cpl A. Burgin	29 Aug 44	La Chappelle St. Ouen, France.
SQMS P. Burke	30 Aug 44	Veron, France.
Lt F. G. Ainslie	10 Sep 44	Zonhoven, Belgium
Lt B.J. Pearson	10 Sep 44	Zonhoven, Belgium
Cpl F. Walker	10 Sep 44	Zonhoven, Belgium
L/Cpl J. Scudamore	10 Sep 44	Zonhoven, Belgium
Tpr F. Johns	10 Sep 44	Zonhoven, Belgium
Tpr C. Lawley	10 Sep 44	Zonhoven, Belgium
Tpr R. Munro	10 Sep 44	Zonhoven, Belgium
Tpr A. Robson	10 Sep 44	Zonhoven, Belgium
Tpr J. Simpson	10 Sep 44	Zonhoven, Belgium
Tpr A. Harratt	11 Sep 44	Bree, Belgium.
Lt A. M. Bryce	14 Sep 44	Meuse –Escaut Canal, Belgium.
Tpr P. Downing	14 Sep 44	Meuse –Escaut Canal, Belgium.
Tpr R. Heathfield	14 Sep 44	Meuse –Escaut Canal, Belgium.
Tpr R. Walker	14 Sep 44	Meuse –Escaut Canal, Belgium.
L/Cpl W. Batchelor	17 Sep 44	Petter, Near Valkenswaard, Holland.
Sgt M. Fox	19 Sep 44	Best, Holland.
Cpl F. Hartley	19 Sep 44	Best, Holland.
L/Cpl F. Harrison	19 Sep 44	Eindhoven, Holland.
Tpr R. Bratt	19 Sep 44	Best, Holland.
Tpr L. Davis	19 Sep 44	Best, Holland.
Tpr E. Morgon	19 sep 44	Best, Holland.
Tpr T. Richards	19 Sep 44	Best, Holland.
Tpr J. Sutherland	19 Sep 44	Best, Holland.
Tpr W. Wain	19 Sep 44	Eindhoven, Holland.
Lt P.J. Ireland	24 Sep 44	Liesel, Holland.
Tpr P. Clarke	24 Sep 44	Liesel, Holland.
Tpr C. Harris	24 Sep 44	Liesel, Holland.
Capt R.H.W.Ellis	27 Sep 44	St. Anthonis, Holland.
Tpr F. Dinham	17 Oct 44	Ijsselstein, Holland.
Tpr H. Clegg	18 Oct 44	Ijsselstein, Holland.
Tpr J. Marsh	18 Oct 44	Ijsselstein, Holland.

2/Lt A.B. Wilson	19 Oct 44	St. Helena Hoeve, Holland
Sgt L. Jackson	19 Oct 44	St. Helena Hoeve, Holland
L/Cpl F. Helliwell	19 Oct 44	St. Helena Hoeve, Holland
Tpr N. Mann	19 Oct 44	St. Helena Hoeve, Holland
L/Cpl W. Banfield	27 Feb 45	Udem, Germany.
Tpr J. Danby	27 Feb 45	Udem, Germany.
Capt R.N. Swanwick	1 Mar 45	Udem, Germany.
Cpl R. Wilkinson	1 Mar 45	Udem, Germany.
Tpr P. Styler	1 Mar 45	Udem, Germany.
Cfn W. Reid	1 Mar 45	Udem, Germany.
Tpr H.Sayers	5 Apr 45	Petershagen, Germany.
L/Sgt F. Crump	7 Apr 45	Leese, Germany.
Tpr J. Beard	7 Apr 45	Leese, Germany.
Tpr D. Powell	7 Apr 45	Leese, Germany.
L/Sgt S. Dibble	14 Apr 45	Winsen, Germany.
Cpl A. Stone	14 Apr 45	Winsen, Germany.
Tpr P. Brown	14 Apr 45	Winsen, Germany.
Tpr E. Hayhoe	14 Apr 45	Winsen, Germany.
Tpr G. Hide	14 Apr 45	Winsen, Germany.
Tpr E. Martin	14 Apr 45	Winsen, Germany.

Died of Wounds

Name	Date	Place
Lt R.J. Pearce	28 Aug 44	La Chappelle St. Ouen, France.
Tpr M. Clark	17 Oct 44	Ijsselstein, Holland.
Tpr W. Statham	17 Oct 44	Ijsselstein, Holland.
L/Cpl J. Whitwam	19 Oct 44	St Helena Hoeve, Holland.
Tpr D. Simmins	20 Oct 44	St Helena Hoeve, Holland.
Tpr H. Cottam	7 Nov 44	Ijsselstein, Holland.
Tpr L. Malley	2 Mar 45	Udem, Germany
Tpr H. Robinson	2 Mar 45	Udem, Germany
Cpl C. Taylor	3 Mar 45	Udem, Germany

Wounded in Action

Name	Date	Place
Lt J.R. Sharpe	19 Aug 44	Moulins-sur-Orne, France.
L/Cpl T. Kelly	19 Aug 44	Moulins-sur-Orne, France.
Tpr M. Frampton	19 Aug 44	Moulins-sur-Orne, France.
Tpr H. Warner	19 Aug 44	Moulins-sur-Orne, France.
Tpr J. Lawrence	21 Aug 44	Gacé, France.
L/Sgt J. Rowney	27 Aug 44	Veron, France.
Capt W.W.M. Robb	28 Aug 44	La Chappelle St. Ouen, France.
Lt B.J. Pearson	28 Aug 44	Haricourt, France.
Tpr C. Elcock	28 Aug 44	Haricourt, France.
Tpr W. Belshaw	28 Aug 44	Veron, France.
Tpr B. Wilson	28 Aug 44	La Chappelle St. Ouen, France.

Capt C. N. Weatherby	29 Aug 44	Haricourt, France.
Capt C.D. Agnew	10 Sep 44	Zonhoven, Belgium.
SSM T. Maddocks	10 Sep 44	Zonhoven, Belgium.
L/Sgt A. Buckle	10 Sep 44	Zonhoven, Belgium.
L/Sgt K. Sampson	10 Sep 44	Zonhoven, Belgium.
Tpr D.Cook	10 Sep 44	Zonhoven, Belgium.
Tpr. G. Gentles	10 Sep 44	Zonhoven, Belgium.
Tpr R. Jeffrey	10 Sep 44	Zonhoven, Belgium.
Tpr R. Kirton	10 Sep 44	Zonhoven, Belgium.
Tpr J. Maskall	10 Sep 44	Zonhoven, Belgium.
Tpr T. Middleton	10 Sep 44	Zonhoven, Belgium.
Tpr J. Pickard	10 Sep 44	Zonhoven, Belgium.
Tpr J. Wren	10 Sep 44	Zonhoven, Belgium.
Sgt G. Marlow	11 Sep 44	Bree, Belgium.
Tpr F. Fellows	11 Sep 44	Bree, Belgium.
Tpr H. Stott	13 Sep 44	Meuse –Escaut Canal, Belgium.
Capt C. Y. Mills	14 Sep 44	Meuse –Escaut Canal, Belgium.
Lt W.R. McM. Winckley	14 Sep 44	Meuse –Escaut Canal, Belgium.
Sgt R. Hayes	14 Sep 44	Meuse –Escaut Canal, Belgium.
Cpl D. Woolfoot	14 Sep 44	Meuse –Escaut Canal, Belgium.
L/Cpl E. Hamilton	14 Sep 44	Meuse –Escaut Canal, Belgium.
L/Cpl F. Sheldon	14 Sep 44	Meuse –Escaut Canal, Belgium.
Tpr R. Ashley	14 Sep 44	Meuse –Escaut Canal, Belgium.
Tpr W. Harris	14 Sep 44	Meuse –Escaut Canal, Belgium.
Tpr G. Horley	14 Sep 44	Meuse –Escaut Canal, Belgium.
Tpr G. Selby	14 Sep 44	Meuse –Escaut Canal, Belgium.
Tpr D. Wright	14 Sep 44	Meuse –Escaut Canal, Belgium.
Tpr L. Manning	15 Sep 44	Meuse –Escaut Canal, Belgium.
Tpr D. Wilson	15 Sep 44	Meuse –Escaut Canal, Belgium.
Sgt R. Nesbitt	17 Sep 44	Meuse –Escaut Canal, Belgium.
Sgt G. Pearson	17 Sep 44	Petter, nr. Valkenwaard, Holland.
Cpl J. McConnell	17 Sep 44	Meuse –Escaut Canal, Belgium.
Cpl W. Shirvill	17 Sep 44	Petter, nr. Valkenwaard, Holland.
Tpr J. Dick	17 Sep 44	Petter, nr. Valkenwaard, Holland.
Tpr S. Laurence	17 Sep 44	Petter, nr. Valkenwaard, Holland.
Tpr H. Richardson	17 Sep 44	Meuse –Escaut Canal, Belgium.
Tpr H. Vosper	17 Sep 44	Meuse –Escaut Canal, Belgium.
Sgt D, Gibson	19 Sep 44	Best, Holland.
Sgt M. Hollis	19 Sep 44	Best, Holland.
Sgt A. Yeomans	19 Sep 44	Zon, Holland.
Cpl E. Kingston	19 Sep 44	Eindhoven, Holland.
Tpr J. Johnston	19 Sep 44	Best, Holland.
Tpr W. Lee	19 Sep 44	Best, Holland.
Tpr P. King	22 Sep 44	St Oedenrode, Holland.
Lt M. Roderick	23 Sep 44	Zomeren, Holland.
Sgt A. Spanton	23 Sep 44	Zomeren, Holland.
Tpr E. Angel	24 Sep 44	Liesel, Holland.
Tpr H. Brown	24 Sep 44	Liesel, Holland.

Tpr S. Burrows	24 Sep 44	Liesel, Holland.
Lt J. H. Blackett	27 Sep 44	St. Anthonis, Holland.
Tpr R. Clark	27 Sep 44	St. Anthonis, Holland.
Tpr R. Fisk	27 Sep 44	St. Anthonis, Holland.
Tpr G. Hughes	27 Sep 44	St. Anthonis, Holland.
Tpr R. Stiff	27 Sep 44	St. Anthonis, Holland.
Lt/Sgt E. Peachey	28 Sep 44	Sambeek, Holland.
L/Cpl B. Simmonds	28 Sep 44	Sambeek, Holland.
L/Cpl R. West	28 Sep 44	Boxmeer, Holland.
Lt D. K. H. Eves	15 Oct 44	Vierlingsbeek, Holland.
Tpr A.Adkin	15 Oct 44	Vierlingsbeek, Holland.
Tpr A Berry	15 Oct 44	Vierlingsbeek, Holland.
Tpr C. Green	15 Oct 44	Vierlingsbeek, Holland.
Lt T.D. Seigne	16 Oct 44	Overloon, Holland.
Capt M. Jennings	17 Oct 44	Ijsselstein, Holland.
Cpl D. Jacks	17 Oct 44	Ijsselstein, Holland.
L/Cpl T. Walling	17 Oct 44	Ijsselstein, Holland.
Tpr M. Beigal	17 Oct 44	Ijsselstein, Holland.
Tpr H. Buchan	17 Oct 44	Ijsselstein, Holland.
Lt M. Mather	18 Oct 44	Ijsselstein, Holland.
Tpr D. Griffiths	18 Oct 44	Ijsselstein, Holland.
Tpr H. Meredith	18 Oct 44	Ijsselstein, Holland.
Lt R. Payne	19 Oct 44	St. Helena Hoeve, Holland.
Cpl W. Shirvill	19 Oct 44	St. Helena Hoeve, Holland.
Cpl J. Sutcliffe	19 Oct 44	St. Helena Hoeve, Holland.
Cpl E. Wingfield	19 Oct 44	St. Helena Hoeve, Holland.
L/Cpl A. Galsworhty	19 Oct 44	St. Helena Hoeve, Holland.
Tpe W. Baybutt	19 Oct 44	St. Helena Hoeve, Holland.
Tpr A. Bradwell	19 Oct 44	St. Helena Hoeve, Holland.
Tpr A. Burge	19 Oct 44	St. Helena Hoeve, Holland.
Tpr W. Durham	19 Oct 44	St. Helena Hoeve, Holland.
Tpr W. Hill	19 Oct 44	St. Helena Hoeve, Holland.
Tpr D. Keller	19 Oct 44	St. Helena Hoeve, Holland.
Tpr R. Marshall	19 Oct 44	St. Helena Hoeve, Holland.
Cpl D. Martin	20 Oct 44	Ijsselstein.
Tpr F. Overton	20 Oct 44	St. Helena Hoeve, Holland.
Tpr F. Campbell	24 Oct 44	Veulen, Holland.
Cpl W. Willaims	28 Oct 44	Deurne, Holland.
Tpr L. Bending	28 Oct 44	Deurne, Holland.
Tpr D. Christie	28 Oct 44	Deurne, Holland.
Tpr J. Davies	28 Oct 44	Deurne, Holland.
Tpr D. Gordon	28 Oct 44	Deurne, Holland.
Tpr H. Horner	28 Oct 44	Deurne, Holland.
Tpr J. Keenan	28 Oct 44	Deurne, Holland.
Tpr C. Leeves	28 Oct 44	Deurne, Holland.
Tpr J. Slinn	28 Oct 44	Deurne, Holland.
Tpr C. Watson	28 Oct 44	Deurne, Holland.
Lt J.F. Finnimore	6 Nov 44	Ijsselstein, Holland.

Tpr R. Garroway	7 Nov 44	St. Helena Hoeve, Holland.
Tpr H. Harding	9 Nov 44	St. Helena Hoeve, Holland.
Cpl G. Webster	10 Nov 44	Veulen, Holland
Tpr C. Griffiths	10 Nov 44	St. Helena Hoeve, Holland.
SSM W. Hague	30 Nov 44	Broekhuizen, Holland.
SSM A. Sara	30 Nov 44	Broekhuizen, Holland.
Sgt A. Seawright	30 Nov 44	Broekhuizen, Holland.
Tpr D. Dewar	30 Nov 44	Broekhuizen, Holland.
Tpr W. Lee	1 Dec 44	Broekhuizen, Holland.
Cpl L. Whelpdale	4 Dec 44	Broekhuizen, Holland.
Tpr Carrington	8 Feb 45	Lommel ranges, Belgium.
Tpr D. Crabtree	8 Feb 45	Lommel ranges, Belgium.
Tpr D. Graham	8 Feb 45	Lommel ranges, Belgium.
Tpr D. Lewis	8 Feb 45	Lommel ranges, Belgium.
Tpr Rae	8 Feb 45	Lommel ranges, Belgium.
Lt J.A. Cruickshank	13 Feb 45	Kelpen, Holland.
Tpr Sutton	13 Feb 45	Kelpen, Holland.
Tpr C. Shepstone	28 Feb 45	Udem, Germany.
Capt T.A. Adams	1 Mar 45	Udem, Germany.
Lt M.R.Caroe	1 Mar 45	Udem, Germany.
Sgt A. Scott	1 Mar 45	Udem, Germany.
L/Sgt J. Yeomans	1 Mar 45	Udem, Germany.
Cpl R. Davies	1 Mar 45	Udem, Germany.
Cpl J. Howard	1 Mar 45	Udem, Germany.
Cpl D. Martin	1 Mar 45	Udem, Germany.
Cpl K. Rumley	1 Mar 45	Udem, Germany.
L/Cpl J. Hibbert	1 Mar 45	Udem, Germany.
L/Cpl G. Kelly	1 Mar 45	Udem, Germany.
L/Cpl L/ Lowe	1 Mar 45	Udem, Germany.
Tpr F. Frost	1 Mar 45	Udem, Germany.
Tpr C. Gardner	1 Mar 45	Udem, Germany.
Tpr F. Holloway	1 Mar 45	Udem, Germany.
Tpr G. Hughes	1 Mar 45	Udem, Germany.
Tpr W. McOwen	1 Mar 45	Udem, Germany.
Tpr R. Salisbury	1 Mar 45	Udem, Germany.
Cfn E. Cuthbertson	1 Mar 45	Udem, Germany.
Lt R.F.Eyles	2 Mar 45	Udem, Germany.
Sgt R. Storr	2 Mar 45	Udem, Germany.
Cfn J. Chatfield	2 Mar 45	Udem, Germany.
Maj M. S. Balmain	3 Mar 45	Udem, Germany.
Cpl M. Lucas	3 Mar 45	Udem, Germany.
Cpl G. Wilson	31 Mar 45	Burgsteinfurt, Germany.
Tpr J. Higginbottom	31 Mar 45	Burgsteinfurt, Germany.
Tpr H. Worsley	31 Mar 45	Burgsteinfurt, Germany.
Lt R. F. Leslie	2 Apr 45	Teutobegerwald, Germany.
Sgt J. Waite	5 Apr 45	Petershagen, Germany.
L/Cpl R. Norman	5 Apr 45	Petershagen, Germany.
Tpr J. Boyes	5 Apr 45	Petershagen, Germany.

Tpr L. Morris	5 Apr 45	Petershagen, Germany.
Tpr R. Rees	7 Apr 45	Leese, Germany.
Tpr R. Riley	7 Apr 45	Leese, Germany.
Cpl T. Walker	8 Apr 45	Schneeren, Germany.
Tpr I. Finch	8 Apr 45	Schneeren, Germany.
Lt E. A. Moore	13 Apr 45	Winsen, Germany.
2/Lt F.N. Cory-Wright	13 Apr 45	Winsen, Germany.
Sgt J. Kennedy	13 Apr 45	Winsen, Germany.
Lt/Cpl A. Cannon	13 Apr 45	Winsen, Germany.
Tpr H. Bradley	13 Apr 45	Winsen, Germany.
Tpr R. Eddie	13 Apr 45	Winsen, Germany.
Tpr R. Grainger	13 Apr 45	Winsen, Germany.
Tpr A. Wilding	13 Apr 45	Winsen, Germany.
Tpr S. Woodford	13 Apr 45	Winsen, Germany.
Sgt W. Burgess	14 Apr 45	Winsen, Germany.
Sgt J. Burton	14 Apr 45	Winsen, Germany.
Tpr H. Boag	14 Apr 45	Winsen, Germany.
Tpr S. Haygarth	14 Apr 45	Winsen, Germany.
Tpr R. Henderson	14 Apr 45	Winsen, Germany.
Tpr A. Lister	14 Apr 45	Winsen, Germany.
Tpr D. Parker	14 Apr 45	Winsen, Germany.
Lt D.H. Tavener	17 Apr 45	Barnsen, Germany.
Tpr R. Clark	3 May 45	Bad Oldesloe, Germany.

1. The following tables contain selected data drawn from Appendices A and B of Major G. Courage DSO, The History of 15/19 The King's Royal Hussars 1939-1945, Gale & Polden Ltd, Aldershot 1949, pp. 251-257.

Piano Concerto No 8 Beethoven